em
ov
orr
lep
arc
his
ene
nes
ic
e c
___
Le

Saints
AND
SINNERS

Saints
AND
SINNERS
SOUTHAMPTON'S
HARD MEN

GRAHAM HILEY

First published by Pitch Publishing, 2016

Pitch Publishing
A2 Yeoman Gate
Yeoman Way
Worthing
Sussex
BN13 3QZ

www.pitchpublishing.co.uk

info@pitchpublishing.co.uk

ISBN 978-1-78531-194-9

Typesetting and origination by Pitch Publishing
Printed by TJ International, Padstow, Cornwall

Contents

*For Martin, Catherine
and Tim with love*

Acknowledgements

OVER THE years, Saints have had more than their fair share of hard-men and larger-than-life characters, loosely termed Sinners for the purpose of this book.

The aim was to bring together a collection of hilarious, insightful and even poignant anecdotes and memories as well as look at the physical and mental toughness needed to play at the top level.

Some of the candidates were obvious: Mark Dennis, Francis Benali, Terry Hurlock, Neil Ruddock and the man who was the inevitable answer to the increasingly pointless question: 'Who was the hardest player you ever encountered?' – Jimmy Case.

Then there are survivors of the infamous 'Alehouse Brawlers', as they became known, Denis Hollywood, Brian O'Neil and Terry Paine soon followed by Jim Steele and a host of other hard-men who thrived in the days when there was more leeway with tackling.

If you will forgive one self-indulgence, I have also included the legend that is Rickie Lambert – simply because I wanted to.

Sadly, some hard-men and characters are missing. John McGrath, Jimmy Gabriel, David 'Docker' Walker, Peter Osgood, Alan Ball and Kevin Moore died far too soon while some others now have dementia.

It is a wretched disease which also afflicts my own father, Peter, who was immensely proud of my previous books but who, sadly, will not be able to read this one.

Here, I must thank Saints' FA Cup-winning manager Lawrie McMenemy, not just for providing the foreword but also for his long-standing support of the Alzheimer's Society. I also need to thank all the players who gave up their time to be interviewed, recounting their stories with brutal honesty – just as they played.

It is one of life's great mysteries how this collection of colourful characters could be hard as nails on the field but, to a man, the nicest people off it.

No book like this could ever be compiled without research and, as always, I am eternally indebted to the dedication and thoroughness of the club historians David Bull, Gary Chalk and Duncan Holley, whose methodical attention to detail is quite remarkable. In particular, their excellent works *In That Number* and *All the Saints* were invaluable.

Other books which provided essential information include Jeremy Wilson's *Cult Heroes*, Alex Crook's *Match Of My Life* and the collected autobiographies of some of those featured, most notably Matthew Le Tissier, John Burridge, Jimmy Case, Perry Groves and Neil Ruddock.

The photos come from my good friend and excellent freelance photographer Paul Watts (pbwpix.co.uk) and from the *Southern Daily Echo*. I must thank sports editor and fellow Pitch author Simon Carter plus Saints correspondent Adam Leitch, as well as Jez Gale, who had the unenviable job of actually finding the pictures.

I am extremely grateful to Paul and Jane Camillin, Dean Rockett Duncan Olner and Graham Hales at Pitch Publishing for their understanding with deadlines and for giving this project the go-ahead. I also have to thank Simon Williams at Southampton Football Club for his help, along with John May at Southampton Solent University for his advice, football knowledge and assistance with legal stuff.

Last but not least, I must thank the love of my life, my wonderful but long-suffering wife, Theresa, who shrieked with horror at many of the anecdotes – the parental guidance warning is dedicated to her! And I must thank my children Martin, Catherine and particularly Tim, who had the daunting task of proofreading the entire book.

I hope you enjoy reading it as much as I loved writing it.

Graham Hiley

Foreword

by Lawrie McMenemy MBE

EVERY SUCCESSFUL side needs a mix of saints and sinners – or, as I always described them, road-sweepers and violinists.

Any manager will tell you that you have to get that blend right – you can't have too many of one and not enough of the other. They both need each other.

You need the skilful, crowd-pleasing ball-players but you also have to have the tough-tackling hard-men in order to let them perform.

Sometimes you have to have a quiet word with the violinists and explain that they would not be as good without the road-sweepers to clear the way.

And sometimes you have to explain to a road-sweeper that he is not a violinist and he should stick to what he is good at!

Over the years, Southampton have had their fair share of saints and sinners – fantastic players like Matthew Le Tissier or real hard-men like Jimmy Case.

He was probably the toughest player I have ever worked with. He was a natural hard-man who really knew how to look after himself – and his team-mates.

He was my last signing for Southampton and not a bad legacy to leave. I wish I could have signed him a few years earlier because he would have made a huge difference to the team.

He was hard as nails but he could really play too. He had won as many medals as anyone in the game and was one of the best players never to play for England.

Yet I got him on a free transfer. In those days, you paid £25,000 to the selling club and they would pass it on to the player tax-free as a kind of signing-on fee, but effectively it was a free transfer.

I had been looking for that sort of midfield enforcer and Jim's contract was up at Brighton. He came down for a meeting and sat sideways on to me, which I thought was strange. But I didn't realise that, under his long hair, he was sporting the biggest hearing aid I had ever seen.

But, like a lot of hard-men, he was one of the loveliest guys off the pitch. He was not too bothered about the money. I used to joke that when we were talking about football he would put one ear towards me, and when we were talking money he used the other.

He didn't ask too much about the contract, only whether he could continue living in Brighton as his wife's mother had just moved down to be near them.

I said that was fine but I knew he liked a night out, so I told him if I heard about him stepping out of line then I would make him move up here. As it turned out, he moved to Southampton soon afterwards and he was still there when I left.

He was a fantastic influence on a lot of the younger players I was bringing through, the likes of Alan Shearer, the Wallaces and Matthew Le Tissier. He had 100 per cent respect in the dressing room because he was not a loud-mouth, just a naturally aggressive good-quality player.

I put him in there with the younger legs to give us that blend of youth and experience and it worked well.

We didn't have the budget to buy international players when they were at the top of their game, but we were able to get them towards the end of their careers – players like Alan Ball, Peter Osgood, Peter Shilton, Frank Worthington.

They all had a touch of quality but they all knew how to look after themselves – and they often played just as hard off the field.

As a manager, you had to know how to handle that side of them. At that stage of their careers, they didn't need coaching – but they certainly needed managing!

I didn't need to tell them how to strike a ball – that was second nature to them. But I needed to keep them in check in other areas.

These days, the game has changed. Managers are more like coaches rather than running the club from top to bottom, as was the case with the likes of Brian Clough, Bill Shankly, Bill Nicholson, Sir Alex Ferguson and myself.

My big challenge was trying to manage a team with a few rascals in it. You can't treat everyone the same. Some you could tell off in front of the rest of the team; others would have to be spoken to in private. Some would need a cuddle, some would need a kick up the backside.

You did what you needed to do in order to get the best out of them.

An example of that was the time I called Brian O'Neil in to see me. I told him I had heard he had been out the night before and asked if he had a good time. He said yes and I said I had heard it was more than just a good time. He said it had just been an ordinary night out.

I said I heard he had chinned someone. He said he hadn't… but then looked into my eyes, realised the game was up and asked how much I was going to fine him.

I said I was going to let it go… but to be more careful in future and that he owed me. He went out and played one of the games of his life in the next match.

Along with John McGrath, Brian was one of the players I inherited when I took over as manager. They were two of the hardest competitors I have ever worked with.

John was a commanding old-fashioned centre-half. The ball might go past him or the player might go past him. But it was very rare that both went past him!

He would regularly drink a jar of honey before a game. I think someone had told him it would give him extra energy. He would then headbutt the lockers and take to the field.

He had the biggest thighs I had ever seen. They were like tree trunks. He would roll his shorts up as high as they would go to show them off to the man he would be marking.

And if the teams swapped ends after the toss, he would make a point of running past the opposition centre-forward to ask if his health insurance was up to date!

It was because of John that Bill Shankly dubbed Saints an alehouse team. Liverpool's Alun Evans had beaten two men and was flying down the touchline. The full-backs were out of position, so John had to come out of the middle… and actually shouted a warning that he was on his way!

Next thing, Evans had cleared the running track and ended up in the paddock.

In those days defenders got away with a lot more than they do now and, as a manager, you would certainly expect your centre-back to test out the striker's bottle early on.

Brian O'Neil was the same. In those days, we had a young Mike Channon up front. He was wonderfully gifted. He floated across the ground, which made him a target for the O'Neils of the opposition.

He was regularly kicked up in the air, causing the trainer to run on. We didn't have physios in those days. Your leg was either broken or it wasn't. None of these niggles and tweaks, just a wet sponge and some smelling salts in case it was a serious injury.

The players would crowd round to see how he was and Brian would push through and ask: 'What number was he?' And he would sort him out!

After he left, I brought in Mark Dennis from Birmingham. Ron Saunders was manager at the time and he said that, as I was a pal, he would warn me that Mark was prone to take the hard-man image to extremes.

Even so, I met with him and he acted like the perfect gentleman. He called me Sir and asked about my family. It was like talking to an angel, so I signed him.

I soon found out he was quite happy to kick not just the opposition, but also his own team-mates!

I remember his first touch on his debut was to take a throw-in and the ball slipped from his grasp. The striker charged on to it and Peter Shilton had to come flying out to rescue the ball. As he lay on the ground, he asked: 'Who the hell have we just signed?'

But, like a lot of the game's hard-men, he is a lovely guy and he helps a lot of the ex-players.

Jim Steele was a real hard-man but he was also a gifted footballer and was named man of the match in the 1976 FA Cup Final, when we also had David Peach and Peter Rodrigues. They knew how to handle themselves but they were good players too.

Even some of the strikers could put it about on the field. Peter Osgood – God bless him – was not averse to dishing out a few bangs – even to the likes of Norman Hunter.

I remember one incident between them which ended with Hunter literally chasing Ossie round the pitch after Peter had whacked him.

Gordon Hill was the referee and just stood there with his hands on his hips, waiting for it to end and to see who kicked who. I don't think I ever saw Ossie run as fast as that – and the ball was nowhere to be seen.

But again, Ossie could play. I remember we went down to ten men against Pompey and Ossie had to drop back into the centre of defence and he was superb. He could handle himself and was not averse to throwing a few elbows. He told me afterwards he could play for another 20 years at centre-back because he could just kick people. We went on and won that game. I am very proud that, in my 12 years as manager, we played Pompey five times and won the lot.

Then you had Keegan, Channon and Ball, who were not exactly sinners but they were all tough with an inner strength.

There is a big difference between being a hard-man and a wrong 'un. I could live with having a few rascals in the side as long as they were not villains.

I did have a couple of wrong 'uns. I won't name names but if you read my recently published autobiography then you might work it out!

We certainly had our share of rascals but I always knew where they were and what they were up to. In fact, I used to warn them that if they wanted a night out they should go up to London, where I would be less likely to hear about it.

It got worse after we won the FA Cup in 1976 because everyone wanted to know us. We were invited everywhere and fans were delighted if they could buy players a drink.

A couple of nights after we had beaten Manchester United at Wembley, we were invited to a casino-type place, where the drinks were flowing, supporters were having their pictures taken with the cup and everyone was letting their hair down.

The club secretary, Keith Honey, had had a frantic few weeks, so it was his chance to unwind. He had a few drinks and ended up being helped home, leaving the players on their own.

Next morning the phone rang and it was the chairman, George Reader. He said: 'Manager... where is the bloody cup?'

I said it was with Keith Honey and he said: 'No it isn't... we've lost the FA Cup.' I was in my office at the time and the team were just starting to come in. I could hear footsteps outside my office and some clanging. I waited and then it went quiet.

I opened the door and there was the cup, lying on its side. I went down to the dressing room and the players were all there, reading their newspapers and looking entirely innocent.

It turned out that Jim Steele and Peter Osgood had been the last to leave, so they took the cup with them and put it in the boot of Ossie's car.

They stopped at one of these all-night burger vans and, of course, everyone cheered them and wanted autographs. The owner said the drinks were on him and asked: 'Do you want it in a mug or a cup?'

Ossie went to the boot, lifted out the trophy and said: 'Put it in that!'

He then took the trophy home and slept with it!

There is no manual which teaches you how to manage that sort of situation – nor the one which blew up after a UEFA Cup tie at Norrkoping. We drew 0-0 but went out on away goals after a 2-2 draw at The Dell.

Afterwards, the players went out and everything seemed fine until Mark Wright and Steve Moran were arrested at the airport and falsely accused of rape.

They had not done anything wrong and were completely cleared. In Mark's case, it was mistaken identity as he was not even with the girl.

Some players had been chatting to a nurse, who did not have a problem with it. But when she went home and got in very late, she told her flat-mate about it.

I don't know whether she embellished the story but this other woman persuaded her to report it so I had to deal with the police and the players, who ended up spending a couple of nights in the cells.

Alan Woodford, one of the directors and a well-known local solicitor, stayed behind with them and sorted it all out.

I had to talk to their families and reassure them everything was OK and I also had to deal with the press. It was well before the internet and social media, so I thought we had managed to keep it quiet. But in those days, the journalists travelled on the same flight and noticed that the two players were missing.

Of course, it was a massive story, although it was never as bad as it was made out to be. When the players flew back, the reporters were waiting for them. We managed to smuggle them out of the airport and I put them up at my house.

Thankfully, it did not affect their careers but it was certainly a tough time for them and for the club.

The other time I had to keep the press at arm's length like that was when Bruce Grobbelaar was accused of match-fixing in *The Sun*. He was cleared in court but, of course, there was massive media interest.

I had to give the press enough to keep them happy, but I had to keep them away from the training ground so that Alan Ball could keep working with the team.

So, it is certainly fair to say that Southampton have had their fair share of hard-men and characters. There is a common theme in that they are among the toughest players in the game – and yet they are also the nicest guys off the field.

They all have hearts of gold – and legs of steel.

Mind you, I still would not want to meet any of them on a dark night… especially after they have had a few drinks.

But they all have great stories to tell and this book will give an insight into some of the best and hardest men ever to play for this great club. Enjoy.

Inside Foreword (geddit?)

by Matthew Le Tissier

YOU MAY be wondering why Matthew Le Tissier is featuring in a book about Saints and Sinners. In fact, I am wondering that myself... I am probably only here to help sell it!

Let's be honest, I was never the toughest character on the pitch. I did receive a lot of yellow cards but they were more for arguing than anything else, though I did manage to pick up two red cards.

The first, amazingly, was for violent conduct in an FA Cup quarter-final replay at Norwich in March 1992. We were 1-0 up and heading for a semi-final against Sunderland, who were in the second tier at the time. But then I lost my head... and my best chance of playing in the FA Cup Final.

Just after I played the ball down the line, Robert Fleck raked his studs down my Achilles so late that neither the referee nor the linesman saw it.

Stupidly, I retaliated. The crowd's roar prompted the referee to turn round just in time to see me give Fleck a forearm smash... with a kick on the shin for good measure. I didn't even wait for the red card, I just kept on walking. Even I was not going to argue with that decision.

Afterwards, I sat in the dressing room absolutely furious with myself for letting him goad me into putting us a man down. It wasn't long before we were two men down as Barry Horne joined me – and that was the cup run gone.

The second red card came in October 1995 in a live Sky game against Liverpool. I probably only made two tackles in the whole of my career and both were in this match.

Dave Merrington was the manager and he decided to use me as the holding midfielder. The theory was that I would sit in front of the back four and spray killer passes around. The flaw in that plan was the role also required some tackling. My first yellow card that night was for a foul on Ian Rush. Normally, I wouldn't have gone anywhere near him – except possibly to compare noses. We were 1-0 up at the time and I mistimed the tackle. It wasn't malicious, I just didn't have the pace to get there before he played the ball.

Then in the second half, I did it again. We were chasing the game at 2-1 down and I went through a defender just after he had played the ball and Dermot Gallagher gave me a second yellow. He told me later he felt awful having to send off a club legend, but I can't complain. It was a fair decision and that's all I ever asked for.

But although I was never a hard-man myself, I played alongside plenty. And I was glad of it.

If there wasn't a lot of protection from the referee, it was good to know you had a minder like Jimmy Case, who really looked out for me when I first got into the side. If anyone kicked me, Jimmy was right there. It might have taken a while – he was clever like that – but you knew that he would dish out his own special form of retribution.

He was probably the hardest player I ever played alongside, not just because he was tough but because he was calculating and clever. That sets him apart from the likes of Mark Dennis, who was not clever or subtle. And I would have to say the same about my good friend Francis Benali.

It was not just that Jimmy knew how to do it without it looking bad, but that he knew when to do it – he would sometimes wait until the following game or even the next season.

He must have had a little black book and when the fixtures came out he would go through them and match names to games – you're getting one there, you're getting one here…

Thankfully, I never played against him – it was bad enough facing him in training! I remember being on the receiving end of a few whacks just to keep me in my place as a young lad.

I could be a bit cocky, you'll be surprised to hear. I remember once we were playing defence against attack. We had to take on four defenders and Jimmy sitting just in front.

He was the only one closing down so we had plenty of time and space and I was messing about. Jimmy didn't like what I was doing. I laid the ball off and three seconds later he gave me a real whack and said: 'Don't take the piss, son.' I got the message.

Just think what he would have done to me if I had ever played against him, especially if I had tried to nutmeg him – and knowing me I would have done.

But it was great to have him alongside me, as well as the likes of Glenn Cockerill and Barry Horne, who wasn't celebrated as a hard-man but he was strong in the tackle.

After Jimmy, I guess the next hardest player I played with would be Terry Hurlock. He wasn't quite as subtle as Jimmy, but he was another I was pleased to have on my team.

I remember facing him when he was at Millwall and I was frightened every time he came over my side of the pitch. With his long hair and menacing snarl, I didn't want to go anywhere near him.

But he wasn't just a thug, he could play a bit. He won Player of the Year at Rangers and you don't do that by just grafting and kicking. I realised when I started training with him that he had a lot of ability, which got overlooked at times because of his image.

The other thing which people did not realise is that he was an absolute diamond off the pitch, a gentle giant who would do anything for anyone.

Then we had Neil Ruddock, who was only a young kid but already a huge personality. Even in his early 20s, he had a presence on the pitch and in the dressing room.

I was good mates with him back then and he didn't mind laying one on me in training if he felt it was needed, though generally he didn't try and do me when we faced each other.

He was still strong in the tackle and let you feel it but he didn't really go for me, although he did catch me at Anfield when we lost 4-2 and I scored twice. I had already gone through and slotted the ball past the keeper when he finally caught up and raked his studs down my ankle. I made sure I did not show that it hurt me – but it did!

He was another player who didn't control his temper very well, as Craig Short found out when Neil lumbered 50 yards to headbutt him!

But even then he was a massive personality. We had a lot of them in the dressing room back then. It was Chris Nicholl's first big job and I don't think he was prepared for that.

We had some big established players and a few strong youngsters coming through, most notably Alan Shearer, who was mentally the toughest player I ever encountered.

He had a determination like you would not believe. He just wanted to get better and he worked so hard on every aspect of his game. And he had a strong personality too.

Even as a youngster, he was ready to offer an opinion and he was not afraid to battle with the likes of Kevin Moore, Russell Osman and Kevin Bond in training. They were hard players, but he would set himself against them in training.

They were senior pros but he could look after himself. He was no respecter of reputations, as he showed when he scored that hat-trick on his debut against Tony Adams' Arsenal. Being a hard-man is not just about kicking people, it is about being mentally tough too, and Shearer had that… and still does.

But if you are looking at physical players who could lose it in the heat of battle, then look no further than a couple of left-backs: Mark Dennis and Francis Benali. Mark is the only footballer I knew who would sharpen his metal studs before a game. I found it really scary. He had the longest studs ever.

If I could ever get away with moulded studs, then I would. If I had to have studs, I used the shortest ones possible. I used them for grip. Denno used them as part of his armoury. I can still remember the noise they made as he walked across the tiled floor. I would not have wanted to have been on the receiving end. I did face him when he went to QPR, but I just got rid of the ball as quickly as I could that day.

Mind you, he did provide the assist for a goal. I was in the box as a corner came across and he cleared it off the line and the ball hit my thigh and went in. I decided against thanking him!

He had a short temper and didn't really know when to dish it out and when to bide his time. If he hadn't been like that – and but for the form of Kenny Sansom – then he would definitely have played for England. He was one of the best crossers of the ball I ever saw.

And then there is Franny with his 11 red cards, which is impressive for a centre-forward turned full-back. He is such a nice guy off the field but a monster on it.

I have known him since we were 15, so I got to recognise the signs when the red mist was coming down. Even though he was one of my best mates, I felt I did not know him at all when that happened.

I could be speaking to him and he would look right through me, and I would know the next chance he got he was going to smash into someone. It is odd knowing someone so well and yet not knowing them at all on the field.

The really funny thing is that his lovely wife, Karen, still thinks he was unlucky with his red cards and that he never meant to hurt anyone. It is the funniest conversation!

I guess she just sees what a lovely, gentle guy he is at home and can't imagine he would do anything that bad, but he would kick his own granny if that is what it took to win.

She is right in one sense. Franny is the nicest bloke you could wish to meet. I have never seen him drunk, he is a devoted husband and father and a loyal friend.

And, of course, his charity run was absolutely phenomenal. I am totally in awe of anyone who can run one marathon, let alone two a day for three weeks. It would have been impossible to have imagined him winning the Barclays Spirit of the Game award when he was piling up all those red cards.

He followed a long line of tough full-backs here. I never saw Denis Hollywood or Brian O'Neil play, but I have been told the stories. Yet when I have met them, they are the nicest blokes.

This book features a lot of good friends and good footballers but I see from Carlton Palmer's chapter that he was a bit upset by some comments I made in my autobiography. I'm not going to get involved in a slanging match. Like the rest of the book, it makes for a good read.

It is a recurring theme that the hardest players are often the nicest guys off it. I don't know what that says about me… I was not a tough guy on the field, so I guess that makes me a complete bastard off it!

Denis Hollywood and Brian O'Neil

PICTURE THE scene: Mick Channon, former England international and now a successful racehorse trainer, is staging a posh party for the great and the good of the racing world.

The champagne is flowing, canapes are being handed out to sporting and entertainment celebrities and he introduces two of his former Southampton team-mates to Scouse comedian Jimmy Tarbuck.

Instantly, the television star taps the side of his glass and calls for hush across the crowded room.

'Ladies and gentlemen, I would like to introduce you to two of the dirtiest bastards I have ever seen on a football field… Denis Hollywood and Brian O'Neil!'

Even now, 40 years since they last kicked anyone in anger, there is still no more fitting epitaph for two of the hardest but most likeable players ever to pull on the red and white stripes.

Hollywood chuckles: 'It still has a good ring to it. We did put ourselves about – but they were good times. We played hard on and off the field and loved every minute of it. We have some great memories.'

And the pair still share that close bond today, collapsing into fits of laughter as they sit in Hollywood's pristine kitchen reliving the good old days. For two hours, it is like watching a slick comedy routine as they fall about helplessly at shared memories and 'do-you-remember-whens'.

21

Inevitably, the starting point is the fabled tour to the Far East, already well documented but still as fresh as ever to the duo.

O'Neil laughs: 'I remember going for a night out with Ken Jones when we were on tour in Japan. He said he was going to drink me under the table, so we went to a bar and got some beers in. We really went for it.

'I drank so much I slumped forward and my head hit the table. Ken shouted "I've won, I've won, you Geordie bastard!" I just about heard him and slurred, "Two more beers!" and we kept going. In the end, I won.'

Denis laughs: 'Jimmy Gabriel had been talking to a couple of Americans and saying that Brian was the best midfielder in the country – then they looked across and saw him slumped on the table having wet himself!

'Brian was in a right state when we came out of the bar and no taxi would take him. So we had to hide him in a doorway while we flagged one down. Eventually, we got him back to the hotel and negotiated this revolving door.

'Terry Paine came up to him, pointed and said "O'Neil, you've pissed your trousers!" Mick Channon said, "I don't know why you're laughing, Terry…. they are your trousers!" He threw them away after that.'

O'Neil, of course, was famous for borrowing other people's clothes, including football boots, never owning a pair in his life and frequently rummaging in team-mates' wardrobes for clothes to wear.

For this interview, he is wearing a Sheffield Wednesday training top, courtesy of his son-in-law, a certain David Prutton.

'I never owned a pair of football boots, maybe one pair, I'm not sure. But generally, I just used to borrow some. Sometimes they did not even match or were different sizes.

'I was watching a match recently and saw some players wearing one pink boot and one blue one – so really I was ahead of my time. Brian O'Neil – trend-setter. Who'd have thought it?

'One day I arrived at The Dell a bit late, so I just picked up the first boots that came to hand and put them on. They were John McGrath's and they were massive – at least two or three sizes too big. All I could do was side-foot the ball… but I did score with a "well-placed side-foot shot!" I had no choice but to hit it like that!'

It was one of his 19 goals in 171 appearances for Southampton, who paid a then club-record fee of £75,000 to bring the Bedlington Terrier from Burnley to The Dell in May 1970.

O'Neil had already established himself as one of the best midfielders in the country having been named in England's original World Cup-winning squad before missing out to Nobby Stiles.

He was still at the top of his game when Ted Bates lured him to the south coast, where he continues to live. It was a relationship which proved fruitful for both the player and his often frustrated and bewildered manager, who could only turn a blind eye to the antics of his latest capture.

'I was not just a hard-man. I could play a bit too. I had a football brain and I could score goals. I even made it into the original squad for the 1966 World Cup, but I got cut from the final party – as Mick Channon loves to tell anyone who will listen.

'Ted just let us get on with things and I would run through a barn door for him. He was a gentleman and I knew instinctively that I could play for him right from our first meeting.

'I was at Burnley and came in to Turf Moor one day and the chairman Bob Lord said, "O'Neil, come with me." So we got in his Rolls-Royce and drove up to the top of the moor, where a little fella got out of his car.

'Bob asked if I knew who it was and I said it was Ted Bates. Bob said Ted wanted a word and I could tell immediately that he was a gentleman and I knew he would suit me down to the ground.

'I was just pleased to get out of Burnley because I could not play for Jimmy Adamson. Ted asked me to come down and I said I would be there next day. I didn't even bother to discuss terms.

'These days, it is all agents and image rights and crap like that. I just wanted to play. It wasn't about money at all. We got £30 per point and you would kick your granny for the £60 win bonus.

'We all loved Ted. On Friday nights, before an away game, he would often sort out an outing to the pictures. He would ring up and book a block of 16 seats and in those days they used to have an interval when a woman would come round selling ice-creams.

'Ken Wimshurst used to say to Ted, "Please daddy, get us an ice-cream... pleeeease!" Ted said he didn't mind paying but wasn't getting them, but Ken would keep on saying "Please daddy" until Ted went and queued.

'They were great times. It was a family club where everyone knew everyone from the office girls to the directors. We played for fun and we enjoyed it – we were all mates together.

'No one was jealous of anyone else, we were close to the fans and went to the same pubs. Football was different then. Nowadays there is so much money at stake that it is all too serious.

'If one of the lads was doing a charity event, we all used to go. Nowadays I think clubs almost have to force players to do community events. You shouldn't have to do that.

'You could have a laugh with the fans then. I used to run out and put my hand down my shorts and count "One... two... three!" The supporters loved it. I tell you, that Southampton crowd took some beating. The Dell was such a small ground that the spectators were right on top of you.

'Nowadays you have big screens but then it was The Albion Band entertaining the fans and they would march off just as we ran out. Terry Paine always used to volley the ball right at them as hard as he could, forcing them to scatter.

'And then there was the time, I ran out wearing a battered old trilby for a £5 bet with a mate of Mick Channon's. I never did get the fiver. Nowadays that would be a booking before I had even kicked off.'

Both agree that with millions now at stake on every result, the game has lost some of its soul. Players are perceived as aloof, detached from the fans behind their remote-controlled iron gates, and often not even socialising together.

Hollywood adds: 'First and foremost, we were all great mates. We won together and lost together and drank together. We would go to the Gateway pub in Northlands Road and chat with the fans and no one gave us any bother.

'Brian was just up for a laugh and was always showing his privates there. One night, the woman behind the bar said he was being filthy and she was going to call the police. She came back a few minutes later and said she had reported that Gerry O'Brien to the police. Poor old Gerry wasn't even there!

'These days someone would have a mobile phone in your face so modern footballers hide away more. I am just glad they weren't around when we were out on the town. I dread to think what sort of pictures they would have got!'

For all the advancements in the modern game, Hollywood is not convinced it is a better spectacle than the days when a meaty challenge could provoke almost as big a cheer as a goal.

'Football is now very different. There is no tackling, no physical contact. Is it any better? I don't know. It is all about possession – like a chess match at times.

'Some of the foreign players have marvellous skill – but will they run through a brick wall the way we did? We would get hurt but we would just get on with it. There was none of this tweaking something. Your leg was either broken or it wasn't.

'I remember the time Campbell Forsyth broke a leg. Three of us collided and the trainer, Jimmy Gallagher, ran on with a sponge. That was all you had in those days – and he told Campbell, "You'll be OK in a minute!" Campbell screamed "Fuck off, it's broken!"

'I wouldn't say I was dirty. I would call myself robust. I played 300 games and only got sent off once. That was when I was about 17 and it was at Swindon.

'I fell on the ground and the other player hit me, so I hit him back and got sent off. I vowed never again.

'I never set out to hurt anyone – too badly. I just wanted my side to win. I thought I was fair but tough. That's the way football was. There were plenty of opponents waiting to kick you if you did not stand up for yourself.

'I didn't verbally abuse the opposition. I would just give them a look. And I never moaned at referees. In those days, you accepted the decision and never argued back.'

Both players will tell you – with a twinkle in the eye – that they were hard but fair. Yet both landed in hot water with the FA within weeks of each other in 1971, with O'Neil collecting a then record ban of nine weeks.

Ironically, it was surpassed by his son-in-law some 34 years later, when Prutton was suspended for a record ten games after pushing referee Alan Wiley in protest at a red card.

O'Neil laughs: 'I always say to him that at least I never pushed a ref. I got called before the FA after I had put Jeff Astle into the enclosure... although I thought he made a meal of it.

'He said a few words at the hearing – nothing in my favour, I know that. I got a nine-week ban and afterwards I said to him, "If I ever see you again, I will go out of my way to get you."

'But it was like that in those days. You had to look after yourself and your team-mates. I had a reputation because I would not take any prisoners – and that followed me around.

'But certainly if anyone ever got Mick Channon, I always made sure I got them back for him. Everyone would be crowded round wanting to see how he was. I just asked, "What number was he?" But I never went over the top or injured anyone badly – I was just hard.'

Around the same time that O'Neil collected his nine-week ban – in those days suspensions were set in weeks not games – Hollywood was handed an almost equally draconian sentence.

He recalls: 'At the time, the FA were based at Lancaster Gate and I ended up travelling up with Jimmy Gabriel, who was a real hard-man. He never got the credit he deserved because he could play. He would bring the ball out of defence, beat the striker, draw the man and pass it to Brian, who used to have a free run at goal.

'I remember when Jimmy stuck the nut on Allan Clarke of Leeds. Clarke went down and Jimmy saw the referee out of the corner of his eye and went down too – and got sent off on the stretcher.

'We went up on the same train and Jimmy had reams and reams of paper with things he was going to say and evidence he was going to present. I thought, "You've wasted your time there, son, you've got no chance. You headbutted him right in front of the referee."

'We got to Lancaster Gate, which was quite intimidating. Jimmy went in first and came out punching the air because – somehow – he had got off. Apparently, the referee had got all the facts wrong in his report. I went in next and I was only up for six bookings or something relatively trivial – but suddenly they started talking about a three-month ban. I turned to Ted Bates and said, "You've got to help me here." In the end, I got seven weeks while Jimmy got off.

'Depending how the fixtures fell, seven weeks could mean seven games or a lot more – or a lot less if there were postponements.'

It was quite possibly a case of reputation preceding the pair following the infamous insult from Liverpool legend Bill Shankly, who labelled Southampton an 'Alehouse' team after their 1-0 defeat at The Dell in September 1970. It was the Merseysiders' first defeat of the season after Alec Lindsay was bullied into conceding an own goal.

The quote became embellished to read Alehouse Brawlers, a tag which stuck. Certainly there were plenty of drinkers in the side and they knew how to scrap – but they could play too.

And while the victory was more deserved than Shankly's sour grapes suggested, both players concede he might have had reason to be unhappy with one particular challenge by John McGrath on Liverpool striker Alun Evans, who was left concussed and swallowed his tongue.

O'Neil laughs: 'I remember the game where we got labelled Alehouse Footballers or Alehouse Brawlers as it became. As I recall, John McGrath tackled Alun Evans two-footed – in the chest. He should have been sent off but it was just a drop ball or something. I thought their player was dead!

'But it was a harsh label because we murdered them that day. They were a good side but we played them off the park and could have won by more. The fact is Shanks did not like getting beat and he could not take it.

'The tag stuck. It was an awful thing to say and even now people will ask if I was one of the Alehouse Brawlers. We were proper men but we could play. They had a great side but did not like teams who stopped them playing.

'We played at Anfield and I remember going for a challenge with Emlyn Hughes, who chickened out. I said, "If I don't get you now, I will get you in the tunnel." It was just mind games really but he would shit himself. Emlyn would come up to our team hotel on a Friday night to have a word with Hughie Fisher. I remember him saying goodbye and then rushing back in a few minutes later squeaking "They've only gone and stolen my car."

'Being a footballer, he would not walk more than a few yards so he parked it on the pavement outside the hotel and someone had nicked it. He said he wasn't too bothered about the car but he had £800 in the glove compartment.

'He and a couple of their players had opened a supermarket and he was supposed to give them their share the next day – and it was a lot of money back then, when we used to get £30 per point.'

Hollywood adds: 'That Alehouse comment was an insult. It was disgraceful really. It was just because we had beaten them. I can only recall one bad incident and that was the tackle on Alun Evans by John McGrath, or Jake as he was known.

'It certainly left their lad in a bad way and Shankly was furious as he got stretchered off, but I don't think he was right to tar us all with that particular brush.'

Sadly, McGrath died suddenly on Christmas Day 1998 after carving out a successful career first as a promotion-winning manager at both Port Vale and Preston and then as an after-dinner speaker. His hilarious repertoire of anecdotes and quips largely centred around his own image as a goliath in stripes, hitching up his shorts to show off his thighs to the man he would be marking.

There was no doubting his physical presence on the field, where opponents would literally bounce off him – always assuming they had not been intimidated into steering well clear of the imposing figure built like the proverbial outhouse.

O'Neil laughs: 'John McGrath was incredible. He was a big hard lad who used to put deep heat on his bollocks to get himself fired up. He would cover himself with oil, put vaseline on top of his head, drink a jar of honey straight down and then headbutt the lockers before taking the field. He would put his shirt on and the hairs on his chest would come through it!

'I would wind him up beforehand asking who he would be marking and then saying whoever it was would be certain to get a couple of goals. It made him even more determined not to let them score.

'He was a great character both on and off the pitch. We went on tour to the Far East and big Jake was in the front row at a snake-charming demonstration. He was mesmerised by it. The snake-charmer had warned everyone not to make any sudden movements as the snake would have them... and Jake was completely motionless.

'Then I came out of a bar pissed and yelled "Oi Jake!" He was too scared to move and just managed to growl "Fuck off!" out of the corner of his mouth. So I shouted again... and he fainted!

'John was sharing a room with Jimmy Gabriel and the beds were only a foot or so off the floor. I said, "It's a pity about that guy last night." John asked "What guy?" and I said some bloke had died, a snake had got him.

'Next morning, Jimmy had big black rings around his eyes. He had not slept a wink because every time John's arms touched the ground he would wake up screaming in panic. And I had made the whole thing up!'

By now, the pair are in full swing reminiscing about the foreign tours, which surpassed even the domestic drinking nights, of which there were many.

O'Neil laughs: 'Then there was the time we went on tour to El Salvador to play Chelsea in an exhibition match and found they were in the same hotel. There was a nightclub nearby, so we all went out together. At one point each night the lights would go out and when they came back on, the hostesses would give a little cabaret.

'One night, when the lights came back on, all the Chelsea lads were in a line on stage, kick-dancing... until a security guard with a machine gun ordered them off. There was no mucking about there!'

Hollywood adds: 'We stayed in the same hotel as the likes of Peter Osgood, Alan Hudson, Ron Harris, Peter Bonetti and Charlie Cooke – so you can imagine how that turned out. We would have swimming competitions with bottles of whisky on our heads.

'By the time we played Chelsea in the exhibition match, we knew their lads quite well so we arranged for it to be a draw. The stadium was packed and the first half was quite tame, and Ted said we were making it too obvious that it was going to be a draw.

'On the other hand, Dave Sexton read his players the riot act and, within ten minutes of the re-start, they were 4-0 up. We were probably all pissed anyway... I think we lost 8-3 in the end.

'We had some great trips abroad. When we were promoted to the First Division for the first time, we were all presented with gold Omega watches with a leather strap. We went on tour to Malaysia and Singapore and played some exhibition games against Leicester.

'We were given some fantastic bonuses along with some spending money so, by the time we got to Singapore, I had a lot of cash in my pocket. So I splashed out and bought a genuine Omega gold strap.

'It was one of my most treasured possessions. I really looked after it and only wore it occasionally in case it got lost or damaged. So when we went on holiday about 15 years ago, I hid it carefully in the house to keep it safe. To this day, I can't remember where I put it. I have turned the house upside down but never found it. When I eventually sell the house, there will be a reward if the buyer finds it.

'I remember going out to Seattle to see Tommy Jenkins when he was there with Harry Redknapp. They had to have a set quota of American players and Tommy said the keeper was useless. But he was loaded.

'One weekend, he took six of the single lads to Vegas. We stayed in a fantastic hotel with adjoining suites, there was champagne on arrival – the works. And he paid for everything. He wouldn't let us pay a dime.

'About a month later he was arrested for fraud and got ten years in jail. But we had a good time out of it.

'We used to go to Jersey to play golf. One night there was a big banquet, a real posh do with everyone in evening dress, but the bars were open all day there so we had been drinking for hours. Billy Butlin was the guest of honour and Terry Paine introduced him to the lads.

'Brian was slumped in his seat, out of it until Billy got to him. Brian grabbed his testicles and said, "How are your balls, Billy?" Billy just said they were fine and walked off.'

Of course, the wild nights out were not confined to when they were let off the leash abroad. It is fair to say Ted Bates kept the team on a very loose rein at home – as long as they never let him down when it came to matchday.

O'Neil says: 'Vodka and water was my tipple but I have not really drunk for ten or 12 years now. I'm not bothered about it now.

'I had enough for a lifetime when I was playing. We used to enjoy ourselves – but we never let it interfere with our game. We were always fighting fit for Saturday. And as long as we were doing it for him on the pitch, then Ted Bates was happy to turn a blind eye.

'There was a big drinking culture back then. It probably ruined a lot of players, but we knew when to do it. We did not go stupid before a game but afterwards we would murder it!

'We would start off in the Gateway pub and then, if we had won, we would go to the After Eight club in Shirley. And we would drink with the fans. These days you can't even get near players, let alone drink with them.'

Serious for a moment, Hollywood adds: 'That was the culture of the time and it ruined a few players. I think Jim Steele got caught up in it. He should have won a lot of caps for Scotland, he was that good.

'I got caught up with it too. I played in the first team at 17 and played for Scotland under-18s and under-23s and for the Great Britain side at Wembley. I should have kicked on from there, but I didn't.

'I stopped playing at 27. I had moved to Blackpool but it was a disaster and I only stayed a couple of months and then played a bit for Bath and Basingstoke, but I had lost something.

'It was not through lack of ability. It happened to a few players. Tommy Jenkins and Jim Steele could have done more, but then I look at the likes of George Best and think I was lucky to come out of it as I did.'

Hollywood arrived at The Dell via an unlikely route, which took him from his native Scotland via Ilford to the south coast and a whole new way of life.

'I was born in Glasgow but moved to Essex when I was 12 and came to Southampton at 15, which was a big upheaval. In fact, I was so homesick that I ran away from the club and went back to Essex. Ted Bates came up and brought me back.

'Spurs and West Ham had supposedly been interested in me and I desperately wanted to join them. But nothing concrete came of it and this scout Jimmy Thompson sent me down here. My gran had to ask where Southampton was!

'She told me not to sign anything but Ted was very persuasive and I signed there and then. I am very glad I did – and very glad that Ted came up and brought me back.

'I got £7 a week as an apprentice and the most I ever got as a basic wage was £65 a week, with £4 for a win and £2 for a draw. But we also had a crowd-related bonus. If the attendance was over 15,000 we got so much, and then a bit more for 18,000 and so on.

'Of course, when we got to the First Division for the first time, we were suddenly earning a fortune by our standards. We were getting crowds of 31,000 every week and halfway through the season the directors said they wanted to get rid of that clause – and we told them to get lost. Or words to that effect.

'We were all given two free season tickets and a lot of the lads used to sell theirs so that would give them a bit of extra money because we were not on a lot. I tell you, that £4 win bonus was a powerful motivating factor. Nowadays you can pay that for a cup of coffee, but it was a lot to us.

'We used to get an allocation of free tickets to games. I remember asking for more only for Ted Bates to tell me, "You've had your quota. If your friends won't pay to watch you, who will?"

'I started in midfield and that's where I wanted to play. But I was very quick and could win the ball, so Ted moved me into defence.

'I lived with Cliff Huxford in Shirley for three or four years. He and his wife took me in and Cliff would have me out in the back yard practising block tackles for hours. And they hurt because he was the hardest player I had ever come across.

'I was hard but I still maintain I was not dirty. I never set out to hurt anyone but sometimes I would take the man as well as the ball. Then I would just give it to the lads who could do something with it.

'I remember Ted saying "You knock 'em down, I'll pick 'em up!' He knew the value of a good hard tackle, especially early in the game.'

O'Neil adds: 'On a Friday, Ted would set up a Subbuteo pitch and flick players around for tactics. One day, he flicked my figure and said "Brian, you're up against Tony Currie." I said, "I know boss, I have been thinking about it all week."

'He gave a knowing look and said, "Well, just feel him out early on." Anyway, the match came round and I went straight in to hammer him… but I never touched him. He just went over on his ankle and got carried off and I looked over to see Ted beaming, giving a double thumbs-up.

'Ted was comical, we loved him. He had this drill where he would be the only defender and he would play the ball out to one of us in the centre circle and we would have to run through against him and shoot. Of course, we all used to blast it as hard as we could at his balls or his stomach. He would be doubled up and we would be in a heap laughing.'

The players delighted in winding up the manager at every opportunity, with Hollywood recalling: 'Before games in Manchester, we used to stay at a hotel in Wilmslow. It was very classy. The directors and management would sit on one table with the players at another – and Ted would carefully watch what we ate.

'Some people on the next table had some enormous knickerbocker glory ice-creams, so I said, "Let's order six of them and see what Ted says."

'The waitress turned up with a tray of massive ice-creams and Ted's face got redder and redder until he exploded, "It's not a bloody party!" We had no intentions of eating them, we just wanted to see what he would say!'

However, the pranks were not reserved simply for the manager. There were plenty at each other's expense too.

Hollywood laughs: 'I bought this expensive white mackintosh from Tyrrell and Green. It was expensive but I thought it looked good. The lads all laughed and said I looked like Inspector Clouseau.

'Anyway, coming back from one away trip on the train, I hung it on a hook in the compartment – schoolboy error! When we got back to Southampton, I asked Tommy Jenkins where my coat was. He just laughed and laughed.

'Eventually, he stopped giggling enough to tell me, "Me and Bobby Stokes were hanging it out of the window, Den. It was so funny, it billowed like a sail… Then Stokesy let it go and it flew off like a balloon!" I was fuming.

'I didn't think anything more about it, but the following week I turned up at The Dell and there was a package for me – and it was my coat. One of our supporters worked for British Rail and knew roughly where it was and made a special trip to get it back.

'Obviously, it was quite dirty – you would think he would have got it laundered. But it shows how special Saints fans are that he went to all that trouble for me.'

O'Neil then begins another round of anecdotes by recalling the time he was laid up after a cartilage operation.

He laughs: 'I was in the Royal South Hants having my knee done and the lads would bring in vodka or beer. Then, one day, Tommy Jenkins decided to bring a dog in to cheer me up as he knew I loved dogs. Dennis hid his pug in his jacket and the nurses had a laugh about it, but one of them must have told the matron.

'She opened the door, saw the dog lying on the bed and snapped "I hope that's dead." So we hid it in the wardrobe.

'I had a private room which was at the end of an old ladies' ward. One old girl wandered in, so I gave her a vodka and had a chat. She died the next day.

'Denis reckons she was fine before she saw me, probably just visiting! But the nurse said she was on her way out and at least had a smile before she died.'

Both players had their own brush with death when O'Neil drove home one night. Hollywood recalls: 'I put my hands over Brian's eyes while he was driving. It was madness really. I was directing him "Left a bit, right a bit…" It was like an episode of *The Golden Shot*!

'When I was an apprentice, I saved up for ages and bought a car. It was my pride and joy. I gave a few of the lads a lift and left them in the car when I stopped off in Bedford Place. I got back to find they had unscrewed every knob and button in the car – the gearstick, everything on the dashboard.'

That takes O'Neil neatly on to another driving story: 'I once borrowed Tommy Jenkins' car but it stalled by the Cowherds pub on the Avenue. I had had a few drinks, so I was in a right panic when a policeman turned up – but I think he recognised me because he pushed it and helped get it going!'

And from there, they move on to Hollywood giving a rather different sort of urine sample…

O'Neil laughed: 'We were one of the first clubs to get a sauna and Denis Hollywood used to piss on the coals. It absolutely stank. Even the girls in the office could smell it and they complained.

'Ted Bates put up a notice saying the next person to pee on the coals would be hauled before the directors. So we threw away the water in the bucket and Denis just pissed in the ladle, so the next person in there would throw it on the coals.

'It turned out to be Fred Kemp and we were killing ourselves laughing as we saw him being frogmarched up to the office with his hands behind his back like a criminal.

'And then, there was the time we locked Terry Paine in the sauna. We just left him there and wedged the door shut with a broom.

'No one particularly liked Terry, but he was a great player who had a fantastic partnership with Ron Davies. The goals big Ron scored. If he was playing today, you would not be able to buy him. What a player.

'If I won the ball in midfield and pushed it wide to Terry, I would just run back to the halfway line for kick-off because if Terry crossed and Ron was on the end of it, then we would score.

'Terry could be a good laugh but he was tough on the field. Lads who played against him said they could never get him back because he was clever and never went in for a 50-50 ball.

'I remember Terry even did Ron Harris and Chopper never went near him again. But Terry was a great player for Southampton. I would never take that away from him. I get on better with him now after all these years, but at the time he was not that popular in the dressing room.'

Hollywood said: 'Terry could look after himself, don't you worry about that. The likes of Tommy Smith and Ron Harris got a lot of publicity as hard-men – but they were no harder than some of the players we had at Southampton. People like Jimmy Gabriel could teach them a thing or two.

'But the hardest player I ever played with was Cliff Huxford. I don't care what anyone says, he was not nasty – he was not smart enough to be nasty. He had thighs like tree trunks and he lived for Southampton Football Club. He was incredible.

'They were very different times and every team used to have a few hard-men. Leeds had an image of being tough but they were more sneaky than hard. They just had this aura and reputation.

'I had some run-ins with Mike Summerbee. He was a big centre-forward when he started at Swindon, but when he moved to Manchester City they put him out on the right – and increased the width of the pitch to the maximum.

'That brought him on to my flank and there was no way I was going to let him past me. I would always try and get in first – but he could look after himself. He used to stop me in the tunnel and say, "Get your pads on, you little bastard!" He could put the odd sneaky tackle in.

'When City moved Summerbee wide, they made Francis Lee centre-forward. Someone hammered him and he thought it was me. He kept saying, "I'll get you, you little bastard."

'They got a corner and, while everyone was watching the ball, he stuck the nut right on my nose. I was seeing stars – but I never went down.

'In those days, you could get away with anything because there were no television replays. It is probably better now if it cuts out the sneaky fouls. There is nothing wrong with a strong, fair tackle but I don't like the off-the-ball stuff.

'I also used to have a few tussles with Harry Redknapp when he was at West Ham. A few years ago, when I was working for the Civil Aviation Authority, the Hammers were playing Liverpool at Upton Park and my boss wanted to go. I didn't really want to ring Harry, but he kept on at me so I rang and spoke to the secretary, who gave me the number of the training ground.

'Frank Lampard Sr answered and I said, "Hi, it's Denis Hollywood. Can I speak to Harry?" Frank came back and said, "He'll be with you in a minute, he's just putting his pads on!" That was quality.'

Hollywood eventually moved to Blackpool in 1972, with O'Neil staying at The Dell until 1974 as new manager Lawrie McMenemy tried to encourage a bit more discipline in a bid to curb some of the off-field excesses.

He wanted the players to wear suits, which O'Neil hated, arguing that as long as he was performing in matches then it should not matter what he wore to the ground. Not that he was any smarter on the field, with his trademark baggy shorts, rolled-down socks and lack of shin pads, which would be outlawed today.

However, one day, even O'Neil took it to extremes when he reported for training looking and smelling like a tramp.

He laughed: 'I used to help a mate on his farm. He was on his own so I gave him a hand with some electric fencing one morning, so I was a bit late when Mick Channon came to pick me up for training.

'I didn't have time to get changed, so I arrived for training in my filthy old work clothes and wellies covered in shit. Lawrie McMenemy went mad and warned me I would be out if I ever turned up like that again. The lads thought it was funny – but they weren't impressed with the smell.

'Ted was a hard act to follow, but Lawrie proved himself. We thought maybe he didn't know as much about football, but he knew people. He surrounded himself with experienced players who knew what to do and who had something to say.

'He should have been club president really. He was the obvious choice, but maybe the board didn't want someone with a strong opinion. In fact, I would have made him manager when Ronald Koeman left.

'A lot of people had the knives out for him when he came to the club, me included, because Ted had been like a father figure to us and suddenly it was all changing. I really admire the way Lawrie came through it and the success he had. But to be fair, Lawrie never came down hard on us. We were naughty but not bad.'

Without the financial rewards that modern players receive, both worked hard to make a living after hanging up their boots – or in O'Neil's case, hanging up someone else's boots.

Hollywood worked in the docks, then at Fawley oil refinery and finally at the air traffic control centre in Swanwick while O'Neil grafted, digging holes and laying pipes – and helping out at Channon's stables, where he would muck out the horses and help out wherever needed.

Hollywood recalls: 'Brian would often get to Mick's at 5am and do odd jobs like raking the stones outside the house. One morning it was pitch black and Brian heard movement, so he assumed Mick was getting up. So he hid in the bushes and leapt out and shouted "Boo!" But it was Jimmy Tarbuck, who yelled, "You almost gave me a heart attack!" Mick wasn't happy.'

O'Neil did have the odd game in the Southampton Sunday League and despite scoring some trademark thumping goals, there was little sign of his ferocious tackling.

When some of his team-mates complained he had let the other side score too easily, he explained at that level players could not stand up to his tackling. His opponents all had to go to work the following day and he did not want to hurt them.

Now Hollywood enjoys retirement with his wife Irene in Swanwick while O'Neil is devoted to his grandchildren and has high hopes that young Caleb Prutton might one day go into the family business.

He says: 'I called into a bookies recently to see if I could get odds of Caleb playing for England. They wouldn't give me a price but he is brilliant. I have never seen a kid with a left foot like him.

'He has a good pedigree in the family. But with me as a grandad and David Prutton as his father, maybe I should try and get odds of him being sent off for England?'

Terry Paine MBE

AS ONE of the best wingers of his generation, Terry Paine was a constant target for some of the game's destroyers, who were determined to stop him by whatever means necessary.

The likes of Ron 'Chopper' Harris and Norman 'Bites-your-legs' Hunter would think nothing of scything down the more creative players in full flight.

Less common was a wide man who could not only stand up to such X-rated challenges but also dish a bit out in return, which probably helps explain why Paine made 816 appearances for Saints in all competitions.

He made 709 league starts for Southampton, coming off the bench four times, and then made a further 106 appearances for Hereford to chalk up a then-league record of 819 games.

In 17 seasons at The Dell, he missed just 22 fixtures he could have played in. Not bad for a 5ft 7in winger who defenders were continually trying to kick.

He said: 'It is fair to say I could look after myself. In those days you expected defenders to kick lumps out of you, but somehow it was unacceptable if the winger did the same.

'I wouldn't say I was hard exactly. Mick Channon always used the word "cute". He often said I was too cute to get caught. That was a sharpness of mind.

'But I also learned how to jump or evade a tackle. John McGrath used to call me "Pogo" for that reason.

'No one really makes a tackle today but back then anything below the chest was acceptable, so you had to have a bit up top to realise that if you put your foot in then you could get it snapped off.

'The fact that I was on the receiving end of so many bad challenges, and yet still played so many games, shows I must have had some awareness of where everyone was on the field.

'What people don't realise is that if you have got your back to the line, then there is only one place tackles can come from. If you are always facing challenges, then you can't be tackled from behind.

'Today's wide players don't tend to do that, but Ted Bates always used to tell me to get the white of the line on the ball so that a challenge could not come from behind and, if it did, then I would get a free-kick.

'I didn't miss many club or international games, so I was either lucky or good at getting out of the way of tackles.'

He was also very adept at making sure defenders knew he could dish it out, as well as take it. For all that, he was dapper and debonair off the field and skilful and stylish on it. But Paine had a steely streak to his game.

'When you get a reputation it stays with you, regardless of whether or not you have done anything to earn it.

'I used to leave my foot in – there were ways of doing it. Why should some 6ft 4in guy be able to kick you without expecting something back? He might think twice if he knows he is going to get something back.

'If he knows you are a soft touch, he is more likely to come in hard. I never set out to do anyone or to break someone's leg. I just tried to deal with the treatment I was getting and hoped to come out on top.

'Defenders would make sure they would "impose themselves" with their first tackle and I would go in equally hard to let them know they were not in for an easy ride.'

Back then, it seemed every team had a hard-man – Southampton had several. That may go some way towards explaining why Paine stayed at the club for so long – he never wanted to play against any of them!

'The hardest player I ever encountered – and thank goodness he was on my team – was Cliff Huxford, who could run through walls. Even in training, he was tough.

'He was worth so much to us. He was a born winner and a destroyer and he was a vital part of the team. He gave me a bit of protection and really knew how to put a tackle in.

'Denis Hollywood was not far behind. I loved him, he was a hard lad if ever there was one. He and Mike Summerbee hated each other. And then there was "Docker" Walker – he was a real hard-man. They were players you wanted alongside you, not against you.

'There were no opponents I was actually scared of, but definitely a few I was "aware of" and kept an eye out for. It was important back then to have an enforcer in your side.

'It's more difficult now to impose yourself physically, but teams still need a ball-winner. But even those are becoming a dying breed.

'I can understand the need to protect the skilled players and the artists – and I might have benefited from that. But the crowd love a full-blooded tackle. We can't all be ballerinas and tackling should be part and parcel of the game.

'A lot of sly stuff went on and there was a lot of verbal intimidation. I remember playing against Northampton in January 1965 and Mike Everitt said, "I see you're playing for England on Wednesday. If you want to play, don't go past me." I just said OK. We drew 2-2 and I missed two penalties.

'I would say Ron "Chopper" Harris was probably the most brutal. I remember he did his knee in one game, but there were no substitutes back then. If your leg wasn't broken, they sent you back on.

'He got it bandaged up and came back on still hobbling. He ended up on my flank and I still remember him chasing me on one leg trying to get me!

'But there were a few about. Norman Hunter could dish it out. It was very rare that I ever tried to head a ball but, on one occasion he hit me with an elbow. Everything went numb and I had to feel to see if my teeth were still there.

'Nowadays the medical staff take over and pull players out with tweaks and strains or to protect them. Back then, we didn't have people telling us to leave it a week or two – and we wouldn't have listened if they had. I would never pull out of a game unless I absolutely had to.

'We needed the appearance money and hopefully the win bonus. And there were plenty of other pros lining up to take your place. Either we didn't have those kinds of minor injuries then or else we didn't know about them.

'I don't think we had as many of those injuries because studs and pitches were different. These days, studs stick in the ground and players can twist and hurt themselves. There are too many of those sorts of injury for it not to be a factor. Someone needs to look at that.

'In our day, the worst injury you could get was a cartilage problem. You would be out for three months and have a big plaster cast right up your thigh. These days, that is a very quick procedure and you can be back playing within a week or so.'

Despite his willingness to stand up for himself – as he diplomatically puts it – Paine was sent off just twice during his 17 years at The Dell, although he did amass plenty of bookings, mainly for proper fouls rather than retaliation.

'I tried to keep a cool head, otherwise there might be a temptation to do things out of frustration if the game was going against you. There is no point in getting involved in an incident which could see you sent off.

'These days, you see players talking back or making a rash challenge even when they are 4-0 up – it makes no sense.

'I did pick up a few bookings in my time, though, and I remember going before the FA, who were unhappy that I had been booked 47 times, but Ted Bates pointed out that I had played more than 450 games, so I got just a two-week ban.

'The game was different then and referees had a bit of personality, so you could have some banter with them. If you did that and got on with them, then often at the end of the match they would say they would not submit your booking.

'I remember having a go at Clive Thomas during a game and he said he might only get five out of ten for his performance, but he was in charge so I had to get on with it. You can't have a laugh like that now. They had more leeway then to use their common sense more. Now they are being judged and are not allowed to use their own discretion.

'It is not easy for referees because pundits like me dissect every decision on television. I work for Mnet Supersport in South Africa on their Premier League programmes and sometimes I can watch an incident five times from different angles and still not be able to decide.

'So, imagine how tough it is for referees getting one look in real time and from one angle which may be obscured. And there is so much riding on their decisions with millions of pounds at stake, so I have a lot more respect for them.'

The game has changed beyond recognition since Paine gave up his apprenticeship with British Rail to sign for Saints in February 1957. Discarded by Arsenal for being too small, the stocky winger made an immediate impact at The Dell.

On successive Saturdays he made his debut for the club's A team, the reserves and then the first team – a meteoric rise which was not universally applauded by some established senior players, who interpreted his brash confidence as arrogance.

But he had good reason for such self-belief and they soon realised that the emerging youngster was a bit special. Quick, direct and strong, he could deliver a killer cross to provide a plentiful supply of ammunition for the likes of Norman Dean, Derek Reeves and then the legendary Ron Davies, as well as Martin Chivers and then Mick Channon.

Paine's pace and power played a key role in lifting Southampton from the third tier of English football to the top flight for the first time in their history and, not surprisingly, his talents were coveted by a succession of bigger clubs.

But back then, there was no freedom of movement among players so, unlike the modern era, Saints were able to hold on to their stars.

As club president now, Paine understands the market forces which make it so difficult for Southampton to keep their big names, but feels the pendulum of power has swung too far since he first joined the club.

'It is very difficult managing a club now because you are not just making football decisions but business decisions. Clubs get forced into doing things they don't want to because of market forces. If a player worth £30m has only a year left on his contract, you could lose a lot of money if you don't sell.

'Back then, it was very different. I worked for British Rail at their Eastleigh body shop. Thank God football came along because I was useless at it! My dad worked there all his life but there is no way I would have survived. I couldn't even put a screw in.

'In my day, once you signed for a club that was it – unless they chose to let you go. We didn't think of it as being unfair, we just accepted it.

'Then the Bosman rule came in, which is absolutely right but maybe now it has gone too far the other way. The balance isn't quite right.

'I know Spurs came in for me because Harry Evans would tap me up every week – and he was a mate of Ted Bates!

'After we won 5-1 at Man City in the FA Cup when we were still a Third Division team, Jimmy Meadows came to my house, claiming he was just passing through.

'Nowadays agents do all of that. I never had an agent as far as football was concerned. I just had someone to look after my business affairs.

'Manchester United were in for Ron Davies for a long time and only eventually got him when his best days were behind him. It really upset me when he died because we were a partnership. I would cross it, but the point was that it was him on the end of it. Yes, I was good for him… but he was very good for me because he could stick that ball in the net.

'I knew of the interest in me, but Ted Bates was very strong and would not let players go. I got a call to see the chairman, who said there was more chance of the Civic Centre falling down than there was of the club letting me go.

'I might have gone if I had been given the chance, but at least it did not affect my international career. I played all my England games as a Second Division player.

'When Alf Ramsey was manager of Ipswich, they won the Second Division in 1961, but we beat them 7-1 in the FA Cup. I scored and set up a couple and I think it always stuck in his memory to give me a chance.'

The last of Paine's 19 England caps came during the 1966 finals in the 2-0 win against Mexico, a pivotal match which kick-started the campaign after a disappointing opening 0-0 draw against Uruguay.

With no substitutes then, Paine was a spectator as Bobby Moore lifted the trophy. The remaining squad members did not even get a medal, a scandalous ruling which took until 2009 to correct.

'I eventually got a medal, although it took a long time to put it right, but it was the correct thing to do. It didn't really hurt at the time because that was the system and we accepted it. At the time, it was about England winning the final. Medals did not come into it.

'And, of course, it was a fantastic occasion. Even 50 years on, it is still very special. We were number one, top of the world – and it is very sad that it has not happened again since.

'Some players from that era are now ill and others have passed away, but I would love the surviving members of the team to see England win the World Cup again before they go.'

That summer of 1966 was a golden time for Paine, who was also celebrating Southampton's first ever promotion to the top flight.

In the modern era, such success would see him set up for life but the Winchester-born club legend does not resent the massive financial rewards now given to players with far less ability than he possessed.

'Of course I would love to be playing now, but I don't regret the age I played in. It is always hard to compare eras. If I am absolutely honest, I think there were more good players in my day. The outstanding players of the modern game are better – but there are fewer of them.

'A lot of very ordinary players now receive fortunes and it must be difficult in the dressing room if you know one player is on £150,000 while others are on half that.

'I always believe that if you are offered a contract and sign it and are happy with the terms, then you shouldn't worry what someone else gets, not just in football but in life generally.

'Money never really motivated me as a player. When I started, I got £10 a week in the summer and £17 in the winter, plus £2 for a draw and £4 for a win. That didn't really change until the 1960s, when Jimmy Hill abolished the maximum wage.

'At the time, £17 a week was still more than the average wage but we never made enough money to set ourselves up for life, not like today's players.'

As one of the club's all-time greats – his 816 appearances rightly earned him the MBE – Paine's eventual departure was out of keeping with his 17 years of loyal service.

Lawrie McMenemy had taken over from Ted Bates as manager and was keen to rebuild after relegation. In his autobiography he was critical of the winger and his attitude, but Paine is reluctant to get drawn into a row.

'When I did leave, I was very sad. Lawrie McMenemy had taken over as manager and talks about his reasons and feelings in his book. That's fine and I hope he does well out of it.

'Certainly once I got into coaching, I understood things like that better than I had done as a player. We had just got relegated and I can understand now his reasons for letting me go.

'I have been asked by the press if I want to respond, but it was 42 years ago and I doubt I could remember it anyway. I haven't read the comments and it would be water off a duck's back. He has a book to sell, so good luck to him.'

Paine has no regrets about the way his career panned out as he went on to sign for Hereford, gaining coaching experience before moving into the media.

'At the time, I was 35 and wondered where I was going to go if I was not offered a job at Southampton. But Peter Sillett, a lifelong friend, got the manager's job at Hereford. He asked me to go there, so I jumped at the chance to work there as player-coach. If I had known how difficult it was going to be, then I might have thought differently.

'It was a real footballing backwater but we bought Dixie McNeil, who finished as the top scorer in the division for two years running, and we won the Third Division title. But we were never going to survive at the higher level because we had no money.

'After that, I looked for other opportunities and ended up coaching in Kuwait, even though I had once vowed I could never live there when Saints had a stop-over on the way back from a tour to Mauritius. Then John Sillett took over as manager of Coventry and asked me to go and work for him just after they won the FA Cup. It was a great place to work with fantastic facilities and it was a good learning curve for me.

'But unfortunately John fell ill and was out of action for three months, and the club couldn't wait for him to recover, so then I went out to South Africa, which proved to be a big turning point for me.

'I joined Mnet Supersport, which is their equivalent of Sky Sports. We broadcast the World Cup finals in South Africa and I did 42 of the 45 games and then one match a week since – and the popularity of the game has gone through the roof.'

Articulate and forthright, Paine has been a driving force behind the success of football in South Africa and, even at 77, was still going strong as the 2015/16 season drew to a close.

But he still has close ties to Southampton and was named as the club's honorary president in January 2013, pipping McMenemy, who could also have laid a strong claim to the role.

'It is a very great honour to be club president and it means a lot to me. I am following a long line of Southampton greats, so it is very special to be among them, and I jumped at the opportunity.

'Basically, I am on call to come over and do whatever they need. The chairman keeps in touch by e-mail or phone and brings me up to date with what is going on.

'I was very surprised when I was asked, partly because I am so far away, but in some ways that suits as you don't want a club president sitting on the shoulder of the manager or interfering.

'Under Ralph Krueger and Les Reed, we have really come on and it is a pleasure to be around the club. We are progressing well. The 2015/16 season was as comfortable as I have ever been watching the team, even at places like Manchester United.

'I still do *Monday Night Football* for Mnet Supersport, which now goes to 52 countries. We take every Premier League game live and have ten dedicated channels, so you can follow whichever team you support. The Premier League is huge throughout Africa and nations will have their own favourite club if one of their own plays there.

'It is especially nice to see my own club doing so well. I am portrayed very much as a Southampton man – even my caption says I am club president. I am as honest and as neutral as I possibly can be, although my heart will always be with Southampton. I still love the club as much as ever.'

Jim Steele

JIM STEELE not only helped win the FA Cup for Saints, but famously helped lose it for them too.

Man of the match in the 1976 final, which brought a 1-0 win over mighty Manchester United, the burly Scotsman revels in retelling the story which has passed into club folklore.

It was the night Steele and his close pal Peter Osgood took the old trophy on an unlikely tour of Southampton, causing panic among club officials when they realised it was missing.

Steele recalled: 'It was a fantastic time in the aftermath of winning the FA Cup. Everyone wanted to know us. We were invited everywhere and never had to buy a drink, which was great.

'The week after the final, we went to some club and took the trophy with us. Bobby Stokes was talking to the guy guarding it, so Ossie asked if he could take the cup outside for a picture.

'The guard said OK so Ossie took it outside, where I was waiting in the car with the engine running. Lawrie McMenemy had gone home, so there was no one keeping an eye on us and we took it down to the Drummond Arms, where Jimmy McGowan filled it with beer for everyone to have a drink.

'Then we took it into the centre of town and stopped at a burger bar. The owner recognised us and said whatever we wanted was on the house. He asked if we wanted coffee in a mug or cup, so Ossie got the trophy from the boot of the car and we all drank coffee out of it!

'Apparently it was worth a million quid, so maybe we should have kept it. Instead Ossie brought it back the next morning and left it outside Lawrie Mac's office. But by then there was an almighty panic.

'Peter came into the dressing room and gave me a wink to say he had returned it safely, but then we got a message to say the boss wanted to see us. We went up to his office and Ted Bates was standing behind him.

'Lawrie said the club secretary had almost had a heart attack when he found the cup was missing. We thought we were going to get fined, but I could see Ted laughing his head off behind Lawrie, who just told us to fuck off!

'But that's how it was back then. We went out, we had a laugh, got into a few scrapes, but had each other's backs.'

The Wembley win is still the most precious memory of Steele's life and he never tires of telling the story of how an unfancied Second Division club went all the way to Wembley.

'The FA Cup success was a fantastic experience. We had just been relegated and should have gone straight back up, but we got side-tracked by the cup. I wouldn't trade it, though. It was incredible.

'I remember we salvaged a 1-1 draw at home to Villa in the third round with a last-minute goal from Hughie Fisher, who never usually scored. We took the train to the replay and changed in London.

'The journey took us past Wembley and Mick Channon said "We'll be back there in May for the final." We all wondered what he had been drinking – but he was right.

'We won the replay and then started to play really well. We got through to the quarter-finals away to Bradford, which was the only game I missed on the cup run… because I had mumps of all things.

'In those days there was no internet or anything like that, so I wandered round the city centre going into television shops. I had no intention of buying one. I just wanted to know how we were getting on. But Ossie and Jim McCalliog did their little trick of flicking up a free-kick and volleying it in and suddenly we were in the semi-final.

'We beat Third Division Crystal Palace 2-0 at Stamford Bridge. It was quite easy really – despite them having Malcolm Allison and his famous fedora on the touchline.

'We had been lucky to miss Manchester United and Derby, who met in the other semi. Afterwards, their winger Gordon Hill was told they would be playing Southampton and he just said "Who?" That really wound us up.'

It was widely assumed that United had only to turn up to win the game, but there was an understated air of confidence among the

Southampton squad, which contained a lot of big characters and big drinkers, as well as some big-game players.

'Even the Thursday before the cup final, we went out. But in those days, there was nothing else to do. There was no Sky TV or internet or computer games. Just three television channels, which finished at 11pm.

'We had our meal at 6pm and then went to our rooms and had nothing to do, so Peter Rodrigues, Jim McCalliog and I asked Lawrie McMenemy if we could go to the pub to play darts to kill the time.

'He agreed but warned us not to tell anyone else and we headed for the pub and had a few shandies and some darts and then went to bed. It kept us relaxed.

'The next night, we were in bed early ready for the final on the Saturday. On the way to the ground, the team coach ran over a couple of Manchester United fans who had jumped in front of it in an effort to stop us getting to Wembley. People did some crazy things in those days.

'They weren't badly hurt, so the police told us to keep going. But it was funny as hell and again that eased the tension.

'We were so focused and determined that day. We knew afterwards we would have to climb 39 steps to meet the Queen and it would be a hell of a lot easier as winners. That was the last final she ever attended. She probably realised nothing was ever going to beat that experience.

'We might have been the underdogs, but we were really confident. Why wouldn't we be? We had so much experience and so many big-game players with the likes of Peter Osgood, Jim McCalliog, Mike Channon and Peter Rodrigues.

'We were under a bit of pressure for the first 20 minutes, but after that we were fine. When we came in at half-time, Lawrie McMenemy asked what I thought and I said if we score, we win. They were never going to get past us.

'It was a wonderful moment when Bobby Stokes ran through to fire home and I knew then that we were going to win. They never got near us and it was fantastic when the final whistle sounded and all our fans went mad.

'After the final, we went to the Talk of the Town nightclub. Lawrie wouldn't let us go home – probably because he knew we wouldn't turn up for the open-top bus tour if we did!

'It was the most boring thing I had ever seen in my life. It was probably very good, but I just found it boring. In fact, Ossie did a runner and got a taxi all the way back to his home in Windsor to get drunk with his mates.

'The next day, we drove back to Southampton on the team bus and I have to say the journey back was incredible. There were banners and Saints flags on every bridge from Basingstoke onwards and the reception we got around the city was unbelievable. It seemed like the whole of Hampshire had turned out to welcome us home.

'There was nowhere to park in the city centre, so Ossie had to run two miles to get on the bus. He had never run two miles in his life!

'But it was a totally magical day. I have never seen so many people in one place and the party seemed to last for days.'

In essence, it did. The celebrations began at the final whistle on 1 May and continued full tilt until the evening of 3 May, when Channon staged his benefit game against QPR. It could not have been better timed.

'Mick must have had a premonition. Not only did he predict it on the train past Wembley in January, but he arranged his testimonial for the Monday after the cup final.

'You couldn't get near The Dell. There were fans sitting on the touchlines behind the goals three deep. It was mayhem.

'And, of course, most of us were still pissed. I was marking Stan Bowles and I told him not to leave me as I was drunk. After a while, I asked him what the score was and he said "1-0 to us." I asked who scored and he said "I did."

'I reminded him he had promised not to leave me and he said, "I didn't, you were standing right next to me!" We ended up drawing 2-2 and Mick cashed in. He deserved it because he was a great player for us and it was long before the mega-money came into football.

'I got £3,600 for winning the cup. It was less than the other lads because I missed the game at Bradford with mumps. I paid £2,400 in tax and most of the rest of it went on putting my mum and dad and two friends up in a hotel for a week when they came down for the game.

'But it seemed a lot of money when I was on £120 a week – plus £60 for a win or £30 for a draw. You would kick your granny for that £30. I sometimes think I have been robbed blind all my life – but I wouldn't change anything.

'I got £1,000 from the *News of the World* for being the man of the match, so I split it between the whole team. Bobby Stokes won a brand new car for scoring the winning goal – and he couldn't even drive.

'I found out later he sold it and kept the cash. But I can't begrudge him that – he was a great lad. I used to go horseracing with him, Mick Channon and Brian O'Neil.

'I remember one meeting where Stokesy and Brian had bet on a certain horse in the final race of the day and, as it approached the last fence, it was six lengths clear of the horse Mick and I had backed.

'Incredibly, it fell and our horse went on to win. They were furious and said they could have jumped that fence better. We'd had a few to drink, so we told them to prove it – so they did!

'They got on to the course after the racing had finished and literally jumped through the fence. They came out covered in twigs and blood from the scratches.

'We jumped in the car and Mick was doing his famous windmill celebration out of the car window as we drove home. That's how it was in those days. I don't know if modern players bond in the same way.

'I suspect they probably just drink at home now. After all, they can afford a bar in their own place and there is no danger of a journalist seeing them.

'But it built real team spirit. We would go out and have a few laughs and then look after each other on the pitch.

'Once we had to do two laps of the sports centre, so several of us hid in the bushes and then joined the back of the group as it went round for the second time. The trainer, George Horsfall, asked if he had seen me at the end of the first lap and I told him of course he had and he had asked how I was doing – and he believed me.

'Lawrie then told us to make our own way back to The Dell. The rest of the players jogged back, but we jumped on a bus and waved to the rest of the lads as we passed them.

'Lawrie found out and was going to fine us until we pointed out he had simply said we had to make our own way back – he didn't specifically say we had to run.'

Steele easily adapted to the drinking culture and the dressing room banter after joining Saints from Dundee for a then club-record fee of £80,000 in January 1972.

However, he admits the move itself and the new environment were to come as quite a culture shock when he got a sudden call to head south of the border.

'I know it is hard to believe, but I never used to drink... until I came to Southampton.

'I was 21 and fully dedicated as a footballer with Dundee. Then, one day, a taxi pulled up during our training session at a local park. In those days, clubs didn't have their own training pitches, let alone all the other facilities that modern players now take for granted.

'The taxi driver asked the coach if Jim Steele was here and said he had been sent to take me back to Dens Park. Automatically, I assumed it was bad news. I thought maybe one of my parents had died.

'I tried asking the driver, but he said all he knew was that he was to bring me back, so I was really on edge as I walked in to meet a complete stranger. He said, "I'm Ted Bates. Congratulations, you have just signed for Southampton." I was stunned.

'I just looked at him and said, "Where the fuck is that?" Then I rang my wife – we had only been married for three months – and told her we were going to move to Southampton.

'I genuinely had no idea where it was. It was quite a shock when I found out that it couldn't have been much further away.

'But in those days, players had no say in where and when they moved. There was no freedom of contract. You were traded like a piece of meat. There had been talk of me going to Leeds or a couple of other clubs, but Saints were the ones who took a punt.

'Next thing I knew, I was on a plane and heading for Southampton. Ted Bates fixed up a room for me near The Dell and told me to report for training at 10am the next day.

'I was so keen to get going that I was up at eight o'clock and made my way to the stadium. Only the office staff were in, but they showed me to the dressing room, where there was a peg with my name on it.

'I was just getting changed when Ron Davies walked in. He looked me up and down and asked, "Are you the guy we have just signed from Scotland?" I said yes and he said, "That's a hell of a lot of money for a freckle!"

'And he was right. The fee was £80,000, which was a club record, but I like to think I gave them good value. And Ron went on to become one of my best mates.

'I quickly realised he liked a drink – and he was not the only one. There was big John McGrath, Jimmy Gabriel, Denis Hollywood, Brian O'Neil, the little winger Tommy Jenkins and the keeper Eric Martin. We used to hang out together. Even Mick Channon used to join us.

'I couldn't believe it. As soon as training finished, we would be in the pub. In those days the pubs used to close at 2pm, so we would have to drink quickly and then order a couple more at last orders.

'Then, about 2.20pm, Terry Paine would often turn up, probably thinking it was too late for him to have to buy a drink. But we always made sure he did.

'He was not the most popular in the dressing room and I think he knew that. The first thing Lawrie McMenemy did when he came in as manager was to get rid of him. We thought he was just a bit arrogant, probably because he had been in England's World Cup-winning squad, even though he didn't play in the final.

'To be fair, he was a great crosser of the ball – and he was hard with it. He would go over the top sometimes, proving you didn't have to be big to be hard. I played against the likes of Johnny Giles and Billy Bremner and Terry was every bit as tough as them.

'They were proper hard-men. These days, players get a tap on the shin and roll around holding their faces, trying to get an opponent sent off. We dished it out, but we could take it too.

'We all liked a drink, but we knew when to stop – most of the time. I remember Jimmy Gabriel vowing not to drink all week before a game against Arsenal because he wanted to be at his best.

'Every morning at training, I would smell his breath to make sure he had stuck to his word and I have to say I was impressed.

'Then, on the day of the match, I walked in and he was virtually passed out in the corner of the dressing room. I asked what happened.

'He said he had been watching a John Wayne movie the previous night and the main characters had a good drink, so he thought he would have a couple too… and then a couple more… and a few more. But he went out and helped us get a 1-1 draw.

'Jimmy was one of the best people I ever met. It was reported he committed suicide when he drowned in the boating lake on the Common, but I don't believe that. He was not the sort to do that. I was in the States at the time, so I could not get back to investigate, but he would never have done that.

'I never used to drink on a Friday night – despite what might have been reported. I did get called into Lawrie's office and he said I had been seen in a pub the night before a match.

'I told him I was living there. I had just split from my wife and had nowhere else to go, so the former Saints player Jimmy McGowan let me have a room above his pub and I would help out in the bar in return. Lawrie just buried his head in his hands in despair.'

However, it was not the club's drinking culture which earned Ted Bates' side the infamous tag of Alehouse Brawlers from legendary Liverpool manager Bill Shankly.

That came when Alun Evans swallowed his tongue after being sent flying by a trademark crunching tackle.

'It is quite something to be known as one of the "Alehouse Brawlers", as the saying went. Yes we liked a drink and we were hard – but we could play too. And Bill Shankly was just pissed off because we had won 1-0.

'We were hard but we were not malicious. The likes of John McGrath and Jimmy Gabriel and myself would always go for the ball, but we were tough.

'There were a few who would hit the top of the ball and then follow through. Those were the sort of tackles which would break a leg. I would say it was probably deliberate or, at the very least, intended to hurt.

'I only ever did one player and I am not proud of it. It was while I was playing in the States and we faced a Korean team on tour. One of their players had hurt two or three of our men, so I did go over the top and I felt really bad when he was stretchered off with a broken leg.'

Steele by name and by nature, he was much more than simply a hard-man who kicked lumps out of people. He read the game superbly, could pick out a pass and could time his forceful tackles immaculately – when he wanted to.

And even though the game has changed considerably in recent years – and not always for the better – the affable Scotsman insists he would not have looked out of place on the modern stage.

'There were times when I would take the man and the ball, but I was not a hatchet-man. I might have been hard, but there was a lot more to my game. I could play a bit too. I could ping the ball 40 yards and hit Peter Osgood every time.

'If he pointed to his chest, I would play it for him to control and turn. If he pointed above his head, it meant he was going to jump and elbow the centre-half in the face!

'Nowadays players are on a hundred grand a week and can't pass the ball ten yards. I am not sure they could have played in my day – but I could fit in now because I could pass the ball.

'The game has changed beyond recognition. You can't make a proper tackle and players roll around pretending to be hurt.

'There are way too many foreigners coming into the game, which is stifling the development of our own players. No wonder it is hurting the national team.

'I would like to see a cap of two or three foreign players maximum at each club because they are blocking the way for British players to come through.

'I have done a lot of coaching with kids and often they train just once a week. Then they play their match at the weekend and that is the only time they touch a ball.

'The rest of the time, they are on computer game consoles. They can all win the World Cup online, but not in real life.

'In my day, we would be out kicking a ball until it got dark – and even longer on the rare occasions someone had a white ball which we could actually see.

'Kids should be out kicking a ball against a wall, practising their skills, feeling comfortable with a ball at their feet.'

Steele's time at The Dell came to an end less than a year after his greatest hour. And again Manchester United were heavily involved.

The teams met again in the FA Cup and this time United gained revenge, winning a fifth-round replay 2-1 at Old Trafford, where Steele was sent off… on his return from a three-match ban.

McMenemy was far from happy but kept faith with the Scot for the Cup Winners' Cup quarter-final against Anderlecht at The Dell.

Saints were trailing 2-0 from the away leg, but goals by David Peach and Ted MacDougall made it 2-2 on aggregate, with the home side building a head of steam and looking set to reach the last four.

But seven minutes from time, Steele slipped and allowed Frankie van der Elst to run through to win the tie. The classy centre-back made just one more appearance for the club before being shipped across the pond to sign for Washington Diplomats.

At just 27, his career in English football came to a premature end, a move which was made harder by the fact that it was not as financially rewarding as he had been assured.

'I screwed up against Anderlecht in the European Cup Winners' Cup. I know that. The ball ran under my foot and they raced through to score the winner. Anderlecht went on to win the cup and I was on my way out.

'But Peter Osgood and Ted MacDougall both hit the woodwork three times each in that game and no one said anything negative about them. I made one slip and I was finished here.

'I was shipped off to the States. I was only 27 but it was a fantastic experience – even though I think I lost out financially. I joined Washington Diplomats and met their chairman, who told me they had paid a £10,000 fee. I said I was a free transfer, so God knows what happened to that money! I know I didn't see any of it. I got a signing-on fee of £4,000.

'At the time soccer was just taking off in the USA, so I got to play against the likes of Pele and Franz Beckenbauer and alongside Johan Cruyff. Pele was outstanding. He would play the ball off your shin and then dart past you while you were off balance. The first time I thought it was a fluke, but when he did it for the fifth or sixth time I realised just how good he was.

'He gave the game a real lift just by his presence. Just before we played his New York Cosmos side, I was sent to do the press conference with Eric Martin and the former Spurs player Mike Dillon.

'We arrived at the hotel to find the car park full and crowds of fans outside. I asked what was going on and the doorman said everyone was there for the pre-match press conference. I explained that we were doing the conference, but it turned out they were all there for Pele and Beckenbauer rather than us.

'He parked the car for us and we went up to this big room to sit with Pele, Beckenbauer and Brazilian great Carlos Alberto – three World Cup winners.

'We were all given a Budweiser but Pele said he did not drink before a game. Afterwards, he invited us up to his suite and told me how much he loved whisky.

'He produced a bottle and we got through it in no time as he explained he never drank in front of the TV cameras because he is such a role model to the kids in Brazil.

'I loved my time in the States. I stayed on there as an electrician after I finished playing thanks to an anterior cruciate ligament injury I picked up in an indoor match.

'I had a couple of bars there too and I wish I had stayed, but I returned to England because my mum and dad were ill. I should have gone back because it is a great country and they will do well in the World Cup in the next few years. The game is really taking off there and the kids work really hard at it – unlike here.'

Now back living in Southampton and a key part of the 40th anniversary celebrations commemorating the FA Cup win, Steele looks back fondly on his move to the other end of the British Isles and to the friends he made here, most notably his partner in FA Cup crime Peter Osgood.

'I had only been at Southampton for three weeks when we played Chelsea and I tackled one of their players. Peter Osgood said, "I will get you for that, you big Sweaty." I had no idea what he meant until half-time, when someone told me it was rhyming slang... sweaty sock – Jock.

'Funnily enough, he became one of my best mates when he moved to Southampton and we stayed friends even when we finished playing.

'A few years ago, I went to Thailand and Ossie wanted me to get him a long cashmere coat like the ones Jose Mourinho wears. They had them made-to-measure out there and that suited Ossie because he had long arms.

'I got three – one for me, one for Ossie and one for Jimmy Case. Almost as soon as I got back, Ossie was on the phone wanting to know why I hadn't given him his coat. I told him I was living in the Cotswolds, so I hadn't had a chance to bring it down.

'He pestered me, so I made a special trip to bring it down to him and he was thrilled. He kept trying it on and was like a child. He was so excited that it fitted his arms.

'I gave it to him on a Wednesday. The following Monday, he wore it to a funeral – and dropped dead from a heart attack still wearing the coat. I have never worn mine since. But I am so glad now I made that special trip.'

Chris Nicholl

FOR A book on Saints hard-men, Chris Nicholl qualifies on two fronts.

As a player he was a rugged, no-nonsense centre-back who wore his repeatedly broken nose as a badge of honour.

As a manager, he showed that same fighting spirit – especially when he resorted to violence in a bid to control Mark Dennis.

By his own admission, 'Psycho' was a nightmare for managers, especially one as inexperienced as Nicholl, who was cutting his teeth in his first major role.

Dennis made it very clear he did not respect the successor to Lawrie McMenemy, who had seemed to have a much better understanding of what made the volatile left-back tick. He knew the kind of escapades Dennis got up to away from the club and he knew when to turn a blind eye… and when to employ an iron fist.

Nicholl's single-minded determination and fierce work ethic on the training field meant he found it hard to come to terms with what he saw as a lack of professionalism from the flamboyant and hot-headed defender, who was never shy of answering back.

It led to a strained relationship until one day Nicholl snapped. Months of frustration boiled over and the manager thumped him.

Nicholl recalled: 'I get on fine with Mark Dennis now, but back then he was a nightmare for me when I was manager. He grew up as a bit of a rebel. He came from the bad side of London, where there was not a lot of wealth, and he was certainly volatile.

'We played at home to Liverpool in the semi-finals of the League Cup. We drew 0-0 and it was a missed opportunity. They had Paul Walsh sent off and they just closed the game down.

'I was frustrated because it was a game we could have won and I really thought we had a great chance of getting to Wembley. Then I found out that Mark's idea of preparation was to be in a snooker club at 1.30am with his baby girl.

'The next day, I nailed him in front of everyone. I told him he had let us down. I had a right go at him for being unprofessional.

'He stood up and, before he could do anything, I hit him. The rest of the lads jumped in and kept us apart, which was probably just as well. We were both properly wound up. It was a real heated clash.

'It was the best thing I ever did. I think he had a bit more respect for me after that and we got on a lot better afterwards. He understood where I was coming from. He knew I was not happy and I let him know in a way he would understand.

'Nowadays that would not happen. Things are a lot more politically correct, if you like. You can't say or do anything which might offend players or bruise their egos.

'I am trying to imagine the reaction in our dressing room if one of the lads had got the hump because the club didn't give him a birthday cake. He would have been hammered!

'But that's how it was back then. You did have bust-ups and players would come to blows. The game has changed now – and not always for the better.'

Nicholl looks back fondly at the physical contact which was commonplace during his playing days and bemoans the way it is rapidly vanishing from the game.

Referees now have virtually no wriggle room when it comes to applying the letter of the law. They can no longer let the first bad foul go with a warning and the former Northern Ireland international detests the way some players try to exploit that.

He added: 'The game is very different these days. You can't put a tackle in because you know the opponent will fall over. Eventually, players will end up on the stage with all the acting there is. It is totally wrong.

'I broke my nose eight or nine times. Usually, it was me heading the back of someone else's head but occasionally it would be an elbow or something else. But back then you just got on with it, partly because there was only one substitute allowed and partly because that is the way we were. You would judge a defender by the number of times they had broken their nose.

'I was so slow, I had to be tough. My timing was not great but I was OK in the air. That was my job, or at least a big part of it.

'The physical side was a big thing then. I would get bashed and kicked about, but being able to handle it was a huge part of the game. In those days, referees allowed players to get away with more. If you broke your nose you could not worry about the blood or the pain, you just had to go again and win the next header.

'In my day, you would not give the opponent the satisfaction of thinking he had hurt you. I remember playing for Luton and we were drawn against Manchester United in the cup. George Best picked up the ball on the right of his own penalty area and ran diagonally across the field to the right side of our box.

'A lad called John Ryan had been detailed to mark him and must have whacked him hard six times in 100 yards, but Best refused to fall over. He wouldn't give John the satisfaction of that.

'Nowadays players go over at the slightest touch – or even if there is no contact at all. It is not right.'

Nicholl is proud to have been a proper 'old-school' chiselled centre-half, whose strength was winning the ball in the air and getting rid of it.

He did not worry about the kind of silky skills some modern defenders like to show off – though he did famously hit an incredible 40-yard strike for Aston Villa in the 1977 League Cup Final replay against Everton.

After helping Villa from the old Third Division to the top flight, Nicholl was bought by McMenemy, who wanted to tap into his record of being promoted in his first season with every club.

It worked. Saints went back to the First Division and Nicholl was able to claim his double bonus for succeeding where more creative players had failed.

'I didn't really want to come to Southampton at first. I was signed from Villa and we had gone from the Third Division to the First. I was captain and didn't particularly want to go.

'But Lawrie wanted me to join the likes of Alan Ball, Kevin Keegan and then Peter Shilton... all big personalities and tough characters. And I soon found out it was a very different sort of set-up.

'I remember being engrossed in a training session early on when this little voice piped up. "First race 12.15." Next thing, Lawrie had said, "One minute and we finish!" He blew a whistle and while I was still kicking a ball, a fleet of cars sped past full of players off to the races.

'Lawrie loved experienced players and had a lot of them. Alan Ball was one of the best players and captains I ever played with. He had fantastic know-how and a great understanding of the game – apart from the time he tried to play a one-two with me.

'I remember giving him the ball and he gave it straight back. I was stunned, I never expected that. I didn't know what to do with it! I loved being with him and it was so sad to lose him so early.

'They were great days, totally different to what I was used to at Villa. But Lawrie knew how to get the best out of players – and it worked because we won promotion.

'He was shrewd like that. He knew when to turn a blind eye to what was going on off the field because he knew those same players would deliver on it.

'He knew how to handle experienced players and big characters and, if I'm honest, that is something I struggled with a little bit. That was an interesting part of the job and one I was not really prepared for.

'Every player had personality problems of some sort, whether it was girls or drink or poor training. You had to know each player and you had to be strong enough to put your ideas across to them.

'It is just knowing how to manage people. I suppose these days you would call it psychology.

'How did I cope with the rascals? Usually by punching them!'

The biggest of them all – and the hardest man he ever encountered – was, of course, Jimmy Case, whose name crops up so often in this book.

'Jimmy Case was crucial to the side. He was a rascal, but I have only good things to say about him. He was classic old-school, for all the right reasons.

'I was never sure what he was doing away from the club or how he was doing it. But I knew he would never let me down on the pitch.

'There was only one occasion when I felt he let me down and that was a game at Coventry, where I just felt he was not right and I took him off very early in the game.

'But overall, his contribution to the team was so pronounced that you had to admire him. He had been brought up the Liverpool way in the days when they were the best team in the country.

'I was certainly not going to let that kind of experience and know-how go. I had to have that in the team.

'I knew he was a rascal and got up to all kinds of stuff, but as long as he was producing on the field that was all that mattered to me.

'He knew the game, he could play and he was the hardest player I ever encountered as a player or as a manager.

'With his Scouse accent, I could hardly tell what he was saying a lot of the time! But what he did say was never about him, always about the team and what he wanted to happen in order for us to win games. He was a big influence on me and on the rest of the lads. I can't speak too highly of him. I was very lucky to have Jimmy in his prime and to use all the knowledge he had, even though he was a rascal.

'He did his own thing and had his own Scouse way of saying and doing things, which was always entertaining, but he was a proper gentleman off the field and a warrior on it. I could not have asked for more.

'He was my captain and our kingpin. Everything revolved around him. He added so much to the young players, both on and off the field. I won't hear a word said against Jimmy Case.

'I loved having him in the side. He was a minder to our young players coming through. He taught them well in training, led by example and looked after them on the field.

'If anyone ever gave them a kick, they knew they would have to answer to Jimmy. He knew how and when to dish out retribution.

'In those days, you could do it too. There was none of the diving and falling over and waving imaginary cards that you see today. I absolutely hate that.'

Case's experience, ability and steel were crucial to Nicholl's rebuilding programme following the departure of McMenemy, who had specialised in getting the best out of players towards the end of their careers – the only time Saints could afford them.

Despite his intimidating stature, Nicholl found it hard to impose himself on the dressing room of big personalities left to him by McMenemy.

'We had some real rascals in our dressing room. It is probably just as well camera phones weren't around back then. Now everyone has a camera, so players need to be careful.

'Nowadays the press get to hear of far too much – and make too much of it. Back then, the press would sometimes hide things for you, especially if they had come away on tour with us. That helped build a bit of trust between players and the press. You could actually get to know one another.

'Lawrie McMenemy had much more experienced and older players, but I wanted to change things around and put the kids in because we had a great crop being developed by Dave Merrington.

'When I took over I wanted some experience alongside Mark Wright, so I signed Russell Osman from Ipswich. He was a terrific player with great knowledge of the game. He was already an England international and he could read the game superbly.

'We had a lot of kids coming through, so I needed some older heads around them. I signed Matthew Le Tissier and Alan Shearer and Rod Wallace and brought them through and gave them their chance.

'I wanted a mix of youth and experience – and even did that with the goalkeeping position. I signed the veteran John Burridge and promising youngster Tim Flowers from Wolves reserves.

'Tim kept Budgie on his toes and learned a lot from him. Budgie was a nutter – but in the best possible sense. He was devoted to football.

'He even slept holding a football. Goodness knows what his wife Janet thought about that – but then she used to throw oranges at him when he was least expecting it.

'The idea was to sharpen his reflexes, though it reminded me a bit of Inspector Clouseau asking Cato to attack him out of nowhere!

'It meant Tim grew up the right way and had the right feeling for the game and prepared well. He learned a lot about the art and the science of goalkeeping from a man who made it his life's passion.

'So there were some decent signings – this makes me sound as though I was better than I actually was!'

Another hugely successful capture who features in this book was Neil Ruddock, picked up for a bargain fee of just £250,000 from Millwall.

'Neil Ruddock was an interesting signing. He was a real strong character, even as a young lad. He didn't worry about having a go at the experienced pros. He had such presence.

'I remember going up to watch a reserve game at Millwall and saw this big strapping lad who was full of himself. He was only a kid, but he had fantastic confidence. He was great to watch and I loved him.

'I left the ground knowing I had to buy him – and it was well worth it. Russell Osman was a classy defender and Ruddock was ideal to partner him and to learn from him.

'He was big and strong and had such authority that we could even get away with a smaller keeper in John Burridge. I loved what he offered the team and I built around him.'

And then, of course, there was his fellow 'Bruise Brother' in Alan Shearer, one of the toughest characters to come through the ranks, both physically and mentally.

It was Nicholl who gave him his chance, famously throwing him into a debut at home to Arsenal as a raw 17-year-old and being rewarded as the young prodigy scored a hat-trick in a 4-2 win at The Dell.

'People say it was a bold move to give Alan Shearer a debut at 17. If anything, I waited too long.

'We were at home to George Graham's Arsenal side, who were renowned for being hard to break down.

'They had the likes of Tony Adams and Martin Keown, who must have been delighted to find they were facing a young kid making his debut.

'They probably thought they could bully him, give him a whack early on and then enjoy a comfortable afternoon. They obviously hadn't seen the way John Burridge would keep clattering into him in training to toughen him up – and Alan still kept coming back for more.

'As everyone knows, Alan scored a hat-trick that day so maybe I should have put him in sooner – as he kept telling me to do.

'I didn't worry throwing him in. Dave Merrington had brought him through the right way and given him the right messages to instil incredible mental toughness.

'People assume I never had any doubts about his footballing ability, but I told him I thought his control wasn't good enough. So he went away and worked on that.

'I told him I thought his heading could be better, so he worked like fury to improve. I said he had a big backside and he should stick it into a defender to shield the ball... so he did it.

'Alan had the most amazing work ethic and determination. He just wanted to improve and he worked so hard and deserved everything he got from the game.

'I never had any doubts about his finishing, though. That was always a real strength. He had such power in his shots, even for a young kid.

'But it was his mental strength which set him apart. He moved away from his family at 16 and came to the other end of the country, which must have been very difficult. But he stuck at it and developed into one of the all-time greats. I am delighted he had such a good career.

'Back then, he was a bit of a cocky lad because he had such inner confidence. I had to keep his feet on the ground – but that was the same with Rod Wallace and Matthew Le Tissier. They were good – and they knew it. They all had something about them which made them different.

'Matt actually went into the team before Alan. I signed them both when they left school, but Matt came through quicker.'

Nicholl's six-year tenure brought two major semi-finals, a seventh-place finish in 1990 and some exhilarating games, none more so than the unforgettable 4-1 win over champions-elect Liverpool.

There is an inescapable irony that such a dour, dogged defender would abandon those shackles to create a free-flowing football side full of energy and creativity.

But with the likes of Le Tissier, Rod Wallace and Shearer at his disposal, there was little option.

'When Tiss and Rod could cross that well and Alan could finish that strongly, it simplified the game. They had totally different personalities, but it worked.

'We did have an exciting team with a nice balance and blend of experience and kids. It was right to bring them on the way we did. We were a good counter-attacking team with the pace of Rod Wallace and the skill of Matthew Le Tissier, who was a complete one-off.

'He couldn't head the ball or tackle – and he was never going to run 50 yards to close someone down or track back. That was just never going to happen.

'But his ability on the ball was phenomenal. You just had to give him the ball and challenge him to show what he could do. He had such skill that he could win a game from nowhere with a piece of utter brilliance.

'It was quite hard to take for a player like me, who worked so hard just to be able to win the ball and kick it into the stands!'

After six seasons of stability more than success, Nicholl paid the price for failing to emulate the achievements of McMenemy – although his replacement, Ian Branfoot, was to find it even tougher.

'I can't complain about getting the sack. I had six years, which is longer than a lot of managers get – especially considering I was a beginner at it. And we did OK, considering our budget.

'I thought we could have got to a cup final, but we lost a couple of semi-finals and although we were flying high in the table a couple of times, we could not sustain it.

'I had a lot of support from the board, which helped. Ted Bates was brilliant for me. He appreciated it was my first job, so he was a great source of advice. But he also knew when to say something and when to let me get on, so I never felt threatened or under pressure.'

'Ted was very influential in me getting the job. I had a good backroom team in Dave Merrington, Ray Graydon, Dennis Rofe and others. They were all terrific and helped with the transition after Lawrie left, which was a huge upheaval for the club.'

Now Nicholl is enjoying his retirement in the Midlands, regularly playing squash against former Villa striker Gary Shaw and – he insists – usually beating him.

The only downside to life is trying to remember all the good times – or at least the names of those he played with or managed.

Like many ex-pros from that era, he is convinced the damage was done by the physical aspect of the game, though he bears absolutely no resentment.

'I do struggle with memory loss now and I know that has definitely come from heading too many balls during my playing days. It is something I worked on all the time in training when I was with Villa.

'After the session finished, I would get Ray Graydon to keep crossing the ball for me to head. I know now that it damages the brain and there has been a lot of research into it.

'These days, you hardly ever see heading sessions in training. People know the risks. But I don't regret anything. I enjoyed almost every minute of my career and I would not change it.'

Jimmy Case

THROUGHOUT THIS book, one name crops up constantly in answer to the question: 'Who was the hardest player you ever encountered?'

Jimmy Case. The name is usually spoken with a shudder as memories stir of eye-watering tackles which had often been preceded by a threatening whisper.

It let any offending opponent know that retribution was on its way. Not immediately, maybe not even during that same game – but it would happen. And it would hurt.

The original hard case, Jimmy was invaluable to the young Saints coming through under Chris Nicholl. The fledgling talents of Matthew Le Tissier, the Wallaces and even Alan Shearer were all able to flourish because of the intimidating presence of the menacing midfield minder. If one of them took a whack, Case would dispense his own form of justice – but quietly, discreetly and ruthlessly.

He explained: 'I was good at going under the radar and at looking out for my team-mates. I would see things develop and if someone was intimidating the likes of Matthew Le Tissier or Danny or Rod Wallace, they would have me to answer to.

'I remember Steve McMahon put in a challenge on a young Jason Dodd, which I thought was too brutal. He was only 19 and McMahon topped him in the first minute. Later on, I clattered him so hard that the pigeons flew off the floodlights.

'I used to look after the younger players, I was their minder. My presence would allow the likes of Tiss to operate more freely. If opponents knew I was around, they were more likely to leave him alone because they knew there would be something coming back from me later in the game.

'I would not go steaming in, though. I would wait for the right moment… when they don't know you are coming and when there are no eyes on you.

'I would go in hard and play the ball, but very often the opponent would be injured in the process. That's how it was then.

'It would be the same if someone put in a bad tackle on me. I would not jump up and get angry or protest. All that does is draw attention to you. The referee sees you are blazing so he keeps an eye on you. My expression never changed. I just got on with it… and waited for the right moment. Sometimes it might not even have been that game. Sometimes it might not even have been that season. But I would not forget. I was like a silent assassin.

'I was prepared to bide my time. Sometimes you would even see me laughing and joking. I never let my expression betray my feelings. And I would never complain to the referee even if I took a whack. I didn't want to make myself a target or give the referee that information.

'That way, if I made a hard challenge later in the game, I would get a bit more leeway. I could make out it was an accident or mistimed because, by then, that incident in the first half would no longer be in the referee's mind as much as it would be if I had made a song and dance about it.'

It was a cold, calculating approach which not only ensured that he avoided the referee's wrath, but also had the effect of unsettling the intended victim, who would spend the rest of the match looking over his shoulder, waiting for the inevitable payback.

Case cannot understand the kind of hot-headed instant retaliation which often lands the player who has been fouled in more trouble than the one who committed the first offence.

'These days, you see players have the ball taken off them and then chase after the opponent and nudge them or foul them, which is just stupid. It is much better to wait.

'I was also very good at judging the mood of a game. I could tell sometimes that the next person to make a tackle would be in the book – usually a forward.

'So I would hold back and not make any more tackles until someone had been booked. It was just a case of being clever.

'I certainly would not do what Neil Ruddock did against Notts County and charge half the length of the field to headbutt someone.

'I once had a chat with him off the pitch and said, "Do me a favour, next time there is a bust-up count to ten before you set off. By then, it will probably all be over."

'The next game, there was another incident. I was in midfield and I saw Neil ready to set off. I just gave him a look and he stopped dead and I could see him mouthing the numbers. If I hadn't done that, he would have got involved and he couldn't afford that.

'A lot of players would get involved when they didn't need to and that puts them on the referee's radar.'

A perfect example of Case's willingness to pick his moment came when Arsenal's Paul Davis infamously broke Glenn Cockerill's jaw in September 1988.

Saints had started the season in fantastic form, winning their first three games, and were top of the league when they went to Highbury for a match which was to have far-reaching repercussions.

Case recalled: 'Tiss and Rod Wallace had put us 2-0 up and in control before Davis slyly punched Glenn off the ball. Glenn was not a dirty player, but he was one of those who would get on an opponent's nerves because he never gave in. He was everywhere and was prepared to put his foot in and is as honest as the day is long.

'Some players think they have a divine right to stroll around and run the game and not be challenged – especially at London clubs. I think Paul Davis probably got frustrated because Glenn was putting in little biting challenges to stop him playing.

'It certainly was not the case of Glenn uttering a racial insult, as was later claimed. Glenn is not like that at all. I think Davis just got frustrated and hit him.

'I knew it was him so when Arsenal got their inevitable penalty, that was my opportunity because I knew the referee would be looking at the taker and the keeper.

'I set off from outside the box at exactly the same time as Brian Marwood and whacked Davis on the back of his left calf and then just carried on running into the box.

'There is a clip on YouTube where you can just see me running in at speed in the bottom left corner of the screen. Marwood scored with about seven minutes left to change the game.

'The referee was David Axcell, who hadn't noticed Glenn getting hit and probably thought he was time-wasting, so he added on nine minutes of stoppage-time.

'Of course, the Gunners got an equaliser seven minutes into added time to snatch an undeserved point. The other annoying thing for me is that ultimately won them the title ahead of Liverpool.

'Everyone remembers the incredible finale to the season when Arsenal had to win 2-0 at Anfield in the last game – and got an injury-time winner from Michael Thomas to steal the crown.

'But if there hadn't been so much time added on against us, they would never even have been in a position to do that.

'Apart from my own retribution, Davis also got hammered by the FA with a then record nine-match ban. It was the first instance of video evidence being used retrospectively.

'I wouldn't do things like that very often, just when it was deserved. The referee had done nothing, so I took the law into my own hands and gave him a proper whack.

'Ray Kennedy had taught me that. He told me about when he was playing for Arsenal and they had got a penalty. He was standing on the edge of the area and just as the kick was taken, Peter Osgood elbowed him on the nose.'

Case learned from an early age how to look after himself on the field, first at school and then playing with and against burly dockers in men's leagues.

He learned through painful experience that going into a tackle half-heartedly would often mean coming off worse. So, although he would not intend to injure an opponent, neither would he ever pull out of a challenge.

'I never set out to hurt anyone, it was just that competitive side of the game and that will to win. I had always had it, even as a kid making my way up through non-league and pub teams.

'That was an education – and it really toughened me up playing for Blue Union, a dockers team in a rough area of Garston. They would all be out on a Saturday night, so the dressing room would stink of beer the next day.

'I didn't drink at the time as I was only 16. Then I joined South Liverpool, which was still rough, but I was a better player then.

'It was a real steep learning curve and a big education for me. I was playing against men so I quickly learned when to jump, when to lean in. I was taking shoulder charges which knocked me all over the place.

'But I learned to take the knocks and to ride them – and then to give it out as well.

'If you go in hard, you are less likely to get hurt. I learned that at the age of eight. If you go right through and commit yourself, you are more likely to come out of it OK. It is the ones who hesitate who get hurt.

'My school teachers explained it is common sense. If you start to pull out against someone going full throttle, then it stands to reason you are going to get hit.

'A lot of it is about body position and posture, bracing yourself, being strong. A lot of the time the ball does not even move in a 50-50 tackle, but the two bodies do.

'If you are stronger than him with a better stance, you end up staying on your feet while he will end up on the floor. Sometimes you will both remain standing and have a second go but if you move slightly to one side, the ball will spin out. It is all split-second stuff.

'But honestly, I never set out to do anyone. People often ask me about the Everton player Geoff Nulty, whose career was ended by a challenge in the Merseyside derby at Goodison.

'The truth is we both slid in for the ball, but there were no studs from either of us. We collided knee on knee – it is just that my knee happened to be stronger than his. It was a complete accident. Honestly, that is all there was to it.

'I never broke anyone's leg. It was simply a case of going in with aggression to let them know you were there. I might have given the odd toe poke on an ankle, but that was it.'

Case always had the mantra of 'live by the sword, die by the sword' and he never had a problem with anyone who made the mistake of trying to take him on at his own game.

'You soon get to know which players are genuine, the ones who can take it as well as dish it out. And you get to know the ones who will try to top you.

'Andy Gray actually said he was thinking of doing me in a game for Everton and set off to do it. He admits it was a stupid idea but he came flying in. I evaded the challenge and next minute he had studs up the inside of his leg.

'I walked away and, as he was being stretchered off, I stood there waving and saying "Bye bye, Andy".

'Bryan Robson was hard but fair. We had some right tussles, which made it all the more harsh that when I was sent off for Saints at Old Trafford, it was for a nothing challenge.

'I was chasing after him and if there was any contact, it was maybe the width of a sock. He stumbled and went over. Even if it was a foul Kevin Moore was back, so I was certainly not the last man.

'But George Courtney was the referee and everything was about him. He made up his mind instantly to send me off and he would not even look at the video afterwards. He decided he was right and that was it.

'As Robson got up, I shook his hand and said it was not his fault. But that cost me three games – and those are matches you never get back.

'Another ridiculous red card came at Newcastle when there was a bit of pushing and shoving. I went in below the radar, in and out quickly. But another player was sent off for a second bookable offence.

'We appealed and went up to Lancaster Gate. We were called in and the three men in judgment asked us to state our case. I stood up and said we are claiming mistaken identity.

'They looked at us in disbelief as I was standing next to Danny Wallace, who is short and black. I took the booking and Danny – rightly – got off.

'It was important that he did because, in those days, a sending-off was a real black mark against you when it came to playing for England. Nowadays it does not matter as much, but back then you needed a clean CV to get an international call-up.

'Maybe that's why I never played for England!'

Even now, it seems incredible that Case never collected a coveted cap. Widely regarded as the best player never to play for England, he was everything that his country needed then – and now.

He was far from simply a clogger, although England certainly needed an enforcer in his mould. He could also play a bit with a range of passing, which could open the tightest defence.

During his time at Anfield, he would frequently be the only player training at Melwood during international weeks. And even during his time at The Dell, there were calls for him to get a belated but deserved call-up.

'I would love to have played for England, but I don't feel bitter about anything or anyone. It just did not happen for me.

'When Ron Greenwood took over as England manager he took seven players from Liverpool, so maybe he thought he could not pick me as well.

'But it meant there were weeks when I was pretty much training on my own because I was the only one not on international duty.

'Liverpool used to win loads of trophies at the time, so the manager Bob Paisley was asked by journalists why England were not successful when they had so many Anfield players. He said, "They don't play Jimmy Case, do they?"

'I don't have any hard feelings. Although I would love to have played for England, I would also have been happy just to play one full season for Liverpool. Everything else was a bonus.

'I was not just a hard-man – I could play a bit too. But back then, it was a more physical game and crowds would love a good 50-50 challenge. It could give the stadium a real lift.

'That is something which has been lost from the game. Everything is about passing and intercepting now. Back then, you were usually allowed one tackle. Referees would have a chat and warn you that the next one would land you in the book.

'And there were more characters back then – the likes of Frank Worthington, Stan Bowles, Alan Ball and so many more. Fans loved watching them because they gave everything and that is what people want to see.

'I don't think there are any real hard-men left now. Even if they have the physical attributes, there is very little they can do with the rule changes which have come in.

'The diving is appalling, but it has become part and parcel of the game. It is almost a non-contact sport.

'I could have played in the modern game because I could pass the ball – but I would have had to have modified my style. I had the skill – and most of the game is about brain rather than brawn and I had the intelligence to be able to read the game and pass the ball.'

Those qualities, though, were not enough to persuade Ian Branfoot to keep Case after he succeeded Chris Nicholl as manager.

It was the first – and biggest – mistake that Branfoot made, setting the tone for much of what followed during a turbulent two-and-a-half-year spell in charge.

Case could have been his biggest asset but Branfoot did not see things that way and let him go, sparking fury among the fans.

'What I do know is that Branfoot did not give me a chance. I guess he had his own reasons, but the first thing he did when he came in was to release me. That hurt me.

'The worst thing was he made out that he was doing me a favour by "rewarding" me with a free transfer. I said to him, "I have been here longer than five years, I am over 34 – I am *entitled* to a free transfer. You have given me eff all." And I turned round and left.

'He probably just saw me as an old pro who could not run as much as he wanted, so he decided to get rid of me without even seeing what I could do.

'He said I could not keep up with play and might not be suited to the long-ball game he wanted to play. I said I was not keen on that style of play – in fact, I hated it.

'But I could have played it. No one could ping a long pass like me. I used to do it all the time. I would spray it left towards the corner flag because I knew Rod Wallace had the pace to get there and I could play it right direct to Matthew Le Tissier because I knew he would not bother to chase it if I didn't find him.

'There was one match when he clearly did not want to run and when I passed the ball to his feet, he gave it me back. I shaped to switch it to Rodney and then thought I wasn't having that, so I gave the ball back to Tiss.

'Again, he played it back to me and again I went to play it left to Rodney before turning back. This time I played it to Matt's chest, so he had to work.

'Amazingly, he flicked the ball over the defender, darted past and crossed for Shearer to score. Sometimes he just needed a challenge. I think there were times he found the game too easy and needed to be tested.

'So I could have played the long-ball game, even though I didn't like it. And I did think, with all my experience and skill and service, that I deserved a chance.

'He said I would not play enough, but I went to Bournemouth and played 49 games for them at the age of 39.

'Maybe he saw me as a threat or thought I was too big a character in the dressing room, but I could actually have been an asset to him. The worst thing was he didn't get to know me and that was a mistake.

'I wasn't after his job. I didn't want to be a manager or even a coach. I just wanted to play. I know managers do look after themselves and get rid of anyone they perceive as a threat, but I was not like that.

'It was a shame the club sacked Chris Nicholl. I got on well with him and he was building a good side. We had a lot of good youngsters coming through with the likes of Tiss and Rod Wallace and a certain Alan Shearer.

'You saw even then that he was going to be a top player – and not just because of the hat-trick he scored on his debut against Arsenal.

'You could see he had skill and finishing ability, but he also had incredible mental strength.

'Even when he lost his way a bit and the goals dried up, he would stay behind after training to work at it.

'I would knock the ball in for him to strike and, of course, he developed into one of the best strikers this country has ever produced.

'Some forwards would worry where their next goal was coming from, but nothing fazed Alan. He kept doing the same things which had got him goals before knowing they would come again.

'He was so focused, so strong. People would try and turn him over, but he just kept going. He had pace, a directness and a real single-mindedness to know exactly where he was going to put the ball.

'You could put him away through the middle and that was it. I had confidence in him – and he had confidence in himself.

'At the time, we had a good blend of youth and experience and it is a real shame we did not quite manage to win any silverware because we were not far away.

'The fans deserved that because they were amazing and we got close with a cup semi-final against Everton, which we should have won, and then another against Liverpool, when Mark Wright broke a leg.

'We played good, attacking, entertaining football and I would have loved us to go on and win something. We were probably just one or two quality signings away from doing that.

'We could have really pushed on. It was just the purse strings which held us back, which was a shame.'

Case may not have won silverware with Saints, but he is still the most decorated player to pull on the red and white stripes (or the Danish pyjamas kit for that matter). With three European Cups, four league titles, one UEFA Cup and a League Cup to his name, Case can point to his medal collection as evidence that he did not simply run around kicking opponents.

He had an exquisite range of passing, a deft touch for a hard-man and a ferocious shot, which brought him Liverpool's consolation in their 2-1 FA Cup Final defeat by Manchester United in 1977.

He guided Brighton to an unlikely FA Cup Final in 1983 before becoming Lawrie McMenemy's parting gift to Southampton.

'My time at Southampton was as good as any in my career. I enjoyed every minute. My relationship with the fans was great and I have no regrets at all about coming here.

'Lawrie said he bought me as a stop-gap and I stayed for six years. I think he later said that I was probably his best buy in terms of value for money as I cost just £30,000 and played some of the best football of my career.

'I moved to central midfield and really enjoyed it. I was a lot more involved than I had been on the wing and I became an important part of the team's function, which was very satisfying.

'I was fortunate to have a lot of very exciting youngsters around me and their potential was highlighted with a 4-1 home win over Liverpool, who went on to win the league. We were fantastic that day and could have had seven.

'We had a very young side out that day and if the kids had not been as good as they were, then we would have really struggled. But they had fantastic ability and helped to prolong my career.

'I was more than happy to take on the role of minder – on and off the field. Coming back from away trips, they would play cards and I would prepare their meals and then clean up. It helped pass the journey. I still tidy up to this day.'

Case was equally down-to-earth when it came to re-negotiating his contract. Not for him the inflated demands of today's pampered superstars or the media tantrums at the insult of 'only' being offered more in a week than most fans earn in a year.

'Contract negotiations were never a problem between me and Chris Nicholl. We would have a cup of tea and get it done in a few minutes. I would bring the match programme, show him how many games I had played and explain why I had missed the others and that was that. I was not bothered about money. I just wanted to play.

'Chris was a proper pro and I got on really well with him. He trusted me because he knew whatever I did off the field, I would never let him down on it.'

Case certainly enjoyed the odd escapade with the club, using foreign trips as a way of encouraging togetherness among the squad.

Pre- or post-season matches were a way for the players to let their hair down, away from the prying eyes of the media – unless they were out drinking too. Back then, it was a case of 'what goes on tour, stays on tour'.

With no camera phones then and no social media, players were able to enjoy a few drinks, which forged an unbreakable bond.

'Things were different off the field too in terms of drinking and socialising. Nowadays there seem to be more dressing-room cliques than bonding but, in our day, a few drinks would bring the lads together. We would all socialise together and enjoy a beer after the match. We had some fantastic trips abroad.

'I remember one trip to Portugal, where I had had a few and I needed batteries for my Walkman. I loved my music, so I was determined to hunt some down.

'None of the other players would open their doors to me – and I can't blame them. They were probably terrified.

'I was climbing over balconies and banging on doors. Eventually I ripped a door off its hinges. All kinds went on when we were away.

'Drinking sessions definitely brought the lads together. One year, I won the *Daily Star* Player of the Year award. I got a nice set of decanters in a wooden holder and £1,500… so I put my credit card behind the bar for the lads to share it.

'I also used to organise the Christmas parties, usually fancy dress. We would fine players for wearing a dodgy shirt or being late on a night out and all those "fines" used to pay for the Christmas do, which would be carefully arranged for a Monday night. I would tell Chris Nicholl when it was and he would know to cancel training the next day!

'One year, we had two sittings for the meal. The youngsters sat down first and the first-team players waited on them because they had been looking after our kit all year.

'One cheeky youngster almost got thumped, though, when he beckoned Peter Shilton over and said, "My man… I say…"

'Another year, I was telling Chris Nicholl the date of the party and out of the blue he asked how much we had in the kitty and said he would match it out of his own pocket. We only had £700 but instantly I told him it was £1,100, so we had a lot of cash that year.

'Even at Liverpool, if a new player joined us for a drink and ordered an orange juice, we would immediately say, "He'll never make it." Mind you, Kenny Dalglish did that and he did not turn out too badly!

'He was the best player I played with. Tiss was on a par in many respects because of what he was capable of doing with the ball. He was a joy to watch. But Kenny's work-rate was higher. He would help you all the time in terms of positioning to ensure you always had three options at all times.

'He would make himself available to you, so you did not have to pass it backwards. Tiss could be very frustrating as well as exhilarating. I remember playing in Francis Benali's testimonial and he was determined to turn it on for the crowd, so he tried to beat every opponent.

'The trouble was each time he lost the ball Graeme Souness and I would have to track back and try to win it. After about ten minutes, Graeme turned to me and said, "How the fuck did you ever manage to play with him?" The problem was that Graeme was Saints manager at the time!

'In terms of pure talent, though, there was no one to touch him and without a doubt he should have played more for England.

'I could not understand why Glenn Hoddle did not pick him. They were similar players in many ways, so you would have thought Glenn would have appreciated his talents and given him a bit more leeway.

'The thing about Matt is you actually expected him to produce something from nothing because he did it time and time again, so I cannot understand why he did not get more of a chance with England.'

So, if Dalglish and Le Tissier were the best players then – to return to the chapter's initial question – who was the hardest player he came across?

'Graeme Souness was the toughest player I ever encountered. It depends how you define "hard" but as well as strength and steel, he also had a presence.

'It is that presence which gives you a reputation and which intimidates opponents. He certainly had that. He could give a glowering stare, which frightened the life out of a lot of players and that was half the battle won.

'I first came across him when he was a youngster playing for Middlesbrough. I had no idea who he was, but I remember him going to knock the ball up the line. I stepped between him and the ball and made myself strong.

'I didn't elbow him, I just flicked him and popped him on the nose. He threw me to the floor. There was a great picture in the paper the next day of me on the ground. He had a hand around my throat and was just about to punch me.

'I looked up at him and said, "Go on… and you're off!" But there weren't many who would do that to me, so I knew then he had a bit about him. And then he came and joined us at Liverpool.

'The other hardest player I played alongside was Tommy Smith. I used to watch him from the terraces when I was a lad. I saw how he conducted himself, how he got stuck in, how he played the game.

'He played midfield for a while because although he was hard, like me, he could pass the ball. He could dribble and, of course, his tackling was second to none.

'He was my full-back when I made my debut and that was a fantastic experience for me. And it really meant something to get a "well done" from him for a tackle.

'He was a proper hard-man along with the likes of Stuart Pearce. By contrast, Vinnie Jones never came near me on the pitch.

'Recently, we were on the same table at a black tie dinner and he said he would never go to my side of the pitch.

'I bumped into the old Wimbledon player Terry Phelan in a wine bar in Manchester and he recalled a time he was playing at Southampton. At half-time, he was getting some iodine rubbed on some stud marks across his chest.

'Vinnie came over to him, winced at the wound and asked who did it. Phelan said, "Who do you effing think?" And Vinnie just forgot any thoughts of retribution!

'Fair play to him, he got himself off a building site and made a career for himself both on the field, and as a hard-man in movies.

'Terry Hurlock is another with that intimidating factor about him. He was all hair and muscle and put himself about.

'I remember one challenge with him when he had gone sliding in on someone and was on the floor. I slid in with my left foot and did not really care where the ball was going, but I knew my right knee was going into his thigh.

'But Terry was one of those who could take it as well as dish it out, a proper player. He was brought in by Ian Branfoot to replace me. He was younger than me, but could he run further than me? I don't know.'

It clearly still rankles that his happy times at The Dell were brought to a seemingly pointless and premature end. After playing 40 times for Bournemouth, he made a handful of non-league appearances before returning to Brighton, where he made 32 more appearances, including a brief spell as player-manager.

After hanging up his weapons of mass destruction, Case moved into the media working as a pundit and presenter for the club's own radio station The Saint and then for BBC Radio Merseyside.

He also acts as an Anfield ambassador and still keeps his hand in as a trained plumber and electrician, even working as a roadie just for the fun of it.

'I do like my music. I was fortunate enough to see Coldplay when they were just starting out because the drummer, Will Champion, is a big Saints fan.

'And I have been a roadie for Echo and the Bunnymen at a few festivals and concerts, which is fun. My mate managed them, so I was happy to help out.

'When I was at Brighton, they played the Concorde there. The lead singer, Ian McCulloch, needed another drink on stage and just shot me a look, so I went on and took him a brandy and coke. Of course, all the Brighton fans knew it was me and loved it.

'But I have always been quite down-to-earth. I love my fishing and I am more than happy sitting on a river bank with a cup of tea. My hell-raising days are long gone!'

John Burridge

ONE OF the proudest days of John Burridge's life was also one of the most painful.

It was the moment he realised he had helped turn Alan Shearer into the physical force that would make the young striker one of the world's top players.

The pair regularly used to stay behind after training when Burridge was at The Dell and Shearer was still an up-and-coming young prospect.

Burridge recalled: 'One of his heroes was Andy Gray. I used to play with him at Villa, so Alan was always asking me how Andy jumped, how he used his elbows, how he would bully the keeper.

'Alan had incredible determination and desire to learn and we did a lot of work together, both working out in the gym and jumping for crosses. He needed toughening up, so I worked on him.

'We would go to the gym on a Monday and a Wednesday and we would work on the weights together and that gave him the upper body strength he needed.

'In training I would punch him in the back of the head, smack into him and knee him in the back or the kidneys or the lungs as we jumped for the ball – and he would always come back for more. I expected him to quit but he kept going. You couldn't hurt him.

'I taught him how to clatter the keeper and we did a lot of gym work which really improved him. It was a waste of time trying that with Matt Le Tissier but Alan really got stuck in, even though he was only a young kid.

'One day, we were having a session of one-on-ones. Alan ran through but I just got to the ball first and he jumped over me. I jumped up, threw the ball at him, grabbed him by the shirt and yelled, "Don't ever do that again! Are you going to play like a woman all your life?" He looked stunned.

'I think he was frightened of hurting me but I told him the keeper expects you to smack into him. I told him, "You are allowed to block tackle the keeper in the chest, so don't ever pull out of a tackle again or I'll hit you."

'About seven years later, I was playing for Falkirk and we had a friendly against Blackburn. There was a 50-50 ball and Shearer chased after it. As I dived at his feet, he smashed into me. I lost two teeth and needed stitches in a face wound.

'He stood over me and said, "Well, you told me to do it." I was so proud, despite the pain. And that was only a friendly!'

Burridge never had any doubts that Shearer was going to succeed but even he never imagined just how much of an impact the youngster would make in his first game.

'He was just a kid, only 17. He used to come and babysit my kids, Thomas and Katie, for a fiver. Then, suddenly, he was thrown in against Arsenal with Martin Keown and Tony Adams in the centre of defence. He was very nervous but I had a word with him in the dressing room and reassured him he could do it – and he went out and scored a hat-trick. I remember thinking "Bloody hell!"

'But that was years in the making. It was down to all the fitness work, the conditioning, the training, the battering he took from me and, above all, the mental toughness he had. He was like no one I had ever seen before. He was not the most skilful player by any means, but he wanted it so badly and he worked incredibly hard.

'He was a hell of a player. He was not a classic finisher like Matthew Le Tissier, but he was still a fantastic goalscorer. He could really strike a ball. And he had been given the right sort of education by Dave Merrington.

'As youth team coach, he did a fantastic job for the club. He brought through the likes of Shearer and the Wallace brothers and Le Tissier and gave them the mental toughness to handle the top flight.

'Le Tissier was incredible… when he had the ball. He would be first out for training in the morning and the last one to come in, provided he had a ball at his feet. Ask him to do any running and he was useless.

'It took me a while to realise what he was like and, in one of my early games at Manchester United, I remember screaming at Chris

Nicholl, "Tell that fat bastard to run with their full-back." Poor Gerry Forrest had to handle two players on his own – but Tiss was brilliant going forward and we won 2-0.

'That was around the time Chris Nicholl tried to make him eat pasta before games and his form dipped. Russell Osman, Jimmy Case and I led a deputation from the senior players and pleaded with Chris to let him go back to his previous pre-match meal of a McDonalds.

'He could do incredible things with a football. You would not see him for much of the match then he would strike an amazing goal from nowhere then go back to picking his nose and scratching his arse... but he would win us the game.

'I had no idea how good Southampton's academy was until I joined. Then I watched Dave Merrington work the youngsters, toughening them up, driving them on, teaching them good habits and skills. He masterminded that academy.

'He was different class.

'And they have continued to do it with the likes of Gareth Bale and Theo Walcott and Alex Oxlade-Chamberlain and so many more. With the possible exceptions of Porto and Atletico Madrid, I would say they are the best-run club in the world because they keep churning the players out.'

That fulsome praised is tinged with more than a touch of frustration for Budgie, as Burridge is commonly known. He is disappointed to see that Saints have continued to sell their best players, just as they did when he was at the club.

'It is so sad when you look at the amount of top-quality players they have let go over the years. You will never get any success if you do that.

'It is all the more annoying when you see what Leicester did. That could have been Southampton if they had kept all their players. They could certainly have got to the Champions League.

'Saints are a bigger club than Leicester, so they could have done it if they had held on to their talent. Their recruitment over the years has been superb and that is the secret of running a club well. The manager only gives you about ten per cent. The rest is down to the players.

'Before I came to Southampton, I had no clue they had so many good youngsters. That came as a big surprise to me when I signed. It was not what I was expecting at all.

'I had played there many times and it was always against old guys like Alan Ball and Peter Osgood, players who were coming to the end of their careers, and Lawrie McMenemy got a bit more out of them.

'That's what I thought I was joining. I thought I was coming to a ridiculous little stadium with a stand that looked like a double-decker bus. When I first walked out there as a Southampton player, I realised it was a great little ground… for the home team. It was so intimidating for the opposition – but not half as scary as Jimmy Case!

'Now, he *was* a hard-man! And he was clever too. I have never seen anyone do it so well. If Gerry Forrest or Derek Statham was having a hard time against a winger, he would go over and tell them to play in midfield for a while.

'He would wait until the ball was in the air and everyone was looking at it then *crack*, he would whack the winger round the back of the legs. And by the time everyone looked round, Jim would be 30 metres away.

'Fans that had seen it would be laughing but the referee would not know what happened or what to do. His timing was perfect.

'And he would still have time to issue a warning: "Stay down, I'll be back in ten minutes!" And then he would just vanish from the scene of the crime.

'Of course, back then we didn't have as many cameras. There was just the one which followed the ball and maybe one behind each goal. Nowadays you couldn't do it because there are so many cameras that one of them would pick it up.

'But Jimmy didn't boast about it and he would never get into an argument with the referee or the opponent. I called him a silent assassin who did his job and disappeared.

'He was not a shouter. He was quiet in the dressing room and in training he knew what he had to do and just did enough. But he was a real leader and a proper captain.

'He would look out for the rest of the lads off the field, as well as on it. We would get on the bus after a win at Old Trafford or Anfield and Jim would put a little apron on and start looking after the lads.

'Back then, you could drink on the bus so the first thing we would do after an away win was stop at an off-licence. Chris Nicholl and Dennis Rofe would get off the coach and come back with bottles of wine and some cases of beer.

'We had already had a couple in the players' lounge and with a long journey back, we were ready for a few more. The lads would get stuck into the beers while Jim would come round and sort out the food.

'He would say things like, "Well played Budgie, some good saves. Beef or chicken?" And he would heat up a microwave meal and serve it. And if you had had a really good game, he would give you extra. And he did that for all the lads.

'Afterwards, he would clean up all the rubbish, tidy the tables and the coach would be left spotless. Everything had to be clean and neat for him. He was a tidy player too. He could pick out a pass and put the ball on a sixpence.

'Then, at the opposite end of the scale, you had Neil Ruddock, who was louder and nowhere near as subtle as Jim.

'I had no idea who he was when we signed him from Millwall, but I soon found out he would kick his own grandmother. He was a big strong lad and when he cleared the ball, it stayed clear.

'He was a good footballer too, a better player than a lot of people think. But he did like to kick people. He would smack someone on the halfway line and be very apologetic to the referee.

'He would say, "Yes sir and sorry sir." Then he would run towards me with his back to the referee and he would be giggling away.

'We had some great characters in the side. Nowadays footballers are all up their own arses, but we used to go out to clubs together as a group and it built a great team spirit.

'I loved my time at Southampton.

'When Chris Nicholl bought me from Sheffield United, he said he needed me for two or three years at the most. He explained he had a brilliant young keeper coming through by the name of Tim Flowers, but he wasn't ready yet.

'I knew Tim. I had worked with him at Wolves. I brought him through. He stayed at my house and I treated him like a son. I would give him bed and board and give him a lift to reserve games, then I would sit behind his goal to encourage and monitor him.

'Tim was a smashing kid and good young keeper. I really liked him and was delighted to work with him again.

'Chris asked me to help get him ready and said as soon as he was then he would take over from me. I said that was no problem. I knew where I stood.

'But it was a tough assignment for me because I had to replace Peter Shilton, who was such a legend, but I think I did OK. So, after a couple of years, I went to Chris Nicholl to ask for a rise.

'I said, "I know what Shilts was on and I know what I am on… at least give me half of what he was on." He was very apologetic and said the directors would never allow it. Some things never change.

'Southampton never paid a lot, which is one reason they kept losing their best players, and it's a trend which has continued to this day.

'I loved my time at Southampton. It was a great club, I had a good rapport with the fans and there was never any real pressure. As long as they stayed up, they were happy. And it was a beautiful place to live, near enough to the bright lights but out of the spotlight.

'I am not ashamed to admit I was a mercenary. If I could get more money, I would move. Saints would not pay me more, so I joined Newcastle.'

That switch was eventually to give Burridge the ultimate payback for one particular clash at The Dell during a 2-1 Littlewoods Cup home victory over Tottenham.

He recalled: 'We were hanging on and Spurs got a corner with a minute or so to go. I held on to the ball trying to use up a bit of time and Ossie Ardiles went to grab it off me.

'I gave him the slightest nudge and he went down holding his face and screaming that I had elbowed him, trying to get me sent off. So I decided to let him have it.

'I had a lovely little trick where I would sharpen the two studs at the back of each boot so they were like arrows. I knew when the officials checked our boots before a match normally, they just ran their hands quickly over the front studs. That was all they had time for.

'They would have noticed the front ones, so I would just do the ones at the back and then, when the referee was not looking, I would bring my boot down on the striker's metatarsal and break it.

'It sounds bad but in those days it was live by the sword, die by the sword, and I could just as easily have been on the receiving end if I had shown any signs of weakness.

'I did not do it often but if a striker was trying to bully or batter me, then I would make sure the referee was not looking and then give them a little kick with the back studs.

'When Spurs finally took their corner, Ardiles tried to stamp on me so I had a look round and thought "Right, you are getting it" and I stamped on his metatarsal. He went down screaming in agony. We cleared the ball and the final whistle went.

'As I ran to the fans at the double-decker end, he chased after me calling me an animal. He was still behind me as we headed for the dressing rooms. We had to climb this flight of steps, which were hazardous enough in studs at the best of times, and I could still hear him mouthing off behind me.

'The Spurs boss was Terry Venables, who had managed me at Crystal Palace and knew what I was like. He was waiting at the top of the stairs and tried to pull Ossie away from me.

'I said, "Let him go, I'm ready for him." Neil Ruddock was behind me yelling at me to hit the little c**t. Ardiles pushed me and I almost fell down the stairs, but just managed to stop myself. He was still shouting, so I hit him. It was just after Britain and Argentina had gone to war and I yelled, "We beat you in the Falklands, we have beaten you tonight… now fuck off!" I shouldn't have said it, but my head had gone because he had pushed me so far.

'I told Terry to get him away before I did real damage. Spurs complained but it was all swept under the carpet. Chris Nicholl accepted my explanation and I thought that was an end of it.

'But football has a funny way of biting you on the bum when you least expect it and a couple of years later, when I was playing at Newcastle, they sacked Jim Smith.

'His successor was kept hush-hush, so we had no idea who we were going to meet when we were called to the dressing room. When I saw Ossie Ardiles walk in, I knew I did not have long left at the club.

'He went round every player and shook their hand, but when he got to me he walked straight past and blanked me. I was dropped from the team and told I was not welcome around the club. The only thing was he did not have the guts to tell me himself, he let other people do it.'

At the age of 40, many players might have thought their career would be over – not Budgie. He was barely a third of the way through the 29 clubs he would eventually play for.

His 12th club turned out to be Hibernian, where he won a Scottish League Cup winners' medal but, perhaps more crucially, he also completed his coaching badges while north of the border.

That was to prove pivotal in his future, but first there was the small matter of becoming the oldest player ever to appear in the Premier League. He was working as Newcastle's goalkeeping coach when he was asked to join Manchester City on loan as emergency cover for Tony Coton, never expecting to play. Once again, the footballing fates conspired as Coton got injured and Burridge came off the bench – against Newcastle.

In those days, there was no rule barring players from facing their parent club and, of course, Budgie played a blinder to keep a clean sheet in a 0-0 draw which severely dented his employers' title hopes.

He went on to make four appearances for City, the last coming on 14 May 1995 against QPR at the age of 43 years and 162 days. It is a record which still stands today and one he is very proud to hold.

By the time he finally hung up his boots in 1997, after a spell as player-manager at Blyth Spartans, Burridge was 46 and had played 771 league games in England and Scotland, turning out for a record 15 Football League clubs.

After 30 years in the professional game, retirement not only left a massive hole in his life but almost cost him his life.

Many footballers struggle to come to terms with the isolation and emptiness of retirement but for a hyperactive, larger-than-life character like Budgie, it was as though his very reason for living had been wrenched from him.

He had clung on to his playing status as grimly as he did the football he would regularly clutch in bed each night.

Suddenly he had no reason to get up, no club to go to, no training to prepare for. And he seriously contemplated suicide.

Without the buzz of football, the adrenaline-rush of running out in front of a crowd, Burridge was struggling to make sense of the only life he had known since he was 15.

He slumped into a black pit of despair, shutting himself away from his loyal wife, Janet, and from the concerned colleagues who tried to help.

He said: 'If I had been thinking clearly I would have seen I had plenty to live for, but I convinced myself that my family would be better off without me.

'I shut myself away in the bedroom for days on end crying. I did not shave or eat, I was a complete mess. I thought I would be better off dead and was seriously contemplating suicide.

'Thankfully, my wife, Janet, recognised the danger signs. In desperation, she rang Kevin Keegan, my old boss at Newcastle. Between them, they got me the help I needed.

'They say it is men in white coats who cart you away, but in my case it was three men in green boiler suits who broke the door down and jabbed a needle in my arse. I woke up in the Priory and stayed there for five months.

'There was one moment I will never forget. We were doing group therapy and I stood up and explained I was suicidal because I had been a footballer all my life and could no longer play.

'The next person was a woman who had lost both her children and her husband in a road accident. That really shook me and put things into perspective for me. I realised there were people with far worse problems than me.

'I felt a bit pathetic by comparison, but I came out with a much more positive attitude.'

There is an inescapable irony in Burridge being sectioned. All through his playing career, he had been labelled crazy for some of the things he did – and yet now many of them are commonplace in the game.

Of course, not all of them caught on. You never see a goalkeeper play a full match in a Superman costume these days – sponsors and stuffy FA rules would never allow it.

Nor do you see goalkeepers regularly doing handstands or swinging from the bar to entertain the crowd as part of their pre-match routine.

'I might not have known exactly why I was doing it but the principle was sound,' laughed Burridge. 'Instinctively, I knew I needed to do those stretches. Now everyone does it… though maybe in a less flamboyant way.

'People thought I was crazy, but I wasn't. I was just totally dedicated. I didn't drink, I ate, slept and breathed football and I was a fitness fanatic.'

That was never more evident than when Saints arrived at Elland Road. The players had to walk past the Leeds United gym and the door was open so they could see Vinnie Jones working on the weights in a bid to psych them out.

Burridge marched in, pushed him out of the way, moved the pin to the maximum load – and pumped iron.

He laughed: 'I worked so hard on my fitness but I knew instinctively what I needed. I couldn't see the point of me going on the long endurance runs we used to do in pre-seasons.

'I never needed to run that sort of distance in a match. What I needed was short sharp bursts and sprints. But I was told I had to join in with the others, which seemed a waste of time.

'When I started working with other keepers, we tailored our fitness work to what we actually needed. Nowadays everyone does it.

'I used to get someone to sit behind my goal and count the number of saves and passes I made, and I would analyse them all and look at what I could have done differently or better. Today, clubs use Pro Zone and all sorts of scientific data to do the same thing.

'I had hypnosis tapes, which I would listen to before a match to get me in the zone and to pump me up. These days, clubs employ psychologists for that.

'So, although they called me crazy, I was actually ahead of my time in many ways – though even I would never have worn one pink boot and one blue, like some players do now. If anyone had tried that in our day, they would have got slaughtered.'

After leaving the Priory, Burridge decided to make a clean break from English football and moved to the Middle East. He spent ten years working as goalkeeping coach for the Oman Football Federation helping the national keepers. He has since worked as a TV pundit and goalkeeping coach around the Middle East, unearthing the gem that is Ali Al Habsi.

It was a move that not only re-energised his life but almost cost him it in a freak accident. He was cycling home one day when a van door swung open without warning. As he swerved to avoid it, he was hit by a car.

He said: 'It was doing 120 kilometres an hour and it smashed straight into me. I was dragged 50 metres and very nearly died. It is probably just as well I was so physically fit because I took a real battering.

'I was unconscious for days. I had a broken back and needed 147 stitches in my face. I had 14 damaged teeth and my collarbones are all metal now. I thought I would set off airport scanners but I don't.

'Thankfully, I made a full recovery and life is good now. I live in a beautiful place in a fabulous country. The only problem is that it is like a furnace from May to September.

'The rest of the year it is like Spain, it is beautiful. But for those few months it is 47 degrees, so you can't go out. You have to wait until the evening to go training.

'That's why I was surprised when Qatar bought the World Cup and said it was going to be a summer tournament. It is only the size of Hampshire!

'It was not just the matches because they could have built air-conditioned stadiums. It would have been the rest of the time away from the games. People would have died.

'But it is a beautiful place to live and I feel very lucky to be here – in every sense.'

Mark Dennis

IT SAYS a lot about Mark Dennis that when he tells people he has had three brushes with death, the general reaction is: 'Only three?'

Like many of the game's hard nuts, the steely left-back known as Psycho played with the philosophy of 'live by the sword, die by the sword' – except in two of the instances it was a knife.

Dennis laughed: 'I have almost died three times, so I guess you could say I am lucky to still be here. Twice I got stabbed and once I suffered a haematoma after a game at Manchester United. We drew 0-0 and Mark Hughes gave me a dead leg. I should have gone off but I played on.

'After that, we went straight to Newcastle for our next game. I should have taken something to get the swelling down, but like an idiot I thought I would be OK. I woke up about 4am in absolute agony.

'My thigh had swollen up like a tree trunk. It was three times its normal size. I thought it was going to split. I was rooming with Mark Wright, who called an ambulance. Next thing I knew, I was in hospital on a drip having lost three and a half pints of blood.

'There was a gaping wound where my leg had been cut open. It was so wide they could not stitch it, so I could see the inside of it.

'I was in the Freeman Hospital, which was only the second to have performed open heart surgery, but I just wanted to get home.

'I kept on at Lawrie McMenemy to get me home and had a row with him about it. They wouldn't move me – but then my wife, Jane, came up to visit and charged it all to the club, which Lawrie wasn't happy about.

'She undid my drip and took me down the pub for a drink. It was mad. I could have got an infection and lost a leg or worse but it just seemed like a laugh at the time, so I went with it. When Lawrie found out, he went ballistic. Two days later, I was on a plane back to Southampton. I never thought I would make a full recovery, but I did.'

At this point, Dennis drops his trousers to show off a spectacular scar from his left hip to knee and laughs at the memory of his former partner sneaking him out of hospital. He admits that turbulent relationship was frowned upon by the club.

'We married too young really and ended up drifting apart. We became more like brother and sister. It cost me a lot to divorce her, but it was the best £20,000 I ever spent. It was a lot of money back then. The club paid half, probably because they were just so glad to get me out of that relationship.'

Dennis still shudders at the thought of his two other narrow escapes with death, adding: 'I was stabbed with a carving knife after a late night out.

'It must have penetrated about four or five inches. The mistake was taking it out of my shoulder. I shouldn't have done that. I lost three pints of blood, but fortunately I lived round the corner from Solihull Hospital.

'Ron Saunders was the manager and I didn't dare tell him what had happened when I went in all stitched up on the Monday. I told him I had been working in a greenhouse when a window broke and a big shard of glass fell on me. I never pressed charges, but there was no apology.

'They say the first cut is the deepest. It was for me. The second time I got stabbed, it wasn't as deep but could have been even more serious.

'It was a row over a taxi after a PFA do in London. I was waiting for a taxi with Warren Neill and this random guy jumped in and said it was his taxi. I said it wasn't and we had a scuffle and, as we wrestled on the ground, he pulled out a cut-back knife and stabbed me in the throat. A quarter of an inch more and I would have been dead. I still have no idea who it was. Jim Smith stood by me 100 per cent and I repaid him by helping us go top of the league and winning the player of the month award.

'The first stabbing was kept quiet, but the second made the press. There were lurid headlines along the lines of "Dennis slashed". They built it up to look like I had been attacked with a machete. It was ridiculous.

'I did lose a lot of blood and it did not help that Mark Wright had wound me up about the whole AIDS epidemic. People did not know a lot about it in the early days, so it was scary. We went to a party and Wrighty told me one of the guys was gay and that I had drunk out of his glass. I didn't sleep for three nights worrying.'

Remarkably, none of those near-death experiences included Chris Nicholl, who would cheerfully have strangled him on numerous occasions while he was manager at The Dell.

The pair literally came to blows, although strangely gained more respect for each other as a result of the bust-up which gave Dennis a scar which he still wears to this day.

Now the pair get on famously, sharing an understanding which was sadly lacking as Nicholl, in his first management role, struggled to handle the volatile left-back.

Dennis joked: 'I had my ups and downs with Chris. I get on great with him now – though he is still as ugly as ever. His nose is even more bent than mine!

'The problem was Chris took over a side which had just finished as runners-up to Liverpool and reached the FA Cup semi-final. The dressing room was full of stars – and he couldn't handle them. It was only a matter of time before it all kicked off.

'He was a nutter – though I am hardly one to talk. His hero was Chris Bonnington, the mountaineer. We lived in the same road and I used to walk past his house and see him climbing up the outside of it. He would have all the gear and be scaling it – he always said I had him climbing the walls!

'To be fair, he was an excellent player, a great defender. But I thought he had the personality of a tennis racket. I told him that – and he thumped me. It was fair enough, I suppose.

'I shouldn't have done it – and certainly not in front of the rest of the lads. I have never seen Nick Holmes laugh so much – and he never laughed at anything.

'We are on good terms now, but back then it was quite fraught and he sacked me.

'I won the case and got reinstated but I ended up having to move on, which really upset me because I loved the club, I loved the fans and I loved the area.

'That's why I still live here now – ironically still in that same road where Chris used to live.

'The big bust-up came after a story was leaked to the papers and Chris went on the warpath demanding to know who had done it.

'I was always taking the mickey, so he thought it was me. He got it into his head and no denials would shift it. They never did discover who it was.

'Anyway Chris could get aggressive and kept saying, "It was fucking you!" and I rose to the bait. I jumped up and said, "When you were a baby, were you fed with a catapult?" That was it. He went for me.

'He flew at me and landed a punch above my eye. I still have the scar now. I went to hit him back but ended up thumping our trainer George Horsfall, who had leapt in to try and separate us. I felt bad about that because he was a lovely guy.

'I went outside – and then stupidly went back in to try and have another go. Chris was in the shower and slammed the door so I could not get at him. The other lads grabbed me and Andy Townsend marched me down to the snooker hall to calm me down.

'I was hauled into a meeting with the board and I said I could not play for Chris again. I had a week off but the story got in the press, which made the situation worse.

'Ted Bates came round to see me and brought Chris so he could apologise – but my dad wouldn't let him in the house. I said I didn't want to play for him again – and three days later the club sacked me.

'I phoned the PFA and spoke to Gordon Taylor. I had played with him at Birmingham and we got on well. He said to leave it to him. Two weeks went past, during which time I had reporters door-stepping me because it was now a big story.

'The upshot was that I got reinstated, which was a big blow to Ted and to the board. But I knew then I was not going to play so when QPR came in for me, I went.

'The only reason I left was because Jim Smith was manager there. I had worked with him at Birmingham and I knew he was a top man so I went, even though truthfully I never wanted to leave Southampton.

'I had three great seasons there playing alongside some great players. We finished third in the top flight working with Peter Shreeves, who was the best coach I ever played for. He was superb and it was a shame he did not replace Jim instead of Trevor Francis, otherwise I would have stayed longer.

'When I signed, I walked in to be greeted by one of the coaches – Bobby Campbell. He had been manager of Pompey when we won 1-0 there in the FA Cup in 1984 and he gave me a funny look. I just said "Hello Skate!" and he laughed and gave me a big hug.

'That was a fantastic win for us at Fratton. I got hit on the head by a coin and, in the time added on for that injury, Steve Moran scored the winner. Three sides of the ground were totally silent and the other went mental.

'It was fantastic. The atmosphere had been evil. Danny Wallace had bananas thrown at him and actually ate one on the touchline, prompting Lawrie McMenemy to say afterwards, "We have had a great day. We have got two pounds of fruit, five pounds in loose change and a win!" That was quality.

'Poor Lawrie was wearing a beautiful suit and when he reached the dressing room it was covered in phlegm from being spat at. We were crying with laughter, but he was fuming and kept saying his wife would kill him. He was more worried about the suit than the result.

'We were told we couldn't leave because it was all kicking off, with fans fighting and coaches being stoned, but Mick Mills refused to stay in the dressing room and said he was going to find a bar.

'I went with him and I walked past the TV presenter Fred Dinenage in the corridor. He was a big Pompey fan and I just said "All right Fred?" and he snarled "Fuck off!" It was vicious and, at that moment, he meant it.

'I saw him recently at Solent University, where we were both speaking to students, and he remembered it and was really apologetic.'

It still seems wrong that Dennis never played for England – a glaring omission along with that of Jimmy Case.

With a cultured left foot, incredible strength in the tackle, a ferocious determination and swashbuckling style, Dennis was widely rated as one of the best left-backs in the country. All that was missing was temperament.

'It does hurt that I never played for England, but the only person to blame for that is me. You live by the sword, you die by the sword.

'I am sure my disciplinary record went against me. I never really got on with refs, you will be surprised to hear. There were a couple who were OK. You could have a bit of banter with Roger Milford, even though he loved himself so much that if he was made of chocolate he would eat himself. He was always looking after his hair.

'I liked Clive Thomas. I remember hurting Gerry Gow, who had done me the previous season. Early on, I smacked him with a tackle which was a sending-off really. Clive came over and I put my arm round him and said, "Sorry, I got there as quick as I could." He smiled and I am sure he changed his mind from red to yellow.

'But you can't do that with referees these days. There is no contact, no banter – and for all the technological help they get, I'm not sure they are any better.

'And they never come out and explain or defend their decisions. If a manager or player makes an error they have to talk about it on TV, but the officials just hide away.

'I couldn't stand Keith Hackett. He sent me off when I was playing for QPR at Spurs. Jim Smith had told me to put Nico Claesen into row Z. That's how the game was then.

'I put in a fierce tackle and got booked. Argentinian midfielder Ossie Ardiles had a word and tried to get me sent off. We then took the lead through Mark Falco and Ardiles tried to nutmeg me. I closed my legs and won the ball. I grabbed his shirt and he threw himself over.

'Hackett had the red card in his hand before he had even come over to see me. I went mad and my team-mate Dean Coney had to haul me off.

'It was not long after the Falklands war and Jim leapt from the dug-out and shouted, "We should have shot you with the rest of them!" He was sent to the stands for that.

'It was a massive story in the press. I was hauled before the FA, who decided to make an example of me and hit me with a 52-day ban, which was a record at the time. I also got a £2,000 fine while Jim got a £1,000 fine.

'The QPR chairman David Bulstrode paid the lot because he was so angry.

'On my way out, Hackett wagged his finger at me and said "Naughty boy!" I almost hit him.

'In fairness, I was 90 per cent wrong in all my sendings-off – apart from that one. It still rankles now. I think I got 12 red cards, but I lost count.

'I got one for fighting with Martin Keown at The Dell. We both deserved it, but now we have a laugh about it. We agree it was nothing personal, just business.

'John Fashanu and I both got sent off at The Dell and we ended up having a fight as we were going up the stairs to the dressing rooms. I took my boot off and hit him with it.

'But for all the talk, Fashanu and Vinnie Jones never went near Jimmy Case, who was the hardest player I ever played with.

'I remember one Christmas party when Jimmy turned up stark naked and literally swung on the chandelier to make his entrance. Peter Shilton thought it was disgusting – but then we thought the same about him. No one really liked him.

'There was one bust-up I had with him which cost me a front tooth. We played Athletic Bilbao in a pre-season friendly and he was always on at me about not being dedicated enough. He said I should have had 50 caps for England.

'We had a row and he told me to put my caps on the table. I told him to put his friends on the table. Later on, we were in a nightclub and I pulled this bird. I was on the dance floor with her and he started having a go at me.

'I said, "Just because you can't get a bird, you ugly bastard" – and he went mad. He waited behind the door on the way out and hit me. I went down and my tooth came out. He ran for the lift, but I got there just in time and put my foot in the door to stop it closing.

'I piled into the lift, the door closed and I went for him. There was no escape. Next morning, he had a split eye and I had a split lip and my tooth was killing me.

'Lawrie said he wanted a word. I got fined and Shilts didn't. At breakfast, he growled, "I never hit you hard enough." I grabbed a fork and went for him again – and lost another week's wages.

'I used to wind him up by saying "Cor! Tina!" after he was caught with his pants down in the back of a car with a girl called Tina.

'I remember the *Echo* said something on the lines of it being a bad week for Peter Shilton. First he came under fire for missing the crosses, now he's in trouble for crossing the missus!

'We used to call him Dracula because he was scared of crosses. That was his only weakness as a player.

'But he wasn't popular and I remember Frank Worthington getting him in such a strong headlock that I thought he wasn't going to survive. Shilts had said something naughty to him and Frank grabbed him so hard, he was going blue. David Armstrong persuaded him to let Shilts go. I told Dave not to interfere.'

Dennis smiles at the memories of the nights out which created a unique and tight bond between the players – though he fears this is another way the game is changing for the worse.

The unlikely title triumph of Leicester City showed what can be achieved by team spirit and a close-knit group of players working hard for each other – and clearly enjoying each other's company off the field.

But too often these days players stay home, away from the all-seeing and unforgiving lenses of the cameras everyone now has on their phones.

However, that does not mean players are any less likely to party – only now they are likely to seek other ways of getting high. A succession of stars have been pictured inhaling nitrous oxide and Dennis is convinced it is only a matter of time before a high-profile name is nailed for taking drugs.

'Players are different now. I don't think they have the sort of team piss-ups that we did. They probably just drink at home now. They all have home cinemas and their own bars, where they can drink or take drugs. I believe in the Premier League that there are at least two dozen players taking Class A drugs. There is no doubt in my mind about that.

'Booze would make them put weight on but Class A drugs won't. It is a no-brainer. They have plenty of money, so the cost isn't an issue – and they can snort as much as they want at home, away from the press or from mobile phone footage.

'I would have been in even more trouble if they had had mobile phones in my day. I dread to think what sort of footage they would have got – it would have been X-rated, that's for sure.

'I have tried cocaine and smoked weed in the past, but it was not for me. I always preferred a drink. And it was cheaper.

'I only earned £1,000 a week at Southampton and £2,500 a week at QPR. The most I ever earned in a week was £3,500. Now I am not saying it is bad money – I know most people would love that sort of salary. But it is only a fraction of what the current players get.

'I only ever played pissed once. That was for QPR, ironically against Southampton on Boxing Day. I was drinking until 4am and was still drunk at kick-off – but I had a stormer and we won 3-0.'

By his own admission, Dennis was a wild child who needed a steadying hand – even though he bitterly resented it at the time.

'I was a nightmare as a player. I needed some guidance. I was an explosion waiting to happen.

'I had a love-hate relationship with Lawrie McMenemy – I loved him and he hated me!

'The funny thing is I did actually like – and need – discipline.

'Lawrie was great like that. He would fine me but then add that if I did the business for him on Saturday then he would give me half of it back. That is good man-management.

'And that's what he was, a good man-manager. He was not a tracksuit manager. He did come out once in a tracksuit and we all fell about laughing. He never did it again.

'But he knew what players needed. Nick Holmes needed an arm round him. I needed a bollocking.'

After playing the last of his nine games for Crystal Palace, Dennis got his life in order helped by the love of a good woman and a bag full of cash.

'I finished playing in 1992 – just when the Premier League started and the big money started coming in. Good timing. I have always been mad on cricket, so I went to the Cricket World Cup in Australia.

'I went for the full nine weeks and saw England lose to Pakistan in the final – I was heartbroken. The whole thing cost me almost £30,000, but I loved it.

'I had some money left over from when I signed for Palace. It was paid in cash. I literally walked out with a suitcase with £25,000 in it and some carrier bags of cash.

'I had received payments when I left Southampton and Birmingham and QPR, but they were all done through the right channels.

'In those days, there was a lot of cash and backhanders going around yet George Graham was the only one who got caught.'

Dennis is well aware he was lucky to come out of his playing career relatively unscathed, despite the brushes with death and the law.

'What kept me sane was the fact I was playing and training with some of the best players in the world, I was going abroad and I was getting paid for something I loved. I feel very lucky.

'Look at Kenny Sansom – the man who kept me out of the England team and is now struggling as an alcoholic. Apparently, he drinks seven bottles of wine a day. I struggle with two on a good day – though I am going to have to cut down.'

He pats his belly and laughs: 'My wife told me I am starting to look like a badly packed rucksack!

'But I used to binge-drink a lot. Occasionally I still do, but nowhere near as much. I have seen a lot of footballers struggle with alcohol from George Best to Claus Lundekvam and, of course, Kenny Sansom.

'It is so sad to see he is such a mess. I am well aware that could have been me. I could have been an alcoholic or dead – and if I had not met Nicki, I probably would have been. There but for the grace of God…

'Now life is good. I have been married to Nicki for 23 years and she is a wonderful woman. She has been my salvation.

'She deals with all our finances and I can't blame her. I have never written a cheque in my life. She is brilliant at that and works her socks off. I am very lucky to have her.

'I feel the luckiest man alive to have a lovely wife and family. Life is so much better now. I don't want to be the Mark Dennis people used to know, so I certainly wouldn't go back to those times.

'I have spent half my life apologising to people for things I have done – and sometimes there is real severe embarrassment.

'I do regret them a bit, but you can't turn the clock back and they were part of me. And you can't put an old head on young shoulders. I have learned now that while it is nice to be important, it is more important to be nice.'

Alan Shearer

WHEN Alan Shearer was thrust into an unlikely Saints debut at just 17 years and 240 days old, it was not simply his goalscoring prowess which convinced Chris Nicholl to take a gamble.

Nor was it the fact that the young centre-forward could clearly handle the physical side of the game which persuaded the then manager to throw him into a clash against mighty Arsenal.

It was the mental toughness the emerging striker displayed which proved he was ready not just for a stunning start, but also for the glittering career which followed.

Shearer repaid Nicholl's faith by becoming the youngest player ever to score a top-flight hat-trick – the first of 283 league goals.

Pundits were quick to praise his finishing and physical power, but Shearer is well aware those qualities matter little without the strength of mind to make them count.

And for that he will forever be grateful to the strong working-class upbringing he received – and to the 'old-school' guidance of Saints' youth team coach Dave Merrington.

Like Shearer, Merrington is a teak-tough no-nonsense Geordie who drilled the club's youngsters with an iron fist – inside an iron glove.

Gone are the days of apprentices who would walk, or at best cycle, to the ground to clean the players' boots, sweep the dressing rooms and gather the sweaty kit.

Now we have academies full of young bright lights with cars, agents and attitude. Heaven help the youth team coach who dares to upset a precious ego who might then take his talents elsewhere.

It is a far cry from the days when Merrington would order the youngsters in for extra training at 6am if he felt they had not given their all in an important game. Or deliver a rollicking which would make the Fergie Hairdryer look as though it was set on warm and gentle!

But Shearer has no complaints about such strong measures, crediting Merrington's no-nonsense honesty for instilling the discipline and mental strength which saw him become one of England's greatest players.

He said: 'Mental toughness is more important than physical toughness in my opinion.

'Dave Merrington was a very hard taskmaster, but very fair and honest. He did not shy away from telling you the truth, which is not often the case in football – or in life.

'But it is my preferred way. At least you know where you stand. There is enough bullshit in football. The best way is to be open and honest, whether you are a player or a manager or a pundit.

'It is no good being offended by criticism. You have to take it and learn from it. Everyone should be told it how it is.

'Honesty is the only way to be. Dave Merrington would tell it how it was and even though it might hurt, you had to take it on board.

'I never had a problem with that. I always knew who I was and where I stood.'

That is a philosophy which has stood Shearer in good stead since his childhood in Gosforth. His father, also called Alan, was a sheet-metal worker who taught his son the value of honesty, hard work and the self-belief to stand up for himself.

'A lot of it comes from my mum and dad. I came from a very working-class background. My dad would get up and go to work in a factory at six o'clock in the morning and he would not get back until six o'clock at night. That taught me a work ethic and a sense of perspective and it really helped me. They were very fair and open parents and I owe them a huge amount.'

Shearer's parents, Alan and Anne, taught him the value of money and of the hard work most people put in to get it. They also taught him to stand up for himself, both on the field and off it.

Even as a young apprentice, he had an air about him which immediately let opponents know they were in for a rough ride. That same approach held firm for his own team-mates, who knew that any slacking or chickening out of tackles would see that same steely gaze turned in their direction.

'I could look after myself on the field. That was partly down to the way I was brought up and the fact that I was taught not to let myself be pushed around – not just on the field but also in life.

'As a schoolboy, I was playing against kids who were bigger and older than me and that certainly taught me to give as good as I got.

'I soon learned not to let myself be bullied on or off the field. It was a big learning curve for me because I was not the biggest at 13 or 14.

'I learned I had to look after myself. If I did not do it, no one else would ever do it. You can't let people push you around, whether it be players, managers, agents or just people in life. If you let people do that, then you have no chance. You need to be strong and stand up for yourself.'

It was that fearsome strength of mind, as well as body, that saw Shearer bounce back strongly from three serious injuries, which makes it all the more remarkable that he is still the all-time leading Premier League goalscorer with 260 – plus his 23 First Division goals for Saints.

He recalled: 'I had some great times in my career – but there were a lot of not-so-great times. I had three very serious injuries, career-threatening injuries.

'You are going to have knocks in life. It is how you deal with them and how you bounce back which is important.

'You will always have negative circumstances and that is when you have to dig deep. You have to handle it. That's what I always did.

'When you get injured, you can either curl up in a ball and feel sorry for yourself, or the first day after your operation you can vow to come back stronger and better than ever.'

However, even someone with Shearer's ferocious determination and mental strength might have struggled to play Premier League football with three toes missing.

And that is the fate which almost befell the future England captain during an end-of-season trip to Portugal, where a boozy prank went horribly wrong.

Neil Ruddock goes into the detail in his chapter in this book but, in a nutshell, a group of drunken players tried to steal Shearer's minibar from his hotel room, knocking over several glasses which shattered on the floor.

Shearer was in the bath at the time and leapt out angrily – and naked. As he chased after them, he trod on the broken glass and almost sliced off three toes.

He recalled: 'I think it was Barry Horne who pulled my minibar off the wall and smashed a load of glass. I was barefoot as I went after them and I cut my toes really badly. One was virtually hanging off.

'I genuinely worried that my career was going to be over before it had even started. It was not a pretty sight, I can tell you. It caused a fair amount of panic.'

Ruddock admits he sobered up pretty quickly when he saw the state of his close friend and 'Bruise Brother'.

Shearer laughed: 'What can I say about Neil Ruddock? He was a character. I think that is the best way of putting it. We certainly had a few "characters" in the dressing room who were not scared to do things both on and off the field.

'What we did have at that time was a great team spirit. We all got on great and had tremendous camaraderie. We would go for a night out and it would not be just one or two of us, but the whole group.

'We had great times – apart from the time I nearly lost my toe. That was a bit too much partying. The worst of it is that I was not even partying!

'We had some fantastic nights out and there are some great stories – but none that I am going to put in this book. In fact, I would not even put them in my own book! But they were great times.'

Shearer came to The Dell as a schoolboy after being spotted by the club's legendary North East scout Jack Hixon, who moved swiftly to snap up the prodigy after Newcastle made the mistake of playing him in goal during a trial match.

The move to the other end of the country also played a big part in toughening up the youngster, who suddenly found himself a long way from home and having to stand on his own two feet.

'I loved my time at Southampton. Moving away from home at 15 was the best thing I ever did. It made me grow up, I got away from some friends and that made me focus my mind,' he added.

'Things just got bigger and better for me. I banged in a lot of goals for the youth team, not so many for the reserves because I went into the first team. Of course, scoring a hat-trick on my debut was fantastic. I was the youngest player ever to score a top-flight hat-trick and that record still stands. I am very, very proud of that.

'Whatever I did between 15 and 21 certainly stood me in good stead.

'It was not just that I made my debut at 17. I have seen hundreds of players make their debuts at 17 and then you never see them at 23 or 24. I went on to play at the top level until I was nearly 36 and that means being strong mentally and physically, working hard, doing all the right things and bouncing back from any setbacks.'

During his illustrious career, Shearer not only won the Premier League with Blackburn but also finished third in the 1996 Ballon D'Or and FIFA World Player of the Year poll.

He owned the Premier League Golden Boot from 1995–97, winning it for three successive seasons. He won the hugely prestigious Football Writers' Footballer of the Year award in 1994 and the PFA Player of the Year in 1995 and 1997.

Yet, as a youngster, he had to win over some doubters at The Dell who questioned whether he had what it took.

He recalled: 'I constantly had people telling me I had weaknesses in my game and that I was not good enough. It simply made me all the more determined to prove them wrong.

'Chris Nicholl was cut from the same cloth as Dave Merrington in that he was straight and honest, and he told me my control was not good enough and that I needed to improve my heading of the ball.

'That was fine. I took it on board. I went away and I worked on it.

'My philosophy was that if someone said I was not good enough at something, I would prove them wrong.

'A lot of people become scared of criticism, not just in football but in life in general. If someone says they are not good enough, they hide or run away from the problem instead of addressing it.

'I got on great with Chris Nicholl. We had our rows and our disagreements, of course. I might have been young and inexperienced, but even then I always had an opinion and I was not afraid to speak up. I remember going to see him to ask for a pay rise and we had an almighty row. He had his view and I had mine and I let him know. But I still respected his opinion.

'I did not get my rise then… but I did get it soon afterwards. That was also his way of keeping my feet on the ground and I realised that.

'I was sorry when Chris Nicholl left. I have a lot to thank him for. He didn't have to put me in the first team when he did, even though I was scoring a lot of goals for the youth team.

'He was an honest man and a good man, another who was tough and hard but straightforward and honest.'

Nicholl's teams had been renowned for playing a fast, slick brand of exciting, attacking football, with the Wallace wingers supplying the ammunition for the likes of Shearer, Matthew Le Tissier and Paul Rideout.

His replacement, Ian Branfoot, opted for a long-ball game, which the fans detested. It brought Shearer 13 goals in 41 league appearances, his best return for the club but more a reflection of the fact he was now a first-team regular rather than thriving under the new manager.

While Branfoot was hated on the terraces, he suddenly found himself the most popular manager among his peers, who were constantly on the phone to offer a variety of cast-offs and cash for the hottest property in the English game.

Legend has it that Branfoot declined to even speak to Sir Alex Ferguson about Shearer because the Manchester United boss had refused to shake his hand after a particularly bruising encounter at Old Trafford.

Branfoot insisted Saints were in the driving seat and would not be panicked or bullied into selling their prize asset. Yet there was a fear among the club's moneymen that one badly-timed injury could cost them their pot of gold.

Consequently, Shearer was suddenly pulled out of a pre-season trip to Scotland in 1992 and wrapped in cotton wool as the club negotiated a then British-record fee of £3.6m with Blackburn.

Sadly, being in the driving seat did not prevent the deal becoming a car crash for Saints, who failed to insert a sell-on clause. It proved a costly error when Shearer became the world's most expensive footballer in 1996.

Even ten per cent of the profit would have netted Saints around a million when he moved from Blackburn to Newcastle for the then world-record fee of £15m.

Even worse was the fact that Saints took a reluctant David Speedie as a makeweight in the deal despite the fact that Branfoot desperately wanted Mike Newell instead.

Blackburn were reluctant to part with him so, despite holding the whip hand, Saints somehow ended up with no sell-on clause and a player who seemingly did not want to join them.

It did not help when Branfoot boasted that Speedie and his former Chelsea strike partner Kerry Dixon would outscore Shearer that season.

Despite an injury-hit campaign, Shearer banged in 16 goals in 21 appearances for Blackburn while Dixon managed two in eight for Saints, with Speedie failing to hit the net at all in any of his 11 games.

Shearer said: 'It was probably the right time for me to move on when I did. I loved my time at Southampton, but I had a great offer from Blackburn and I knew they were going places under Kenny Dalglish and Ray Harford, who had been my coach with England at the Toulon tournament that summer.

'With Jack Walker and Kenny Dalglish there, I knew it was only a matter of time before they won silverware, so it was right for me to move.

'I became Britain's most expensive player, so it was great money for Southampton. They got me for nothing and sold me for a record fee, so it worked out well for both of us – apart from the fact that they did not put a sell-on clause in the agreement. And they did get David Speedie in return.

'But I really did enjoy my time at The Dell and I still have a lot of affection for Southampton. They gave me my chance and taught me a lot and I had a fantastic time there. And I am delighted to see them doing so well, especially considering the number of players they have sold.

'It was a brilliant achievement from Ronald Koeman and the board to do that and still come back stronger. They have a great recruitment process there, not just with youngsters but the players they bring in.

'They keep on producing talented youngsters but they also bring in the right kind of players – and just as importantly the right characters – to replace players when they leave. A lot of clubs are very jealous of the work they do in recruitment because that is possibly the toughest area of the industry now.

'But they have always been strong on bringing youngsters through, with the Wallaces and Matt Le Tissier as well as myself coming through the ranks.'

It was something of a golden generation for Saints, with so many talented players bursting through at once.

It was long before Alan Hansen's infamous prediction that: 'You'll win nothing with kids.' Even so, Nicholl was cute enough to know that the crop of raw talent needed protection.

It came in the form of a marauding, menacing, moustachioed Merseysider – a certain James Robert Case, whose name crops up time and time again whenever the question is posed about who is the hardest player they ever encountered.

'Jimmy Case was brilliant for me when I was coming through. He was a real father figure to all of us.

'He had done and seen it all and won everything at a great club and he was fantastic for passing on advice and experience.

'He was the original hard-man. He saw it as his job to look after us all. If anyone had a go at one of us, you would see him have a word with them – and you knew he would go through with whatever he was saying.

'He was probably the hardest player I ever played with. He was tough as anything and if someone kicked one of us, he would kick them back. I am not sure you could do that today.

'Tackles are becoming more and more extinct. You can't tackle now because you will get a yellow card, so it is going out of the game. In a way, that is a good thing because you want skilful players to be protected, but I do think players get punished too much.

'I would have coped okay in this era. If you are good enough, you can play in any era. You can't tell me that Jimmy Case would not have been a good player in the modern game. He was not just a hard-man. He could pass the ball and shoot, so he would have adapted.

'If you are a good player in the Seventies, you will be a good player in the Nineties or now. You find a way round things, so it would not have bothered me.

'I don't look back. I loved every minute of my career. I was brought up to stand up for myself, so it was never an issue for me and I could certainly put myself about on the field.

'I had big thighs but I was not the biggest when it came to pushing people. But that side of the game never ever fazed me. I gave as good as I got.

'Those physical knocks were certainly more prevalent in my day. I am not so sure that is the case now.

'I had some unbelievable battles with Tony Adams. Sometimes we would come off the pitch with both of us having had stitches, but at the end of it we would shake hands and have a pint or two – or too many in his case.

'It was always important to shake hands afterwards. You could have a right battle on the field, but afterwards it would all be forgotten.

'Adams was the hardest player I ever played against. He loved a battle and could look after himself. In those days you were pretty much allowed one free hit, so any time you went to Highbury you knew that some time inside the first 15 minutes you were going to get whacked from behind.'

Since hanging up his boots, Shearer has carved out a successful media career, establishing himself as a lynchpin of *Match of the Day*'s traditional Saturday night analysis.

It was a steep learning curve for a man who had always been guarded with his comments to the media during his playing days, well aware of the lasting impact a poorly chosen word or phrase might have.

And he admits he found it difficult at first to break free from that self-restraint – although the infuriating demise of his beloved Newcastle United did make that somewhat easier!

Shearer did step away from the cameras in a brief but futile attempt to save the Magpies from relegation in 2009. He answered an SOS and took temporary charge of the team for the final eight games of the campaign, a change which came far too late to halt the plummet into the Championship.

Newcastle made the same mistake again in 2016, leaving it far too late to bring in Rafa Benitez, a failure which prompted Shearer to give full vent to his frustration on air.

He said: 'I love the media work I do. I feel a very, very lucky guy. Not only did I play football for a living but I got to work for one of the most iconic programmes in the world in *Match of the Day*.

'I think I have been more outspoken – or analytical – in the last three or four seasons. When I first started, I did not want to criticise too much in case I got back in the game in some capacity.

'I probably did not want to upset people, but I decided if I was not going back into football that I needed to be more analytical and critical and I have worked hard to improve – as I always have done in every aspect of my life.'

But the measure of this down-to-earth character who has never forgotten his roots is perhaps best summed up by his philanthropy in setting up a major charity in his home city – and donating the entire profits from his testimonial match.

'Now that I have finished playing, my life is still very full. Apart from my media work, I have the Alan Shearer Foundation (www. alanshearerfoundation.org.uk), which is an activity centre and respite home for disabled children.

'It is a highly specialist centre which offers respite, residential and social provision for people with complex disabilities and acute sensory impairments.

'We need to raise at least £250,000 every year to ensure that we can continue to provide free sensory and specialist leisure activities and offer free and subsidised respite breaks for profoundly disabled children and adults.

'That takes a lot of my time. I am very hands-on and take a very active part in the running of it.

'I gave all my testimonial money to the foundation – that was £1.6m. But I don't just give money. In a way, that is the easy bit. I give a lot of my time too.

'It does take a lot of time but it is very rewarding and it is good to be able to give something back.'

Micky Adams

WITH THE apt nickname of 'Fusey', Micky Adams was always an explosion waiting to go off.

By his own admission, he was not averse to throwing the odd punch when his short temper boiled over.

This makes it all the more ironic that he was the innocent victim in the biggest scuffle of his career.

It was also the most highly publicised as a benevolent visit to Jersey descended into mayhem and violence after David Speedie made the mistake of trying to fight Terry Hurlock... with Adams unwittingly caught in the middle.

It cost him a cut eye and a night in the cells – and it was not even his fight.

Ian Branfoot's Saints side were invited to play a friendly on the island, but used the trip as an opportunity to have a few drinks – and to clear the air after their usual poor start to the season.

Adams recalled: 'We had lost 2-1 at home to QPR after taking an early lead, leaving us with just six points from our first eight games of the season. So, the mood was a bit flat as we headed off to Jersey for what was supposed to be a goodwill friendly.

'It was also an opportunity for a team bonding session – and a few drinks.

'It was a chance for everyone to say their piece because it had not been a good start to the season. We had lost Alan Shearer in the summer and had brought in David Speedie and Kerry Dixon, who were struggling in front of goal.

'They were both proven scorers but both struggled for form early on. So, in a bid to put things right and to sort the season out, we had an open discussion about what we could do better and how we were going to start winning games. It was an open forum where anyone could say anything without any come back, but David did not agree with certain things that were said. And he decided to pick on Terry Hurlock.

'It was a brave decision, I have to say. It was also a bad one. If you are going to pick a fight, at least pick one you can win.

'Punches were thrown and Speedo took a bit of a battering. His face was bloodied but the scuffle was split up quite quickly and he went to the toilet to clean up. Our coach, Lew Chatterley, tried to quieten him down. Once he was calm, he said he wanted to apologise to Terry and went back out. I was in the toilet too and as we came out, it looked as though he was going to say sorry, but he hurled himself at Terry again, which was a stupid thing to do.

'Terry gave him another couple of slaps and I jumped in between them and said "Relax, this is nonsense." An ashtray got thrown but unfortunately it hit me on the forehead. And it fucking hurt!

'Even worse, it bounced on to the hotel manageress, who had come to see what all the commotion was about. I was cut, David was cut and the police were called.

'Because I was covered in blood, they thought I had been in a fight. I had to go to hospital for stitches and as I came out they arrested me and wanted to take me in for questioning.

'They were proper old-fashioned cells with bars and when I got there Speedie was hanging out through the bars shouting, "I'm going to get you." Quite why he wanted to get me I don't know. All I did was try to keep the peace and got clobbered for it.

'But he was just in that sort of mood. I was questioned through the night and released.

'*The Sun* had got hold of the story and sent a reporter, who tried to follow us the next day. I guess someone at the hotel must have tipped them off, but it meant there was no chance of keeping it quiet.

'Speedie had stitches and a big lump on his head and when it went to court he was told to get off the island.

'We were all worried about it kicking off and how that might affect us as a group because we had always had great team spirit.

'We were not necessarily the best team, but we always stuck together and had a go.

'David was just frustrated because he was not scoring goals and for whatever reason he was struggling to settle. Strikers can become

Withdrawn From Stock
Dublin Public Libraries

very depressed when they are not scoring and he found it tough. He wanted to do so well and it was not happening for him.'

Maybe it did the trick as Saints lost just two of their next 11 matches and, although they finished just one point above the drop zone, they were comfortably safe before the final fixture.

It was a familiar trait for Adams, who takes great pride from the fact that during his five years at the club Southampton had always secured their top-flight place ahead of the last game of the season, first under Chris Nicholl, the man who signed him from Leeds for £250,000 in March 1989, and then under Branfoot.

While many Saints fans resent Branfoot and his long-ball tactics even to this day, Adams has more time for the gritty Geordie, who was to take him under his wing and lead him into management.

'Ian Branfoot was never the fans' favourite – but he never got the club relegated. We always stayed up because we had such great team spirit under him.

'That competitive togetherness kept us up year after year. There were a lot of times when we were struggling against the drop, but we battled it out because we had a group of lads who would stand up to be counted.

'We worked hard for each other on the field and we socialised as a group off it. We had some good trips and some great times. I enjoyed my stay at Southampton, where we had some really good players. I very quickly realised I would need to raise my game.

'I came in thinking I was a decent player, but the Saints lads were a different level and things were a bit different off the pitch too because Chris Nicholl had his own unique way of doing and saying things.

'I remember my first ever day of training at the club and all three Wallace brothers had a slanging match with Chris. He had had a go at one of them – but they were very close and if you take on one, you take on all three.

'In the end, Chris had to stop the practice match and he sent us all back to The Dell for a team meeting. We all sat there waiting for him to come in and I was expecting him to slaughter the Wallaces.

'He came in and said "Right..." then he completely forgot what he was going to say and walked back out! Coach Dennis Rofe went to follow him but turned and warned, "When he comes back in, don't start laughing." It took him about half an hour to think what he was going to say.

'When he eventually came back in, he picked on Matthew Le Tissier because he had got a letter from the FA for shouting at the referee – as usual. I was gobsmacked. I wondered what I had let myself in for.

'Chris was quite blunt and forthright at times and he would always let us know how we had played before we left the ground after each game. He would go round the dressing room and point to each of us in turn and say things like "good", "not bad", "shit" or "wanker".

'I used to sit there thinking, "Please let me be shit, not a wanker!" He was a great guy but he had one of those personalities.

'I remember one game when our goalkeeper Tim Flowers came off with a wrist injury five minutes from the end of a game when we were hanging on. Afterwards, Chris cornered Tim and asked what the matter was. He said he had hurt his wrist and was going to hospital to see what was wrong. Chris just looked at him and said, "If it is broken, then OK. If not… wanker!"

'If Chris ever called you up to his office, he would have around a hundred Post-it notes on his desk and he would sit there searching through them until he found the right one.

'Once, I was standing there for about 15 minutes as he picked one up and said "No" then tried another, "No, not that one" until he found what he wanted to talk to me about. Then he accused me of eating steak in the hotel.

'But that wasn't me. It was Neil Ruddock. He had a Doberman and sneaked it into the hotel and ordered a fillet steak. He cut it up and gave it to his dog.

'He was lethal. He should have gone on to have won a lot of caps for England because he was such a strong player – and one who enjoyed a good time off the pitch. And invariably, I would be right alongside him.

'The worst scrape was the time we nearly cost Alan Shearer his toes, but I'll let Neil tell that one in his chapter. It is fair to say, though, it was a very scary moment for all of us and almost robbed England of a future star and Saints of a British-record fee.

'Obviously, Alan was a bit special. I was lucky enough to watch his debut as Leeds were down at Bournemouth, so we all came to the game against Arsenal. I couldn't believe what I was seeing.

'Even at 17, he was telling the senior pros what to do and where he wanted the ball in the box. For someone of that age to come in and start ordering experienced players around just shows how mentally tough he was. He would go mad if anyone checked back instead of crossing.

'He was a special player and his finishing was terrific and I really enjoyed playing alongside him. We had a decent team and with Rod and Danny Wallace in full flight, we had a powerful attacking unit, even if we were a bit flaky in defence.

'And, of course, we had the emerging Matthew Le Tissier, who had incredible skill but was lazy, so we had to do all his running for him, which was fine because he had the ability to get us the win bonus.

'In his book, Tiss puts me down as one his favourite players but that is because I would give him the ball and go on an overlap, and he would just use me as a decoy and go and do his own thing.

'That's just the way he was but he could do special, special things. In terms of pure natural ability, he was the best I ever played with. He was frustrating at times, but he could win you the game from nowhere.'

In addition to their undoubted flair, Nicholl's side could mix it. They had some tough competitors and some real characters, with two fondly labelled as a head case and a hard case.

Goalkeeper John Burridge would entertain the fans with his madcap antics in the warm-up, while Jimmy Case preferred to stay under the radar.

'We did have some very good players who would hold their own in any side today and we certainly had players who could look after themselves.

'Jimmy Case was the hardest man I ever played with. I remember one tackle at Everton when Graeme Sharp tried to do him on the halfway line, but Jimmy saw him coming and went even higher.

'Jimmy had a way of knocking players down and stumbling on top of them without it looking intentional. He was a master at that and was always very apologetic to the referee – but we knew.

'And off the pitch, he was immaculate. He was our housekeeper on the coach, making sure all the lads were looked after. The bus driver never had to clean up.

'Then there was dear old Budgie – what a character he was. I remember an end-of-season trip to play Carl Zeiss Jena back when it was still East Germany and there was real tension as we went through no-man's land accompanied by armed guards.

'All the lads were on their best behaviour – apart from John Burridge, who kept asking if the area was mined and, if so, how did they dig up their potatoes?

'Before the game, there was a big gymnastics display on the pitch. Suddenly, I looked round and there was Budgie on the runway. Next thing he had charged down, bounced off the trampoline on to the horse and done a spectacular somersault.

'We all fell about laughing, but the funniest thing was the crowd greeted it with total silence, not a flicker.

'Afterwards, we were not allowed out of the dressing room. Apparently, a football had gone missing and they thought one of us had got it.

'We went mad at them, saying it was our final game of the campaign and we were just about to go to Portugal for an end-of-season break, so why the hell would we nick a ball.

'They were adamant one of us had stolen it. We said we have loads of footballs back at the club. It made no sense for us to have stolen it. So we just sat there with the police refusing to let us leave. We must have been there for 30 minutes until Budgie eventually owned up.'

And, of course, one of the strongest competitors was Adams himself. His volatile temper earned him an unwanted place in the Premier League history books.

'I do have the dubious honour of being the first player to be sent off in the Premiership. It was the second game of the season, away at QPR on a Tuesday night, and I hit Ray Wilkins. Let's face it, who hasn't fancied doing that?

'I don't really know why I did it, I just wanted to let him know I was around. I was having a bad game against him and I just lost my temper. That's why I got the nickname "Fusey" as I had a very short fuse.

'Chris Nicholl had put me in midfield and that was not really my strength. I was not having the best time of it and lashed out.

'I also got sent off at Forest for stamping on Brian Laws after jumping up to avoid his tackle. Chris asked me what I did and I said I never touched him. Then Chris said he would look at the video and I said "OK, I stamped on him."

'Then when Chris left, the club brought in Ian Branfoot, who had previously been a coach at The Dell and who had taken Reading from the old Fourth Division to the Second in his first job as manager. They also won the Simod Cup under him at Wembley.

'The Saints fans did not take to Ian, but I liked him. I enjoyed his company and he was a good coach, one of the best I ever worked under. But he did not suit Matthew Le Tissier.

'He used to drive Ian Branfoot mad. All week, Ian would have him practising set-pieces, driving a corner to the near post or hitting it deep – and then on the Saturday Tiss would completely ignore him and shoot from a corner. He was that confident, he always thought he could score – and he was that good that he could!

'Ian wanted players to run a lot and to be fit. I was not the most gifted of players, so that suited me. But it was not great for Tiss. I needed that discipline and Ian was good for me.'

Adams enjoyed Branfoot's emphasis on a high-energy, physical game, which was never better illustrated than when Saints travelled to Sheffield Wednesday in September 1991.

The left-back recalled: 'Ian asked Alan Shearer and Neil Ruddock to test out the bravery of goalkeeper Chris Woods. When the first corner came over, they took him clean out and he did not come for a cross for the rest of the game.'

Adams' close connection with Branfoot continued until the board finally succumbed to the fans' protests and sacked the manager following a drab 1-0 home defeat by Norwich on the first day of 1994.

That also proved to be the last of Adams' 171 games for the club. His links to Branfoot saw him frozen out by incoming manager Alan Ball, something which still rankles even now.

'My only disappointment about my time at Southampton was the way I ended up leaving the club. I don't think I was treated fairly,' added Adams.

'Alan Ball came in and I was banished to train with the kids. It was not just me but the likes of Terry Hurlock, Steve Wood and Iain Dowie. And then he got rid of us as soon as he could.

'Obviously, I can't now ask him why he did it because he died far too early but I still feel it was a shame because I was never a problem for any manager. I just wanted to play and I gave everything in every game.'

He did, though, leave the club a lasting legacy, spotting a promising youngster playing left-back for Olivers Battery and recommending him to Saints, who quickly signed up Wayne Bridge.

'My mate's lad was playing in a match in Winchester, so he asked if I would like to come along and watch him, so I did.

'The opposition had a little left-winger who was quick, enthusiastic and had a good left foot. He ran with his head down a bit, but he had a bit about him.

'At the end of the game, I introduced myself to his mum and explained I did some coaching with the Saints under-12s. I told her we had a training session the following night and would like him to attend.

'I asked if any other clubs had approached her about him and she said no, so I said to bring him down so we could take a look at him... and the rest is history. He is now a millionaire and married to a pop star... so he does not owe me much!

'To be fair to him, he always mentions me when he is asked how he was discovered. There are plenty trying to claim the credit but I can honestly say no one else knew about him and he always remembers that.'

After a brief spell at Stoke on loan, he linked up with Branfoot once more, this time at Fulham as a player-coach.

'Ian got me on to the coaching staff at Fulham, which eventually led me into management, so I have a lot to thank him for. I did a lot of scouting for him, which meant long days, but it enabled me to learn the ropes.

'When Ian left the club, I got the manager's job. Fulham were 91st in the Football League at the time, but I kept them up and then got them promoted.

'Things were going well and we looked like we might get promoted again but then Mohamed Al-Fayed came in as the new owner. I knew the writing was on the wall for me as he had a lot of money and wanted a big-name manager.

'He went for Kevin Keegan and I could not really argue with that. There was uproar from the fans though because we were doing well and I was just six months into a five-year contract. It was disappointing at the time, but I was well compensated.

'There were a lot of stories that I had made millions, but that was nonsense. And it was disappointing as I had been told I would be there for years. After that, I went to Swansea but only lasted ten days. I fell out with the people there because I had been promised money for new signings and it was not forthcoming.

'I have always had strong principles and if people bullshit me then I am not interested, so I decided to go home.

'Then I went to Brentford and Ron Noades bought the club and made himself manager. How unlucky was I in my first three jobs?

'I had heard rumours and then I got a call to meet him. He asked if I had heard the news about him buying the club. I said I had and he told me, "I am also the manager and you are gone!"

'I went to Forest as assistant to Dave Bassett and learned a lot there before Ron Atkinson came in and memorably went to the wrong dug-out for his first match in charge.

'I got on well with him. His team talks were inspirational but it was a bad time for the club. Pierre van Hooijdonk went on strike and refused to come back, for whatever reason.

'He was a nightmare to coach. The pitch was either too big or too small – every day he found something to moan about.'

His next job was as boss of Brighton, where he again showed his eye for raw talent by snapping up a young Bobby Zamora for just £100,000.

He once more proved his managerial credentials by leading the Seagulls to the Third Division title and laying the foundations for a second successive promotion, although he left to work under Dave Bassett again, this time at Leicester.

When Bassett moved upstairs to become Director of Football, Adams took over as manager, albeit too late to save the Foxes from relegation from the Premier League. However, he did lead them straight back with promotion at the first attempt – despite a transfer ban after the club went into receivership with debts of £30m.

'That was my managerial highlight. It was a real slog to keep people motivated and focused when we went into administration. A lot of things went against us, but somehow we managed to pull it off.'

Continuing financial problems contributed to immediate relegation and, ultimately, the manager's departure.

He returned to his former club Coventry and helped them avoid relegation before joining Port Vale and then his boyhood club Sheffield United and then Vale again, leading them to promotion to League One in 2012.

In October 2014, he was appointed as manager of Tranmere, who were bottom of the Football League – and only one place higher when he left two games from the end of the season.

He then answered an SOS from Irish club Sligo Rovers, steering them clear of relegation before returning to England to be closer to his family, working at the Premier League assessing referees.

He laughed: 'I always assessed referees when I was a player – I just used rather different language!'

Francis Benali

SITTING IN his immaculate study, Francis Benali gazes fondly at the walls covered in memorabilia and pictures of a playing career which encompassed 15 years and 369 appearances, 11 red cards and just one very memorable goal.

He glances up at a signed photo of himself labelled 'Southampton Hall of Fame' and smiles as it is put to him that he was one of the hardest men ever to pull on a red and white striped shirt.

'There are a few ahead of me. Denis Hollywood was hard as nails… Neil Ruddock was pretty tough… Terry Hurlock could look after himself. And then there was the daddy of the team – Jimmy Case.

'I was just breaking through as a youngster and it was fantastic to have him looking after us. He was the enforcer in midfield, our minder.

'If a tackle went in on one of us, he would take it into his own hands to make sure we were protected by dishing out his own form of retribution.

'We were blessed with a few players who could look after themselves if the game went that kind of way.

'I used to watch Jimmy closely and saw how he looked after himself and others. He was very clever. He did not have the instant red mist which afflicted me. He would wait – it might not even be the same game but it would come. He never forgot.

'But he was a wonderful footballer too. He could pass the ball so well and had a ferocious shot on him.

'As I got older, I followed his example in terms of looking out for the others. Matthew Le Tissier, for instance, did not tackle well but he was our jewel and needed protecting.

'He was a friend too, so if there was a naughty tackle on him I would try to pay them back with a challenge of my own. That's how it was then. We had one another's backs.'

It was that togetherness – the famed Spirit of Southampton – which kept the team in the top flight for the entire duration of Benali's playing career.

For much of that time, the club were battling against overwhelming odds, struggling to compete on a capacity of 15,000 against rivals who brought in more revenue from merchandise alone.

Four times in five years during the mid-Nineties, the team stayed up on the final day of the season ahead of bigger clubs whose spirit did not match their spending.

Benali adds: 'We did not have the money or the resources to spend on players. In the final years at The Dell, Manchester United were making more on programme sales than we took in gate receipts.

'We would constantly hear pundits write us off at the start of the season, which hurt both personally and collectively and it made us all the more determined to prove them wrong.

'We knew we were never going to win the title. But equally, over 90 minutes, we knew we could beat anyone on our day, thanks to our spirit.

'There was a lot of talk over the years about the unity and camaraderie which ultimately helped us maintain our place in the top flight. That was down to the characters and the individuals we had, as well as the people who ran the club. We were a family and all looked after each other.

'If one of us was picked on, they would have several others to deal with – although I would usually be the first on the scene… mainly because I was faster than Neil Ruddock!

'We were a tight group with no cliques. We had a lot of home-grown youngsters who were prepared to put their heads in where it hurt.

'The likes of Neil Maddison and Tommy Widdrington would run through brick walls along with Jason Dodd and Alan Shearer, plus a couple of young signings like Tim Flowers and Richard Hall.

'The highs and lows gave us a special bond and forged friendships which have lasted to this day.'

As a Southampton man born and bred, Benali has always known how much the club matters to the city and to the supporters. As 'one of our own', he matched the fans' passion on the field with an intensity which made him a terrace favourite despite the occasional lapses both with and without the ball.

What he lacked in style he made up in steel. He gave everything for the cause, always ready to spill blood – sometimes even his own.

'I was born and raised in the city. I lived in Albion Towers and then moved to Portswood. My school was walking distance from The Dell and I used to go and watch the team long before I signed for them.

'I sacrificed a lot from a very young age. I have never been drunk or smoked. I have looked after my body and I have kept that lifestyle now.

'I didn't go partying because I wanted to give myself the best chance possible to achieve my dream of playing for Southampton.

'I used to hate it when players who had more talent than me did not make the most of it. I saw it as my responsibility to pass on advice to any of the younger players coming through to make sure they looked after themselves.

'I have seen players with a lot of ability who have dropped down the leagues or even out of the game because they did not have the right attitude or application.

'They had the chance of an incredible lifestyle and plenty of money but wasted it, so I would try to shake them out of thinking it was going to be easy. I would always give everything in every match.

'I think that is why I have always had a common bond with the supporters. They know I feel the same commitment and passion for the club as they do.

'I had plenty of bad games and made lots of mistakes, but at the very least they always knew I was trying my hardest. I could always hold my head high knowing I had given 100 per cent even if I wasn't playing well.

'I think that is the minimum you owe to the fans. I know what they feel and I hate it if I ever think players are not giving 100 per cent.

'That's why it was so hard to watch as the team got relegated in 2005. I had taken huge pride in keeping Southampton in the top flight all through my playing career.

'We had come close to going down but somehow we always got out of it, mainly due to our spirit and commitment.

'To then see a few players looking as though they were literally going through the motions was very hard to take. There is no excuse for not trying your best.

'If everyone gives 100 per cent and you don't win, then so be it. If you are not good enough or don't perform on the day, then I can live with that.

'But it looked like we went down without a fight, which I could not accept.'

Benali is fiercely proud that the club was never relegated on his watch. Although the lack of resources meant they never managed to challenge for honours, in its own way simply surviving was a massive measure of success.

'We didn't win any silverware but let me tell you that staying up on the final day of the season felt like winning a trophy. In many ways, it meant more because it affected not just the players but the whole club and the whole city.

'A trophy looks nice in a cabinet – apparently – but that's all it is, something for show. Staying in the Premier League actually affected people's lives for at least a year, the grounds they visit, the teams they watch, the amount of business coming into the area.

'People's jobs and livelihoods depended on us staying up. It meant so much to so many. And as a Southampton lad, it meant more to me than anyone.

'Those were our cup finals and it was an incredible feeling to know how much joy we had brought to thousands of fans both at home and abroad.'

Benali's ferocious determination frequently crossed the line, earning him a reputation as one of the Premier League's most fearsome competitors. Like many of the game's hard-men, Benali is one of the nicest people you could wish to meet off the field.

Once the first whistle sounded, he underwent a transformation akin to the Incredible Hulk, turning from mild-mannered man to monster in less time than it takes to say 'red mist'.

He laughs: 'I never set out to be a hard-man, it just kind of happened, partly through my physical development and partly through my make-up and character.

'As a teenager I started out as a striker, which sounds strange considering I only ever scored one goal for the club. I actually played as centre-forward for England under-15s at Wembley.

'I had a moustache even then, which scared opponents and showed how I had developed physically. I was five foot nine and bigger than most of the players I was facing.

'But then everyone else caught up and grew bigger than me, so I moved further back. But I was always very physical.

'Even in my early years at the club, the game being what it was, I found myself getting into physical confrontations with the centre-back. It was unnecessary but it was just my temperament. If they kicked me, I would get them back.

'The result was I found myself moved into midfield because Chris Nicholl felt it would suit my style better – and that resulted in me going to left-back when Derek Statham got injured.

'I was always pretty quick and agile and I took exceptional pride in my fitness. I only had a limited amount of talent, so I had to make sure I could get around the pitch.

'I made up for any lack of ability with sheer desire, work-rate and effort. That meant I was a bit robust in some of my tackling.

'There were times I overstepped the mark, but more often than not I was just trying to impose myself on an opponent.'

By his own admission, Benali was never the most gifted in terms of inventive talent. But he was more than capable of snuffing out the opposition's flair players.

'I could tackle. I soon realised I was good at that side of the game. I might have lacked a bit on the creative side, but I could stop players and intimidate opponents.

'The defensive side of my game was stronger than my attacking abilities. The first five or ten minutes of any game were crucial for me. In those days, you pretty much got one free tackle, a free hit. It was an opportunity to stamp your mark and hopefully just get a warning.

'After that first challenge, you would have an idea of whether you were going to have a fairly comfortable afternoon or a battle.

'If an opponent was going to be looking over his shoulder and worrying more about me than the ball, then I would have a slight advantage.

'With some players it worked, with others it didn't. I tried it on with a young Roy Keane, who was playing wide right, so I thought I would test him out and flew into a tackle. It's fair to say it did not work and later in the game he came back with one of his own. I knew then I was not going to intimidate him.

'He was probably the toughest opponent I faced along with my former team-mate Alan Shearer. The fact we were friends counted for nothing on the pitch. He was so strong and physical.

'Then there were the likes of Mick Harford and John Fashanu, who would always be looking to leave something on you in a challenge. But then if you dish it out you have to be able to take it, so I had no problem with that.

'It would be hypocritical of me to fly in and then moan when I am on the receiving end. Live by the sword, die by the sword – that was how I approached the game.'

That aggression cost Benali several spells on the sidelines serving suspensions for a series of eye-watering challenges, many of which have become cult viewing online.

'I think I was sent off 11 times in my senior career – not counting the ones in the reserves and the youth team… and the garden with my kids!

'I suppose the most memorable was probably the first when I launched John Fashanu into orbit. Fans joke he came down with snow on him!

'I guess it was quite spectacular, which is why it has had around 60,000 views on YouTube.

'He was a very physical player in a very physical team and I just flew into him, which kind of established my reputation early on.

'But then a senior player did tell me that the odd red card is not a bad thing. It lets people know you won't be intimidated and that you will stand your ground and fight for your team.

'Another one which people remember was the red card for a foul on Nick Barmby in February 1993. It was a bad foul but there was no malice towards him. It was just frustration on my part because of the way the game was going.

'We had been completely in control at 1-0 up until early in the second half, when Spurs scored four in five minutes. I remember a Saints fan saying he had been out for a drive, listening to the game on the radio and quite happy.

'He decided to put his car through the car wash. He put the aerial down at 1-0 up and by the time he came out we were 4-1 down.

'I was just frustrated and when the ball came in from a throw I came through him with a high challenge. It was rash and it achieved nothing because the game had gone.

'All it did was put the team under further pressure and put my place under threat as I had a spell on the sidelines. And I had to go home to Karen and explain why I had had my wages docked – again!

'Another one of pure frustration was when I literally put West Ham's Paolo Futre into row A. He was a tricky player and we had just conceded a goal. I was not having the best of games, which added to my frustration, so I lashed out at him and sent him into the advertising hoardings.

'I hold my hands up – that was not a good challenge. However, there were certain officials who would be looking out for me, a case of my reputation preceding me.

'Most of the red cards were probably fair. If I was a neutral watching it, I would say I had to go. The one I felt was harsh was the one on Norwich winger Ruel Fox, when I was accused of elbowing him.

'I am not like that. I did catch him but I was trying to shrug him off. It was not a deliberate elbow as such. The problem was John Fashanu had cracked Gary Mabbutt's cheekbone a couple of weeks previously, so there was a clampdown.

'Graham Poll sent me off three times in my career – and that was one of them. But I still maintain that was unfair.

'Similarly, I tried to shrug off Dean Sturridge on the last day of the season. I was trying to shake him off, but it was right in front of their fans when they used to be along the touchline in the East Stand. They went mad and I was off again.

'I also saw red in an FA Cup tie at Reading on a completely frozen pitch. Only three games in the country went ahead that day and that was one of them. Heaven knows why because the surface was rock solid. I got sent off for an elbow and then Robbie Slater followed as we lost 3-1.

'The last one was just daft. It was at Bolton, who had a niggly midfielder by the name of Jamie Pollock. He had been getting at me all game and I flared up.

'The trouble was that as the red mist came down, I tried to stop myself. I knew I should not retaliate and I had been trying to learn to control myself, so I did neither one thing nor the other.

'I jumped up and tapped him on the cheek. The referee was right there and by the letter of the law I had to go. It was not hard, there was no damage, but I had raised my hands and struck an opponent.

WINNING TEAM: Ted Bates and
Lawrie McMenemy show off the FA Cup.

TOUGH TALKING: Most of Matthew
Le Tissier's bookings were for dissent.

HOLLYWOOD STAR: Denis Hollywood was a leading man for Saints.

DOUBLE ACT: Brian O'Neil and Denis Hollywood enjoy reliving the good old days.

WORLD CUP WINNERS: Terry Paine and Alf Ramsey talk tactics.

FOREVER A SAINT: Club president Terry Paine visits Southampton as often as he can.

MAN OF STEELE: Few attackers would get past Jim Steele.

IT'S A STEELE: Jim Steele (left) and Peter Osgood (centre) took the FA Cup on a night out!

LOOKING ON: Chris Nicholl in the dug-out.

STRONGARM AND ARMSTRONG: Chris Nicholl and David Armstrong celebrate a goal.

HARD CASE: Jimmy Case is widely rated as the toughest Saints player ever.

ELDER STATESMAN: Jimmy Case was a father figure to the Southampton youngsters.

REFUSING TO BUDGE: John Burridge was a formidable barrier in goal.

DENNIS THE MENACE:
Mark Dennis could be a
problem for his managers as
well as opponents.

HOWZAT: Mark Dennis is
still a big cricket fan.

SHEAR JOY: Alan Shearer celebrates another goal for Southampton.

PLAYING FOR KEEPS: Alan Shearer demonstrates how to go in hard on a goalkeeper.

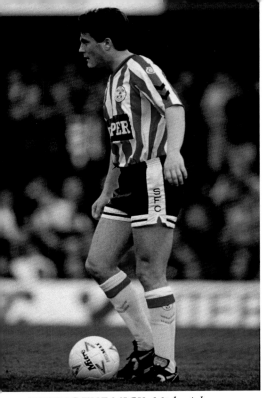

TAKING THE MICK: Micky Adams was a key signing for Saints.

FRAN-TASTIC: Francis Benali has always been proud to play for his home-town club.

PLAYING FOR LAUGHS: Neil Ruddock soldiers on.

TAKE A BOW: Jason Dodd celebrates scoring for Saints against QPR.

ROCKET MAN: Iain Dowie worked for British Aerospace before becoming a professional footballer.

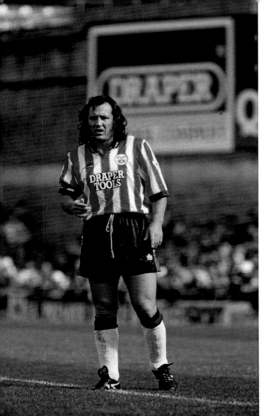

MIDFIELD MARAUDER: Few dared to go too near Terry Hurlock.

BACKING BRUCE: Saints fans rallied to support Bruce Grobbelaar.

CLOWN PRINCE: Bruce Grobbelaar entertained fans with his antics in goal.

GONE IN A FLASH: "Flash Gordon" Watson regrets leaving Southampton.

GETTING STUCK IN: Carlton Palmer shows his combative style against Wimbledon.

BRIEF STAY: Graeme Souness left after just one season as Southampton manager.

REF JUSTICE: Chris Marsden and Robbie Savage argue with the referee.

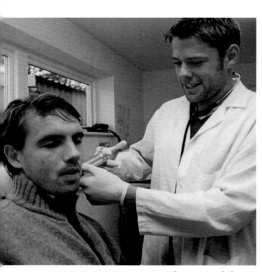

RISKY BUSINESS: Claus Lundekvam allows "Dr" James Beattie to treat him!

JUMPING FOR JOY: James Beattie celebrates another goal.

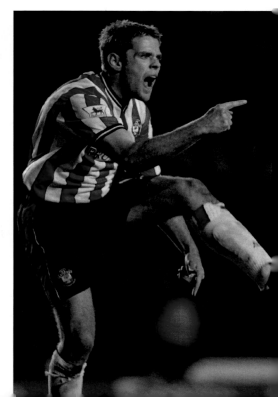

SPECIAL NIGHT: Claus Lundekvam still treasures the memory of his testimonial match.

PRUTTON ON THE STYLE: David Prutton celebrates a goal.

MAKING A POINT: *Michael Svensson cut a commanding figure in the Saints defence.*

FACE IN THE CROWD: *Rickie Lambert treasures the memory of winning promotion to the Premier League.*

'In hindsight, I should have thumped him properly. I might as well have got hung for a sheep as a lamb and I would have felt a bit better if I had decked him. Instead I just felt a bit stupid.

'I did make a concerted effort to try and clean up my disciplinary record, not least because the club was being monitored by the FA.

'As I got older, I learned not to be quite so rash. I was always prone to flying into a tackle, but I did try and control myself partly for my reputation and partly because it was costing me a fortune.

'I had three red cards in one season and under the code of conduct I was fined half a week's wages for the first, a week's salary for the second and the maximum of a fortnight for the third. In addition, the FA clobbered me with an extra ban.

'I had to negotiate with club secretary Brian Truscott to spread the cost, so I set up a monthly standing order because I couldn't afford it all at once.

'I thought maybe if I kept up the payments I could have a free one if I was in credit... but apparently it didn't work like that!

'I do look back now and wonder if any good came from the red cards. I might have played 400 games if I had not been banned so much. But then I would not have been the player I was.

'I knew my style of play meant that opponents would not enjoy facing me and they knew anything they did get they would have to earn. They would not have an easy afternoon.

'That was purely down to my will to win, which was so intense that I would kick my own team-mates in training. Even in a five-a-side game, I was desperate to win.'

It is fair to say fans could become frustrated when a misplaced pass would be intercepted. But they loved the way Benali would chase back to redeem the situation.

Similarly, managers came to appreciate the advantage of having such a whole-hearted competitor in the side, despite any other misgivings they might have had.

A succession of 'replacements' were brought in and Benali saw them all off as one manager after another called on his unyielding commitment to dig them out of a hole. Fittingly, when he finally did give up his place, it was to another local hero in the form of Wayne Bridge. And that made it easier for Benali to accept.

'There were quite a few defenders brought in to replace me, which is a weird scenario. You want the team to do well and to improve but not at your own expense. That can affect your career and your livelihood.

'I was always very welcoming but mindful they could take my place. I saw them all as a challenge and never took my place for granted. I knew I had to keep performing and impressing if I wanted to stay in the side.

'It was Wayne Bridge who finally ousted me and, if I had to give up my place to anyone, I am glad it was him because he was a local lad, a Saints fan and he went on to become an England international.

'I really like him as a person and he was a fantastic footballer who had the attacking flair which modern full-backs need.'

It is not just a need for more enterprise going forward which would make life harder for Benali in the modern game. He is well aware that tighter interpretations of the laws would now make it even more difficult for him to impose himself.

'If I was playing today, I would certainly have had to change my style. I couldn't go flying into tackles the way I used to do. I would have had to adapt to the new rules, which might have made me less of a player.

'It was tough enough staying on the field back then – let alone now. People always ask if I would rather be playing now because of the huge financial rewards.

'Although the money would be nice, that was never an issue for me. I just wanted to play for Southampton and I was lucky that in my era, players could get away with a few more robust challenges than they do today.

'Nowadays you only need to brush against a player and they go down and have a little roll until the referee gets a card out. I really can't be doing with that – just get up and get on with it!

'It seems the art of tackling is dying out of the game, which would have made it tough for me – and a lot of my team-mates. We had a lot of characters who loved a night out as much as they loved a tackle.

'I enjoy the odd glass of wine but I have never been drunk… which made me the ideal candidate to hold the kitty on a night out. The lads knew they could trust me.

'It was certainly entertaining watching them get drunk on trips abroad. Half the time, they were too far gone to know how much was in the kitty, so maybe I should have kept it. I could have used it to pay off some of my fines!

'It meant I missed out on most of their escapades and only heard about them the next day. I knew Alan Shearer had come close to having a toe sliced off and I was in Jersey when Terry Hurlock and David Speedie had their bust-up, but I had left the bar when it all kicked off.

'Terry was a great lad, a really likeable character. He was funny and very generous and would give you his last pound. On the pitch, he was a formidable opponent.

'He looked fierce and he was fierce. He would run through a brick wall for you and if sparks were flying he was always there to back you up.

'He was strong too. You only had to look at him to see how physically powerful he was – but he could play a bit too. He enjoyed a crunching tackle, but he could pick a pass. He was very under-rated. Nowadays we would all have to adapt to the tighter rules.'

Looking back, Benali has only one regret about his career, adding: 'I would like to have scored a few more goals, but at least I got the one. It was the decisive goal in a 2-1 win at home to Leicester on 13 December 1997 – the date is etched on my brain.

'I am still not sure why Matt Le Tissier decided to pick me out with that free-kick – possibly it was the only misdirected pass of his career!

'Whatever, it landed right on my head and the ball flew into the net. I can still hear the roar now. It was a truly magic moment – though not for all those who had backed me to be the first goalscorer in every match for 11 years. When I did finally find the net, it was the second of the game, so they still didn't get a pay-out.

'That was a big highlight for me along with all the final-day Great Escapes, my debut, signing as a pro for my home-town club and, of course, my testimonial, which was a fantastic night.

'It was so special to share it with my wife, Karen, and children, Kenzie and Luke, as well as the rest of my family and friends.

'I appreciate and cherish every day that I played for Southampton. It was always my dream and I realise how fortunate I was to do that.

'I always knew it would not last forever, but it is scary just how quickly it went – a bit like life itself. One minute, I was a 16-year-old apprentice, the next I was retiring.

'I got a great send-off when I came on towards the end of the first Ted Bates Trophy match against Bayern Munich.

'Not many players know at the time when they are playing their last-ever game, but that was the scenario for me. I had made the decision to hang up my boots and turned down the offer of a coaching role, so I knew I had reached the end of the road.

'We played what was effectively a mid-season friendly and Gordon Strachan told me I would play the last ten minutes or so to give me the opportunity to say farewell to the fans.

'Knowing it was to be my last game, I was quite emotional in the build-up. I have never felt like that before any other match. I got an incredible reception, which made me even more emotional.

'At the end, everyone wanted to swap shirts with Michael Ballack, who was their big star at the time. I just wanted to absorb the moment. It was like my wedding day. I just wanted to take in and remember every second of it.

'I had no plans to swap shirts, but then one of their youngsters came over and asked to swap, so I did. I had no idea who it was, but it turned out to be Bastian Schweinsteiger – not a bad shirt to get!

'I am very grateful to Gordon for giving me that chance to say goodbye, but that is typical of the man. He was a great man-manager.

'Gordon was very good to me and I hope he saw the value I brought to the squad after I handed the reins to Wayne Bridge. Even though I was not involved on the playing side, I still tried to have an input in the dressing room.

'I have tried to take bits and pieces from every manager. I tapped into the experience of Gordon and Alan Ball, who was a World Cup winner, and Glenn Hoddle, who was tactically very astute.

'He had great knowledge of the game, but I felt his man-management let him down. He did not keep a lot of players happy – me included.

'His assistant, John Gorman, was always trying to pick up the pieces with the players Glenn had annoyed. It was not a good time for me personally.

'You could see the ability he had as a player whenever he joined in the five-a-sides. If we weren't getting what he wanted us to do, he would demonstrate it. But he found it hard to accept that others couldn't do what he did.

'Of course, I was nowhere near as skilful as him but what disappointed me was that even if I was not at his level, I hoped he would appreciate that I still gave everything.

'Other managers knew what I brought to the team and to the dressing room, but he didn't appreciate that side of the game.

'Tiss was the other end of the spectrum, which made it all the more strange that Glenn did not take him to the World Cup when he was England manager. I cannot for the life of me think why, unless it was jealousy.'

After hanging up his boots, it seemed a natural fit for this articulate and intelligent man to move into coaching to pass on his experience to the next generation.

Benali flirted briefly with a coaching role and with a property business, but is now looking to follow Le Tissier into the media.

'Now I do a lot of punditry and motivational speaking, which I really enjoy. I would love to do more of that… so if anyone reading this wants to book me (apart from referees!), just get in touch with my agent.

'I did take a coaching role when I first retired, which came as a real shock to me. That's why I gave it up. I went from a player's salary to a junior coaching wage and I was working 24/7 – or at least that's how it felt.

'Steve Wigley was a great person to learn from and he was mindful of the time factor and let me have the odd afternoon off. But it was a real shock to go from being a player to working for a living.

'Ultimately, I could not see myself becoming a manager. I had seen the experiences that Dave Merrington, Stuart Gray and Steve Wigley endured when they stepped up and it made me wary.

'I would love to have managed Southampton, but I would probably have had to have left and earned my stripes elsewhere in the hope of one day coming back. That was too much of a gamble and I was not prepared to leave the area I love and uproot my family to pursue an ambition that might never happen. I thought it was highly unlikely I would ever get the job as Saints manager.

'Tiss and I did put ourselves forward when things were not going well after relegation. As ex-players, we were hurting and just wanted to help. Mind you, I'm not sure how much help we would have been. Half the team would have stood around doing nothing and the rest would have been sent off!'

Instead, Benali settled on a path which was to earn him far more national acclaim than his playing career ever did. It was a route which stretched 1,000 miles – and he completed it in just 21 days.

Benali's Big Run (an understatement if ever there was one) saw him run, jog, walk and stagger from Newcastle to Southampton via every Premier League ground.

How he must have cursed Swansea for staying in the top flight! But at least Norwich were not there.

Even so it was a phenomenal feat, one of the great endurance challenges of modern times. It was the equivalent of running two marathons a day – every day – for three weeks.

Benali took almost 1.2 million steps to raise £265,000 for Cancer Research.

'People ask me why I did it… I often ask myself the same question.

'I guess I wanted to inspire others as well as to raise a huge amount for a very good cause. And I also wanted to push myself to the very limit and test my boundaries.

'I learned that the hard way after just one day. I knew it was going to be an enormous physical challenge, but I had no idea how tough it would be mentally.

'The enormity of it hit me after the first day. I pretty much had a breakdown. I collapsed in Karen's arms and sobbed. The thought of running 40-plus miles every day for the next three weeks was too daunting.

'I was physically exhausted, but I could not sleep. My mind was racing. I could not get my head round the fact that, in a few hours, I would be getting up and doing it all again, even though every muscle in my body was on fire.

'Karen kept me going, but it was so tough. In the end, I had to take one day at a time, even one step at a time, depending how I felt. It could be as little as just summoning the reserves of strength just to put one foot in front of another.

'I took it hour by hour, minute by minute… aiming for the next brow of a hill, the next tree, the next house – whatever it took just to keep going. Apparently, I burned more than half a million calories, which is roughly Matt Le Tissier's daily intake!

'But it was an incredible experience and I couldn't have done it without the support of my family and friends. A lot of former players or colleagues turned out to run even small sections with me for moral support. And, of course, I was driven on by the knowledge that this wretched disease has touched the lives of so many people, including my own family.

'The people we met en route helped drive me on to St Mary's, although I would be lying if I said there weren't many moments when I genuinely thought I was not going to make it.

'My daughter, Kenzie, interviewed me in the middle of the challenge and I had a real emotional breakdown. But it was worth it all when I finally completed it.

'The final day was incredible. I knew coming into the stadium would be emotional, but I was unprepared for the fact so many people would come out on to the roads to welcome me.

'They were there in the country lanes, then a few more on the roads coming into Southampton. The closer I got to St Mary's, the more people were there.

'I know some did not even go to the match because they wanted to stand and cheer me on. I was deeply touched by all the support. It made a world of difference.

'Finally, I reached the stadium and I just remember getting a lump in my throat and feeling as though I was going to burst into tears because of the affection and appreciation towards me. It was an amazing way to finish.

'That day – and the entire three weeks – will live with me forever… but not enough to stop me doing it again!

'You forget the hard times and the pain and just focus on the good bits. Karen says it is a bit like childbirth. People can still donate. Just go to justgiving.com and search Benali's Big Run.

'I was very honoured to be named JustGiving's Celebrity Fundraiser of the Year and also to be the first recipient of the Barclays Spirit of the Game award.

'I don't suppose too many people would have put money on me winning that during my playing days!'

Neil Ruddock

IT WAS like that scene from Jurassic Park. You know, the one where the T-Rex is lumbering after the jeep and the glass of water starts to shake.

Fans at The Dell swear the ground shook in a similar fashion as Neil Ruddock set off on a 50-yard run to attack Craig Short.

It was the Friday before Christmas 1991 and Notts County had just equalised in what turned out to be a 1-1 draw. With a minute to go, there was a set-to between Short and Alan Shearer, prompting Ruddock to set off on a revenge mission from the other end of the field. It was the beginning of the end for Ruddock and his love affair with the Saints.

'I was wound up because they had just scored when I thought I saw Craig Short stamp on Alan Shearer, who was my mate, my "Bruise Brother". I couldn't let that go – even though I was at the other end of the field and it wasn't my battle.

'Without stopping to think – as usual – I set off on a 50-yard run. Obviously, with my pace, it took me a long time to get there. Even so, I didn't stop to consider the consequences.

'I still have no idea what I was thinking. It certainly wasn't pre-meditated, it just happened. I had built up a real head of steam by the time I got there and launched a flying headbutt at him. He needed four stitches in a bad cut above an eye. It wasn't big or clever.

'I turned to run away and ran straight into the referee. I knew I was getting a red card, so I just kept going. It was stupid and I knew I had gone too far that time, but I wasn't prepared for the furore which followed.

'I was enjoying a meal in La Lupa when Ian Branfoot rang. There were no mobiles back then, but somehow he had found out where I was and called the restaurant to say I was being fined and transfer-listed.

'It put me right off my dinner. I couldn't eat another thing, I just felt sick. I loved it so much at Southampton and I just sat there wondering what I had done.

'It ruined my whole Christmas because there was a bit of a media witch-hunt, with all the papers saying there was no room in football for a thug like me. I knew I had done wrong, but I had hoped for a bit more support from my manager, especially one who encouraged a physical edge – albeit not that much of one.

'I knew I had let myself and the club down, but from some of the press comment you would think I had killed someone. I was told in no uncertain terms by the club that they regarded my behaviour as totally unacceptable.

'I asked Ian Branfoot if it was his decision to transfer-list me and he said it was, though I suspect he was under pressure from the board. They made it quite clear that we did not do that sort of thing at Southampton.

'It was a very worrying time for me and my family. I knew I was no angel, but that was my first major indiscretion and I thought I might have been given a second chance.

'My old mate Jimmy Case was brilliant. Even though he was no longer with the club, he took the time to call me a few times to keep me from going under. He told me not to take too much notice of what was being written and that I was a good enough player to bounce back. It meant a lot because the club had been very public in their condemnation of me, which made it worse and made it easy for the media to give me a good kicking.

'They made an example of me and the message was rammed home as I was made to train on my own or with the reserves, where the coach Ray Graydon did a fantastic job keeping my spirits up.

'He kept encouraging me and reassuring me that things would turn if I worked hard, so I knuckled down. I think Ian Branfoot was impressed by my attitude and by the time he recalled me I was at peak fitness and mentally tougher.

'First I had to serve a three-match ban, though fortunately I escaped a disrepute charge – despite the media pressure. Then I was made to wait to get my place back but when I did get back in, I had a good run of form and I started getting interest from other clubs.

'Crystal Palace, Tottenham and Wimbledon all wanted me. So did Portsmouth, but I would never have gone there!

'Ian Branfoot took me off the transfer list – but it was too late as far as I was concerned. I had felt unwelcome and suddenly a lot of clubs wanted me.

'As it turned out, one moment of madness got me a dream move to Spurs, so things worked out well for me, if not for Saints, who never really replaced me either as a player or as a character.'

If Saints were disappointed to lose the commanding centre-back, it was compounded when they failed to receive anything like what they regarded as the player's market value at tribunal. The panel set the fee in part according to the wages Ruddock was to be paid at Tottenham – only for him to receive a hefty pay rise soon afterwards.

A more realistic valuation would have been the £2.5m Spurs later received from Liverpool, where the England international won a League Cup winners' medal.

Although he went on to have a hugely successful career, Ruddock admits it might never have happened if the situation had been handled differently.

'If I had not been transfer-listed in the first place, I would have signed a new deal because I loved my time at Southampton.

'It was a shame because I liked Ian Branfoot and on the whole I thought he was a good manager, especially as he encouraged us to socialise together and organised trips abroad for us to do that.

'He even said if I did well for him and the club then I would be drinking in bars all over the world – and that was good motivation for me!

'We had some great tours which often turned into an excuse for a team-bonding session – or piss-ups as we used to call them! Mind you, we almost went too far the night we nearly deprived England of the man who was to become one of their greatest ever players.

'We had gone away to Portugal for a summer trip, which meant we could have a few drinks without having to worry about matches, so we made the most of it. One night, Micky Adams, Matt Le Tissier, Barry Horne and I had all drunk our minibars dry, so we went in search of another.

'We decided to raid Alan Shearer's as he wasn't a big drinker. We barged into his room and, as he was half asleep in the bath, we decided to just take the whole minibar. Barry pulled it off the wall and ran off down the corridor with it while I poured a bottle of vodka over Alan in the bath – as you do!

'The problem was that the minibar had a load of drinking glasses on top of it and they all fell on the floor and smashed. Alan leapt out of the bath in a temper, but the vodka had gone in his eyes so he couldn't see properly and he didn't notice the broken glass.

'Next thing, he had trodden heavily on a shard of glass and collapsed on the floor in agony. There was blood everywhere, which sobered us up pretty quickly.

'Even now, I still wince thinking about the sight of three of his toes cut to the bone and hanging on by a thread, with blood pouring from his foot. I have never felt panic like it.

'He was in serious danger of losing his toes and we knew we had to get him to a hospital quickly. The problem was we were all too pissed to drive – and so were the coaching staff.

'The only one sober was a young defender called Steve Davis, who rushed him to this really primitive hospital where he was left in a room with some car crash victims and wondering if his career was over.

'Thankfully, they managed to stitch the toes back on and he made a full recovery. But it was a really close call – and the irony was that Alan hadn't even been drinking.

'I am just so thankful that we – and Alan – did not pay a terrible price for a stupid drunken prank which went horribly wrong.'

When Ruddock, then 21, arrived at Southampton from Millwall for a bargain £250,000 in February 1989, he thought he could hold his own in the drinking stakes. He soon found out he was just a beginner compared to Jimmy Case, the man who would become his mentor both on and off the field.

'These days, I think players don't tend to socialise together too much but back then I never drank with anyone else. They were my team-mates, my work-mates and my best mates.

'Jimmy certainly taught me how to drink. He was a great organiser on and off the field and set up some fantastic nights out.

'It was quite a shock the first night I went out with him. We played a pre-season friendly in the New Forest and then went out with Jimmy and our right-back Gerry Forrest.

'The pub we went to was closing so Jimmy went round the corner to another pub, got the landlord out of bed and made him open up.

Normally you get chucked out of a pub but here was Jimmy opening it!

'I have no idea how long I kept going, but eventually I fell over. Jimmy took me back to the Park Hotel and poured me into bed. Next morning, I woke up feeling like death and had to go training. Jimmy was fresh as a daisy.

'Jimmy could always find somewhere for a drink. I remember pre-season trips abroad. In those days there was no internet, so we usually had no idea where we were going or what would be there... but when we arrived Jimmy had already got the nights out planned and set up.

'He would always remind me I was a big centre-half so I should drink like one, not like a pussy winger. By the time I left Southampton, I could match him and now I reckon I would probably beat him if we went toe-to-toe... only in a drinking contest though, never in a fight!

'I have never seen anyone put it away like he can. He was number one for me. But he played until he was 41, so it can't have done him too much harm!'

Case was equally influential teaching the young Ruddock the tricks of the trade on the field, urging him to foul smarter, to bide his time and to go under the radar.

It proved a difficult lesson for the hot-headed youngster to take on board, but he soon realised the wisdom of the words.

'Jimmy was definitely the hardest player I ever played with. He taught me how to be a hard-man and how to drink. I'm not sure in which order, though!

'He taught me to be more slippery, more clever. I was raw, just a young lad and very inexperienced. I had a bit of a mouth on me and got wound up, but Jimmy taught me how to deal with it.

'He told me a true hard-man keeps his mouth shut because otherwise referees come looking for you. If they realise you are on the edge and wound up, they will keep an eye on you.

'I used to wear a special strapping on my wrist that I could tighten, so it hurt. If I got angry, I used to tie it tighter and get rid of the aggression that way.

'It was all psychological and Jimmy taught me that. So even before sports psychology became trendy, I was already finding ways of coping and channelling my aggression.

'It is better to stay quiet and bide your time. Jimmy would remind me it is a long career and there will be other opportunities for revenge.

'I remember seeing him clatter a few players and saying, "Why did you do that? He's done nothing." And Jimmy would reply, "Not today… but five years ago he did!"

'I was very lucky to have Jimmy in the team. He would talk me through games. He knew I had a tendency to lose the plot and said he was the same at my age. So he took me under his wing and taught me the game.

'He was a very clever player and it is disgusting that he never played for England, a real tragedy. I think his tough-guy image probably went against him.

'People probably saw that and thought he was just a destroyer, but he could really play. He was a great player before he became a hard-man. He had a lovely left foot.

'He taught me to be as tough as you can but as fair as you can – and never to let anyone know when you were hurt.

'These days, it is the opposite. Players roll around feigning injury and trying to get opponents booked or sent off.

'In my day, you just got on with the game and then rubbed the injury a few minutes later when no one was watching. You never let on you were hurt, either to your opponents or to the ref as he would think you would be looking for revenge and keep an eye out.

'It was just a case of being cute and waiting for your chance for revenge. Jimmy was the best at that. As a hard-man, I always felt you had to be able to take it as well as dishing it out.

'I can't stand all this pretending to be hurt, clutching faces when you have been pushed in the chest and trying to get other players sent off. That's not for me.

'You look at the current laws and it is becoming a non-contact sport, like basketball. Players will get done for travelling soon. It is too much stop-start.

'Players now go over at the slightest touch. But if you are genuinely hurt, you don't roll around.

'I think money has a lot to do with it. It is win at all costs. You look at Diego Costa for Chelsea against Arsenal when he did a fantastic number on Gabriel and got him sent off.

'And then even great managers like Jose Mourinho come out and defend him.

'That is not being a proper hard-man. I would love to see Jimmy Case get hold of him – he would not last long.

'I would never try and get a player sent off. In my day, you wanted them to stay on the pitch so you could kick them again!'

For all his hard-man image, Ruddock was a decent player too. A towering presence in the air at both ends of the field, he was an indomitable defender and a potent goal threat – never more so than when he scored an unforgettable penalty to effectively save Saints from the drop.

A wretched run of 17 league matches without a win had seen Chris Nicholl's team plummet from third from top in November to third from bottom in April 1989, prompting the manager to sign Ruddock in a bid to arrest the decline.

Nicholl could never have imagined, though, just how important his acquisition would prove just six games into his Southampton career as relegation rivals Newcastle visited The Dell for a crunch six-pointer. It was widely assumed that at least one of them would go down, possibly both. And with so much at stake, it was hardly surprising it was a dire game with barely a chance, let alone a goal – until the last minute.

Rod Wallace skipped through and went down as he tried to round the keeper, the faintest contact sending him tumbling for a fortuitous penalty which would ultimately decide the fate of both clubs.

Ruddock recalled: 'Matt Le Tissier and Derek Statham weren't on the field and I could see not too many of our lads fancied it. The ball was like a hot potato. I wasn't a penalty taker – but two things I did not lack were self-belief and bottle. So I picked up the ball.

'You could hear a sharp intake of breath around the goal and I swear a lot of the Milton Road end ducked as I ran up! I think their keeper thought I was just going to smash it, but I placed it and the crowd went absolutely mad and we won 1-0.

'I captured the moment with what became known as the Ruddock Stomp, a celebration which even featured on T-shirts, especially after I scored two in our next match, a 3-3 draw at Middlesbrough.'

Saints stayed up quite comfortably in the end while Newcastle were relegated. But Ruddock had already established himself as a cult hero at the club and had proved he was not just a destroyer.

'I like to think I could play a bit too. I was hard, but a decent player. You don't get to play for clubs with great footballing traditions like Southampton, Tottenham, Liverpool and West Ham, as well as England, if you can't play.

'I captained all those clubs at one time or another. In those days you had to have a bit of toughness, that's just how it was. I became a better player at Southampton and I became a man. It is where I learned the game – and I had a great time too.

'I was lucky to come into a side with a mix of old pros and promising youngsters like Rod Wallace and Matthew Le Tissier. John Burridge was in goal and alongside me I had Russell Osman and Derek Statham, both full England internationals.

'In front of me there was Glenn Cockerill and Jimmy Case, so it was great for me to be playing with such talent. They taught me every aspect of the game, both on and off the field.

'I doubt if it still happens now but in those days the older pros would help the young lads with such things as finding a place to live and settling into the area.

'Even now, when I see those players, I am quick to buy them a drink because that respect is still there.

'And then, of course, there was Alan Shearer. I used to pick him up before he could drive – and he is that mean he has never repaid the petrol!

'He has stopped taking my calls now, probably because he thinks I am going to be asking him for money!

'Obviously, he has gone on and been hugely successful, but in those days he was so broke that he would do anything for a few bob. I remember giving him £20 to sleep on my patio for a night and he was so skint he did it!

'I remember once Alan and I had gone out for a few drinks with Terry Hurlock one afternoon, when Shocksy (as we called Alan) got a call from his wife to say he was meant to be at a presentation.

'We hurried there so quickly that he didn't notice his jumper was inside out – and, of course, I was not going to tell him. So there must be dozens of photos of young kids with medals and Alan Shearer with a v-neck jumper inside out.'

Although he loved his time at Southampton – and the nights out with his team-mates – Ruddock has no regrets about his decision to leave, even though his second spell at Spurs lasted only a year.

'It worked out well for me, even though I fell out with Alan Sugar and ended up leaving for Liverpool. It was hard to get my head round the fact that 18 months after the Craig Short incident, I was signing for one of the biggest clubs in the world.

'I never thought I would end up playing for a club like Liverpool, playing in front of packed houses every week and being unable to walk down the street or go shopping. It was a different world and everything I dreamed it would be. And it all stemmed from Alan Shearer being stamped on and me steaming in to help him.'

Jason Dodd

DURING HIS 16 years with Saints, Jason Dodd never once hid from an opponent. Now a team-mate? That's a different story...

The only player who actually terrified him was Jimmy Case – and the former full-back still shudders at the memory of the moment he thought he was going to take a hammering at the hands of his Southampton colleague.

'Jimmy was a great lad, a fantastic player and a really nice guy off the field. But you would not want to get on the wrong side of him. I remember a mid-season trip to Portugal – they called them warm weather training breaks, but they were just an excuse for a piss-up to bring the lads together.

'Jimmy cut a finger on a broken glass. Really it needed three or four stitches but, being Jimmy, he didn't bother and just went to chuck some water on it. He had to take off his wedding ring, which was a family heirloom – it had been given to him by his nan, I think – and it had a lot of sentimental value.

'Micky Adams picked it up and put it safely in his pocket, but the word went round that I had lost it. I absolutely wet my pants when I heard Jimmy was on the warpath and looking for me.

'I literally hid from him for the next 24 hours as the lads wound me up about what Jimmy was going to do to me. I was absolutely terrified and stayed well clear of anywhere I thought he might be.

'Finally, he caught up with me and just as he was about to lay into me, Micky produced the ring. Of course, the lads were in a heap because I had been stitched right up, but I was genuinely scared.'

Dodd had every reason to be terrified, having witnessed early on in his Saints career just how brutal Case could be – and how valuable he was to have as a minder.

'Jimmy Case was the hardest player I ever played with. He taught me so much because he went about it in a subtle way.

'He was like a silent assassin. He was not loud, he did not go shouting about how hard he was or trying to intimidate people – he just did it. And he was clever about it. He would bide his time if need be.

'I remember in a game at Liverpool, Steve McMahon put in a naughty challenge on me after about 15 minutes. I was able to play on, but it was a really bad tackle which was meant to hurt.

'Jimmy left it at the time but later in the game he just held back a split-second as he went into a challenge. It was hard but fair and McMahon ended up being stretchered off.

'It was a massive learning curve for me. Jimmy really looked after the young pros... you could say he was our minder. He went about it the proper way, not shouting the odds or smashing people or punching them, but he really knew how to handle himself. He was brilliant.

'Jimmy was as hard as they come but, like a lot of the game's tough men, he was as nice as anything off the field. Terry Hurlock was another like that. He really looked out for the young players.

'He was tough as anything but he could play a bit too. The fact that he was Rangers' Player of the Year tells you that. Ian Branfoot did absolutely the right thing getting him in. He was brilliant for the dressing room.

'He was one of the hardest men I ever came across but he just got on with it. I remember a few of the youngsters were struggling to even move the bench press machine as Terry walked into the gym. We encouraged him to have a go and he smashed ten out while we just stood staring open-mouthed.

'Michael Svensson was another that you would not want to tangle with, even in training. We used to come off the pitch moaning about him because he trained as he played. He would always give you a whack.

'He was solid, a natural-born leader. He did not say a lot but led by example. If you were in trouble, you would want him alongside you. His injury was a big reason why the club went down.'

Although not a hard-man in the mould of Case or Hurlock, Dodd soon learned to look after himself on the field, although he admits the step-up came as quite a culture shock.

After signing from his home-town club of Bath – and being famously described by manager Chris Nicholl as 'a cocky fat boy with a Wiltshire accent' – Dodd learned a quick and painful lesson about the realities of the professional game.

The Southampton youth team were playing at Aston Villa in the final of the Southern Junior Floodlit Cup and Dodd went off injured – a little too easily for the liking of gritty Geordie coach Dave Merrington. If you think Sir Alex Ferguson's infamous hair-dryer treatment is bad – this turned the dial up a couple of notches to red hot. And Dodd still winces at the memory.

But it toughened him up and made him determined not to be on the receiving end of anything like it ever again. And he quickly realised he needed to toughen up off the field.

Although he went on to become one of the loudest voices in the dressing room and one of the prime organisers of 'social events', Dodd admits to feeling overawed in those early days.

'In the first 18 months after I joined the academy from Bath, I was too scared to speak. I just watched how the senior players did their jobs and learned so much from them.

'It was a massive learning curve for me. I was very homesick at first and wondered what I had done, jacking in my job. It was quite an intimidating dressing room because there were some proper big-hitters like Kevin Moore, Micky Adams, Glenn Cockerill, Alan Shearer, the Wallaces and Neil Ruddock all wondering why Chris Nicholl had signed this fat boy from Bath!

'I only earned £110 a week and drank soft drinks, so it was quite an eye-opener when I first went on nights out and the lads would send me to the bar to get the drinks.

'It was a real culture shock given where I had come from. But it was brilliant for me as a young kid to have such experienced players around me. It definitely helped me in my career.

'I learned so much in my first two years – how to do things... and how not to do things. I learned a lot on the field and off it.

'And the tours and drinking sessions really helped the lads to bond and to forge the team spirit which got us through and kept us up year after year. I am not sure clubs do that any more.'

When he was finally given his opportunity in the senior side, Dodd could hardly have got off to a better start. After all the hard work, he must have thought playing at the top level was easy.

'I had a good beginning to my playing career. I had 15 minutes in a League Cup game at York, which we won 2-0. It was only a few minutes but it felt like a full game… I was knackered at the end.

'But I must have done OK as I then made my full league debut at QPR, where we won 4-1, with Tim Flowers saving a penalty to bail me out after I had given it away – albeit a harsh decision.

'Then I followed it up with an unforgettable 4-1 win at home to Liverpool, who went on to win the league.

'We absolutely murdered them – it could have been seven. It couldn't have been a better start for me and it got the supporters onside with me.

'And it enabled me to be accepted by the players, who really helped me – mainly by giving me almighty stick, especially when I saw them rubbing deep heat on their legs.

'I thought I would do the same and slapped a load on. Oh… my… God! It felt like my legs were on fire. I spent ten minutes in the toilet trying to wash it off while the lads fell about laughing.

'I am just glad I remembered to wash my hands before I went to the toilet!'

Dodd was given his chance by Chris Nicholl, who had made it his mission to inject more youth into the side – and the rookie defender admits to being intimidated by the Northern Ireland international.

'Chris Nicholl was a real character – a proper battle-hardened centre-back in his time. He believed you could not be a defender if you had not had your nose broken. By the look of him, he had earned his stripes several times over!

'I remember one night we were beaten by Everton at The Dell and he was laying into us. It was quite a big dressing room and he was in the centre having a right go.

'The light switch was outside in the corridor and one of the apprentices must have leaned on it because the room was plunged into darkness.

'The light came back on a couple of seconds later and there was Chris in a proper fighting stance. He thought we had switched the lights off and were going to jump him!

'Chris was like that. He would join in training and smash people. He was scary.

'The night before one away game, we played doubles at snooker and I got drawn with him. And he was useless. I was not bad because

I used to go down the 147 Club three or four times a week, but he didn't have a clue. And yet he ended up abusing me and yelling at me – and I just took it!'

By his own admission Dodd was never going to be a top-calibre player, but he made the most of his ability with intense work-rate and determination.

Those qualities, allied to his reliability, no-nonsense defending and the technique to strike a decent cross or shot, saw him go on to make 453 appearances for the club, scoring 13 goals, including seven penalties from seven attempts.

That total would have been far greater had he not remained in the spot-kick shadow of the legendary Matthew Le Tissier.

The biggest threat to his place came from another emerging youngster in Jeff Kenna, with Dodd often playing in midfield so both could be accommodated.

Although not the most graceful, Dodd's competitive streak and ferocious will to win made it difficult for any of his bosses to leave him out.

'I made sure I was as fit as I could be. I had 13 managers and every time a new gaffer came in, I knew I had to impress him to make sure I kept my place. I had to be on top of my game the whole time, which probably made me a better player. I got on pretty well with all my bosses, but they knew what they were going to get from me.

'I was never going to be a world-beater, but I was a good solid player and a leader. That's why I was captain in later years.

'I was never a problem at all to any manager. I like to think I was someone they could rely on.

'I was loud in the dressing room and on the pitch. But I tried to use it to my advantage. If I put in a hard tackle and left a bit on someone, then I would quickly apologise.

'Or I would try to put players off by chatting. Once, we were playing Arsenal, who had Marc Overmars and Thierry Henry on the left against me. I said to Henry, "Why don't you fuck off to the other flank, you are making me look an idiot." And he did! I couldn't believe it.

'I would try and get in the referee's ear too. Mind you, that was back in the day when you could actually talk to officials. And they would give some back and tell you to shut up and get on with the game.

'I didn't rant but tried to be more subtle. I would talk to them in the tunnel and try to build a rapport. I would tell them if they had any problems on the field they should come to me.

'They don't set out to make bad decisions, so I would try and get onside with them rather than yelling and going mental.

'I wasn't looking to get them to change decisions or show any bias, but just to get a little bit of goodwill. Nowadays it is them and us, but back then there was a bit more communication. I would say my piece – and they would tell me to shut up!'

Inevitably, there were times Dodd fell foul of the officials and ended up being sent off. Mostly they were for the good of the team, but there was one dismissal which still rankles even now.

'I did pick up a few red cards – one for deliberate handball on the line at Newcastle, another for a professional foul in a crucial match at home to West Ham. That was a case of taking one for the team as it saved an almost certain goal and got us a vital win.

'But the most bizarre and unfair sending-off *ever* came playing for the England under-20 side against Mexico in the Toulon tournament.

'It was completely one-sided. We were 6-0 up and even subbed Alan Shearer and Rod Wallace to protect them for the next match. I remember receiving the ball and their lad came to take me out.

'He lunged in and I flew up in the air. I jumped up angrily and he fell to the ground as though I had hit him. But I honestly never laid a finger on him. Why would I? We were 6-0 up… and I was the one who was fouled.

'He rolled around and the rest of his team came steaming in – and I was the one sent off. He stayed on the field. How does that work?

'They had already had three players sent off, so I guess the referee was trying to even it up – or at least felt he could not send off a fourth Mexico player.

'I went into the dressing room and Rod and Shearer asked where the rest of the lads were. They thought the match was over.

'I told them what had happened and, of course, they just fell about laughing. They thought it was hilarious that I had been sent off when it was their player who smashed me. Thanks for the sympathy, lads!

'There were no cameras, so the manager Ray Harford just said to take the ban and he would bring me back for the final. He did and we beat France 1-0, so it worked out.

'Back then, I think it hurt a lot more to be sent off because clubs did not rotate their squads as much as they do now. Players wanted to play every match and if you did not play, you were gutted.

'I am not sure if pros really bother so much now. I think they accept being left out. But back then you wanted to play every match, so if you got a ban, it hurt – and it also meant you might not get your place back.

'There was none of this resting players. There were 38 Premier League games and if I did not play at least 30, I would be gutted.'

Having overcome his initial shyness, Dodd adapted well to the raucous dressing room banter – creating much of it himself. His was usually the first voice visitors would hear on arrival at the training ground. His louder-than-life personality was an integral part of the bond which banded the players together and saw them defy the odds to avoid a succession of survival scrapes.

Dodd's battling spirit would play a key role in keeping the team up and he was devastated when they meekly slipped through the trapdoor in 2005.

New manager Harry Redknapp blamed him for a shocking 5-1 defeat at Tottenham – though he was hardly the sole culprit on a wretched afternoon.

It proved to be Dodd's final game for the club and he watched from afar as the campaign lurched from one disaster to another. It culminated in relegation on the final day, when Saints succumbed without any of the trademark Spirit of Southampton which had seen them defy the odds for so long.

'It was that spirit and togetherness which kept us up year after year. We were not the best team. Often better sides than us went down. But we had a real unity. There were a few seasons when we just had to hang in there until we could move to St Mary's and begin to grow as a club. We had to survive year after year on gates of just 15,000 at The Dell.

'After we moved to the new stadium, the club brought in Gordon Strachan and we did really well under him. We even reached the FA Cup Final and I was absolutely gutted to miss out on leading the team because of injury.

'I tried so hard to get fit but just could not make it. Gordon made sure I was involved on the day and it was a fantastic occasion, even though we lost. But I was desperate to be playing.

'I did get a medal as the FA commissioned three extra for players who had contributed to the cup run, but I was gutted not to have played after so many years of helping the club to merely survive.

'But then it all went wrong. After Gordon left, the club brought in Paul Sturrock but that did not really work out and he left a couple of games into the new season.

'Steve Wigley took over and then, to our astonishment, Harry Redknapp pitched up as manager. We knew he would want to bring in his own players because that is what Harry does.

'But the ones he brought in were worse than the ones that were here, in my opinion. I could see it was all going wrong – we knew in November that we were in deep trouble – but there was nothing I could do about it because I was not playing.

'I just had to get away from there, so I ended up going on loan to Plymouth just to get some games – and I loved it there. But it hurt to see what was happening back at St Mary's.

'I am not sure that some of the new players were too bothered. They knew they would find other clubs and they did not have a real affinity for Southampton.

'In previous dog-fights, the players had busted their balls for the cause but it did not seem to happen. Maybe they did not battle, maybe they were just not good enough.

'The game is all about opinions and, in my view, the players who came in were worse than those already here.

'It was a horrendous final year at the club for me. It was really hard to stomach. After all the battles to stay up, the team looked like it went down without a fight – especially that final game of the season against Manchester United.

'They had the cup final the following week and looked like they were not too bothered and yet we barely put a tackle in. There is no way the likes of Tommy Widdrington, Neil Maddison, Francis Benali and myself would have let that happen in a match we needed to win in order to stay up.

'I could not be around it and, as I was no longer really wanted, I ended up going to Brighton. I had to get out. It was a shambles.

'I was distraught that I had to put relegation with Saints on my CV.

'I didn't play much that season but I was a Southampton player in the year we went down, so it is there and I cannot hide from it.'

Dodd hung up his boots in 2006 after making seven appearances for Brighton. He had a brief spell with Eastleigh before joining George Burley's coaching staff.

His personality and experience seemed a perfect fit but when Burley took over as manager of Scotland, Dodd had a brief spell as joint caretaker boss, with John Gorman overseeing a horrendous 1-0 FA Cup defeat on a frozen pitch at Bristol Rovers courtesy of a goal from future Saint Rickie Lambert.

'I did have a brief spell as caretaker manager culminating in that wretched FA Cup defeat at Bristol Rovers. We just did not perform on the day.

'I have no idea why. We had set everything up right, prepared properly and then the players just did not do it. The pitch was awful and maybe some of them used that as an excuse.

'The biggest disappointment was the cup had opened up that year. We would have had a quarter-final against West Brom and then a semi-final against Pompey. Imagine that – facing that lot at Wembley!

'Not only would it have given us a great chance of winning the cup with a final against Cardiff, but it would have stopped them from winning it. I was gutted.'

Dodd then left St Mary's but returned to coach the under-18s. Adopting many of the old-school values of discipline and hard work taught to him by Dave Merrington, he was hugely influential in bringing through names as notable as James Ward-Prowse, Calum Chambers and Luke Shaw, as well as Matt Targett, Harrison Reed and Sam Gallagher.

Bizarrely, he was sacked in May 2014, along with Paul Williams. It prompted Shaw to angrily tweet his disgust at the decision.

For all the praise heaped on Southampton's famed academy, the next two seasons did not see any young players promoted to the first team who had not been coached by Dodd.

Although his knowledge and experience were missed at St Mary's, he soon found a role coaching at Winchester College, following in the footsteps of another former Saints coach, Lew Chatterley.

'Life is great now. I love the role and there is no stress or pressure. There is no worry about losing my job if the manager changes – and the holidays are wonderful!'

Iain Dowie

AT 6ft 1in and with a bruising build, Iain Dowie always fancied himself as a bit of a hard-man – until he came to The Dell.

There, he encountered Francis Benali, who trained as he played, smashing into team-mates with a ferocity that shocked even this most robust striker after his £500,000 switch from West Ham.

Even for a player as physical as Dowie, it was an eye-opener. But he had just about come to terms with it when – just two weeks later – Terry Hurlock signed for Southampton.

So, a key question…

Who would win a fight between Terry Hurlock and Francis Benali?

'I'm honestly not sure… but I know I would pay good money to watch it! They were proper hard-men.

'In a boxing ring, Terry would probably beat him but he would have to knock him out inside three rounds, otherwise Franny would be too fit for him.

'Franny was wiry, deceptively strong and fit as anything while Terry was a really powerful bodybuilder – he could lift so much weight.

'I always remember seeing him just after he'd been doing a weights session. He was in just his shorts, ripped and his long hair all over the place. He glanced at himself in the mirror and reckoned he looked Robert De Niro in *Cape Fear* – I checked out the pics and he absolutely did!

'Terry was a tough boy. He was from a very different background to Franny, who was softer and more demure as a personality. Don't get me wrong, Terry was still a great lad off the pitch. He was an absolute diamond, maybe a rough diamond, but he was fantastic to have around.

'Terry really cared about the clubs he played for. He was a big personality but he really looked after the apprentices. He would take them out and buy them a beer and take care of them.

'He was a real character. I remember at one point he kept his savings in a cornflakes box under the bed. I saw him a couple of years later and said, "How's the cornflakes box?" He said "Fuck me, big man, I'm down to a variety packet!"

'He was a great lad who would do anything for anyone – as was Franny, who is a good mate now. We get on really well now and I see his daughter Kenzie when she is working at Sky.

'But back then I had a few clashes with him in training. Like me, he loved a tackle. But he was quicker than me and gave me a few whacks. One day, he gave me one too many, so I slung my arm up and he instantly fronted me up.

'We traded blows. He connected well with the side of my head and I got him quite well on the jaw before it was contained. The rest of the lads jumped in to pull us apart. I'm surprised they went anywhere near us considering the way we were going at it.

'I can't remember who it was but at least one of them got clipped on the way into the ruck. They had seen a few scraps in training but even the hardened characters drew a deep breath.

'It could have got very messy because neither of us was going to back down. It was a proper scrap. It is funny looking back on it and we laugh about it now, but at the time it was pretty intense.

'I remember when the Danish midfielder Ronnie Ekelund signed for the club. He was a great player, so skilful. But he couldn't believe what he had walked into. He made the mistake of nutmegging Franny, who had steam coming out of his ears.

'I think the top of his boot connected with the top of Ronnie's head and next thing Franny was trying to drag him off to beat him up! It was a real culture shock for Ronnie, but he soon adapted.

'But that's how it was then. Training was absolutely ferocious. We trained as fiercely as we played and Franny and I had many a clash. It was a different generation then.'

Dowie was originally on Southampton's books as a schoolboy, but drifted into non-league football after being released by the south coast club as a 16-year-old.

He studied for a Masters degree in engineering and worked for British Aerospace, earning him the tag of 'Rocket Man' – though maybe a more appropriate Elton John song might have been 'Saturday Night's Alright for Fighting', given the events in Jersey where Hurlock and David Speedie came to blows.

Micky Adams gives the details in his chapter, but Dowie recalls: 'We were already loaded with beers when we got back to the bar and there was a real spikiness about David, who was frustrated because he hadn't yet scored for the club.

'I seem to recall him asking Terry Hurlock to pass the sandwiches and then saying, "Oh I forgot, you can't pass anything!" That was it… Terry went for him. It all calmed down very quickly and I think it was Jason Dodd who took Speedo into the toilets to help him clean up. But when he came out, he cut loose again and Micky Adams got hit with an ashtray and ended up being taken away by the police, which was so funny because he had done nothing wrong.

'I just remember Speedo being sprawled on this glass table and Terry yelling, "I'm going to hit you so hard you'll think you were fucking surrounded!"

'Then, when it all calmed down, we went and sat in Terry's room and listened to music as though nothing had happened.

'The first training session when we got back was as ferocious as anything I have ever known in football. We put everything in for 90 minutes with no holding back – but that was how we played too.

'I loved playing alongside both Tel and Franny. They were both proper men… in a dressing room of proper men – and, by the way, that includes Matthew Le Tissier, who was never going to smash into tackles but he worked his socks off in other ways.

'It was the best dressing room I have been in with some great personalities like Micky Adams, Glenn Cockerill and Kevin Moore, God bless him. We had some proper characters round the place.

'And then we had Neil "Razor" Ruddock, who was a great lad. Back then, Beaujolais Nouveau day was a big thing each year and I asked him to get me a bottle of 1986 – he didn't get the whole concept of Beaujolais Nouveau! But several bottles later and he was signing the barmaid's breast with a felt tip pen!

'We had good players who could pass the ball, but who could fight if they needed to. They were resilient and honestly believed in each other.

'The dressing room was very open. There were no pariahs. There wasn't one bad apple in the group. If someone didn't comply, they were told. It was a very honest, open environment – I don't think it is the same in the modern game.

'There are too many precious egos now but back then if you didn't play well, you would be told by four or five of the lads. I certainly wasn't shy to voice my opinion. It was a sporting environment which very much kept you on your toes.

'We had some great people, outstanding individuals. And they all cared so much for the club and each other. I know some people feel that wasn't the case when Saints eventually got relegated from the Premier League. And I felt sorry for Roy Hodgson this summer because it looked like there was a lack of passion and tempo from the England team.

'We never had that. We went at every game full throttle. We might have lost if we weren't good enough, but never through lack of effort.'

Ian Branfoot, the manager who brought Dowie back to the club, loved that competitive edge, both on and off the field.

However, the team's more robust style of play alienated thousands of fans, who were screaming for the manager to be sacked almost as soon as he replaced Chris Nicholl, who had encouraged a much more entertaining passing game.

To many, Dowie's arrival epitomised the less cultured approach adopted by Branfoot and the Northern Ireland international had to battle for acceptance as he struggled for goals early on.

'I was on the books at Southampton as a youngster with the likes of Reuben Agboola, and it broke my heart when they released me. But my dad was really supportive and kept reassuring me I would make it and that I would get to Wembley one day.

'I played non-league with Cheshunt and Hendon before being picked up by Luton, who then sold me to West Ham, who were my club so I didn't really want to leave them when Saints came in for me. I had scored four goals in 12 games to help them get promoted, but then Billy Bonds said he wasn't going to play me and I had to go.

'That was tough because he was a hero of mine – and I ended up scoring as we beat them 1-0 at The Dell. To be fair, Billy was the first one to come up to me after the game to say well done. But they ended up being relegated while we stayed up quite comfortably.

'I didn't have a great start at The Dell because Ian Branfoot was under a lot of pressure as manager and I think some fans felt I personified his long-ball game, which wasn't well received.

'I can accept that to some extent because I did like a physical battle, but I think by the end of my time at The Dell people saw there was a lot more to my game than that.

'There were some who did not see what else I brought to the team and the aspects of my game which I worked very hard to improve. I knew my strengths and weaknesses.

'My touch was OK but I tried hard to improve it in training. I was very good in the air and prided myself on being fit. And I was among the top three or four runners at the club – distance not sprints. I was never going to be Usain Bolt!

'I remember one game where I actually bent my run so I was through on goal. I think it was Michael Gilkes ran past me like I wasn't there and a fan called out "Dowie, have you got a piano on your back?"

'I was never quick but I had half a yard in my head and I worked hard. And I was fortunate to play with some very good players who were proud to play for Southampton.

'It was a fantastic club for me and what pleased me was the way I won a lot of the fans round to the extent some of them were chanting for me towards the end of my time there when I was not playing.

'We were never going to press for honours, but we all loved playing there and we never got relegated while Ian Branfoot was there.

'The fans were on his back a lot of the time and it was hard playing in that atmosphere, but Ian never let the pressure transfer to the players.

'He was a proper man. The abuse he took was horrific at times. I experienced some of that myself and it wasn't nice. I remember going to Old Trafford and took almighty stick from the Saints fans.

'My mum and dad and brother Bob were in the crowd and had a bit of an altercation with some of the Southampton supporters about it – and let me tell you, if Bob was involved there was only going to be one winner!

'But Ian took it on the chin. He was a good man who understood the game.

'I liked him as a person. You could have a laugh with him but he would chastise you if you weren't doing it for him.

'I have a great deal of respect for Ian Branfoot. He was straight-talking and honest and would never say anything behind your back. He was always straight with you.

'He used to take dog's abuse as he walked along that touchline, but he never hid. There were many matches when it all kicked off among the fans, but he showed great mental strength.

'He kept us in the division even though we had hardly any budget for new players. Other clubs spent a lot more than us but went down. One thing we did have was fantastic spirit. And we had a wonderful group of players and characters. I loved being part of that.

'Back then, a lot of teams played more direct, even Liverpool, who were the top side. They could be direct at times. When I went into management, my teams didn't play that way but then we did what we had to do in order to survive on the resources we had.

'Ian Branfoot tried to do the right things. But some things went against him. Leaving Matthew Le Tissier out probably defined him. If Tiss was playing now – bloody hell! He would be one of the best in the game.

'It is laughable that the most Tiss ever earned was £3,500 a week. Even then, he should have been on ten times that. He was a fantastic lad, a genius on the ball and he was actually fitter than he likes to admit.

'Yes, he ate crisps and other junk food but he worked incredibly hard when he had the ball. I think I was good for him because I was hard-working and could run all day. I think we made a good partnership.

'I would have to say he was the best player the club has ever had. I know they had the likes of Kevin Keegan and Alan Ball... but Tiss is right up there.

'I was just someone to allow him to perform and to do what he did best. I accepted my role in the team, but I am happy to claim an assist for that great goal he scored against Newcastle.

'The fact is that it was a shit header from me which went behind him... so he had no choice but to juggle it over the defender!'

Similarly, Dowie proved a good foil for the emerging Alan Shearer, holding the ball up selflessly to allow his strike partner to run the channels and to rediscover his goalscoring form.

After hitting a hat-trick on his debut against Arsenal, Shearer managed just four goals in Nicholl's final season but struck 13 times under Branfoot to earn a £3.6m British-record move to Blackburn.

And while the likes of Hurlock and Benali and Ruddock were seen as the main hard-men in the side, Dowie says Shearer was a match for any of them, quickly learning to handle himself in an era where centre-forwards had to stand up for themselves.

'These days the game has changed, with very little contact allowed. In my day, we would go to Arsenal and as soon as the first ball was played up to your feet, you knew you would be taken out by Tony Adams or Martin Keown, Steve Bould or Andy Linighan.

'Similarly if they played the ball down the line, we would take them out. You never got sent off for it, maybe a booking. They were tough tackles, but very few players had any intent to hurt and you just had to deal with those.

'I remember scoring at Palace and my shirt was in tatters because Eric Young had virtually ripped it off. But that didn't faze me. I enjoyed the physical side of the game.

'It was what it was. You couldn't play as a centre-forward if you weren't prepared to mix it with the centre-back and try to dominate them.

'Look at Alan Shearer, he was never shy of doing that. Physically, he was tough as old boots and he could properly look after himself.

'He had strong thighs and an incredibly low centre of gravity. He was like Harry Kane with the ball. He was quick and although you didn't think he could hit a shot like Tiss, he had this unerring knack of finding the corner of the net.

'He was very clever, he was strong and he was the best I have ever seen at heading the ball at goal. He could sense how to attack the ball and he could smash it from anywhere.

'Technically, he was very good too. He was a powerful lad who loved to run in behind defenders. He called it the "Charlie run" at Blackburn. If he shouted "Charlie" it meant he was going to spin and go behind the defender.

'He's a good friend of mine, good fun and a great personality. He has people he trusts around him and if you break that trust, then that's it.

'He grew up in a tough area then came down here, which was not easy at 16, but he had an incredible career. History tells you he is the best centre-forward the Premier League has ever had, but he also loved the physicality of the game. He was a warrior, there is no doubt about that.

'I had a brief time in management with him at Newcastle – too brief really. We should probably have had longer, but at least we had the balls to take it on.

'We had a lot of injury issues and it was a huge disappointment to Alan when we were relegated because the club means so much to him. It is one of the best clubs around. I would love to have played there – but I wouldn't have been good enough.'

Dowie still harbours hopes of getting back into football management having enjoyed his stints with Oldham, Coventry, Hull and Charlton. However, his biggest success came at Crystal Palace, leading them to the Premier League with an astonishing run of 17 wins in 23 games to lift the club from 19th to sixth and a place in the play-offs, where they beat his old club West Ham 1-0 to win promotion.

In recent years, he has worked as a pundit for Sky Sports and in March 2016 he raised a few eyebrows by taking a post with the online housing survey company GoTo.

'It has been hard work – I did 18,000 miles in the first three months, but I have enjoyed it. We do a lot of stuff with Purple Bricks because the founders, Kenny and Michael Bruce, love their football.

'I still do all my match reporting for Sky, which is a lot of fun and keeps me involved in the game – though they never seem to put me in the same studio as Francis Benali...'

Terry Hurlock

IF ONLY *Game of Thrones* had been filmed 20 years earlier, Terry Hurlock could have followed Vinnie Jones to Hollywood.

With his flowing locks and fearsome warrior image, the former Southampton midfielder could have claimed the Iron Throne with just a stare.

But his opponents would always know he could back it up with ruthless action if need be.

A young David Beckham came up against Hurlock while on loan at Preston and readily admitted he stayed well away from him. Matthew Le Tissier employed similar tactics when Saints faced Millwall at The Den.

And, when Neil Ruddock was asked his favourite animal, he had no hesitation in joking: 'Terry Hurlock!'

Although an understandable verdict given his intimidating persona, it does him a disservice because Hurlock was no thug, despite the fact he is regularly named in run-downs of the top 20 hardest footballers of all time.

Not only was he a far better player than many gave him credit for, but away from combat he was widely acknowledged as a top man who would do anything for anyone.

He laughs: 'I always had long hair. It wasn't just an image that I was trying to cultivate. I kept it that way until it started falling out!

'I think my reputation did precede me with referees. It was everything, I suppose: the hair, the image, the disciplinary record – or just the fact they wanted to get me in the book so they could say they had booked Terry Hurlock. I might be wrong but I think there was an element of that, especially in Scotland, where it seemed I was booked every five minutes.

'I don't think I ever got done for dissent. I always regarded those as a waste when you could pick them up for a tackle instead!

'I'm not saying I didn't deserve a lot of the cards I received, but definitely not all of them, especially when I was playing for Rangers.

'I was hard but I was fair. There were occasions I mistimed tackles and plenty of players came off worse in a 50-50 challenge, but I never set out to hurt anyone. I wouldn't do that.

'I always went in hard but I never set out to do anyone. That's not to say I wouldn't want to meet them in the bar afterwards!

'I got done plenty of times – but you just accepted it and got on with the game in those days.

'The rules are even stricter now, with referees handing out bookings for the slightest contact, but I do think I would still have been able to play at the top level because I would have learned the game very differently.

'It is hard to adapt and to change the habits of a lifetime when they start clamping down on tackles halfway through your career – even now, I still want to put my foot in if I ever have a kick-about.

'I used to love a tackle, as long as it was hard but fair. These days, the slightest nudge and players go down. I do wish I could play now, though – I was too early for all the money.'

These days, even very ordinary players seem to command a weekly wage in six figures, which will see them living in luxury long after they are forgotten by the fans.

Hurlock though makes a living working in the mail room for the RMT rail union, his friendship with the late Bob Crow helping him to secure the post, so to speak.

Until his death in March 2014, Crow was the outspoken general secretary of the National Union of Rail, Maritime and Transport Workers – and a big Millwall fan.

'Bob's sister used to work with my mum. He got in touch with me because he wanted something signed and we became friends.

'I asked him to bear me in mind if he ever had any jobs going, so he asked me to come in for an interview and I got through and started working in the post room. It was nice to get a bit of regular money at my age. As long as I have enough to get by and for a couple of beers, then I'm happy.

'I found it difficult after I stopped playing. I did all sorts of jobs just to make a living. I had a pub which did well but then it all fell apart when I moved to Rangers because I couldn't spend enough time there.

'I never earned that much as a player, but if I had used my loaf and had a bit more luck with my property then it might have been different.

'When I signed for Rangers, I bought a house but lost a lot of money on it and virtually ended up giving it away.'

That story is recounted by Hurlock's former Saints team-mate Perry Groves, who recalled: 'Terry told me the estate agent had done him up because he showed him this fabulous spacious house with four bedrooms, bathrooms, fitted kitchen – not so much Beckingham Palace as Hurlock Hall!

'Terry and his wife, Kath, said yes on the spot without bothering to look at the garden. It was only after they moved in that they noticed a noise coming from there and opened the door to find a huge electric pylon going "Zizzz, Zizzz, Zizzz!"

'Tel said "No wonder the agent never opened the back door when he showed us round." Tel used to worry that visitors would get some sort of radiation sickness and lost a bit of money when he sold it to come to Southampton.'

Hurlock, a £400,000 bargain from Rangers in September 1991, was one of the first signings made by Ian Branfoot, who was already under pressure from the fans for allowing Jimmy Case to leave.

Whatever the merits of releasing Case – and even now it seems bizarre – there is little doubt that Hurlock was as close as possible to being the ideal replacement.

Many, though, judged him simply on his caveman appearance, claiming that he personified the more physical approach demanded by the new manager, whose long-ball style was so loathed by supporters brought up on an entertaining passing game.

It was a tag that Hurlock never quite shook off with the more ardent purists, even though he was to become a cult hero on the terraces.

'My downfall was taking Jimmy Case's place. He was a hero to a lot of fans and they didn't take to me because of that. But that was out of my hands. I just tried to do the best I could for Southampton. It wasn't my fault that Jimmy had gone.

'I have spoken to him a few times and we ended up good mates, which is good because he was a hero of mine. You could not hurt him – he would go straight through you, but he could really play too.

'I loved Southampton, though it took a bit of time to adapt. No disrespect to Saints, but it was a bit different to being at Rangers!'

During his year at Ibrox, Hurlock was named as the club's Player of the Year as he led them to the Scottish Premier League title and the League Cup under the equally combative manager Graeme Souness.

But he struggled to cope with referees, who seemed to regard booking him as some kind of medal of honour.

'I used to get booked every other game up there, so I kept losing my place through suspension. And, because we kept winning every week, I couldn't just walk straight back into the team.

'I found myself in the reserves or being used as a squad player and I got a bit fed up with it. They were just starting to tighten up on the rules, so you could hardly touch opponents – and then Southampton came in for me.

'I was no spring chicken at 33, so I asked Walter Smith – Souey had gone to Liverpool – if it would be OK if I went. He wasn't happy, but he understood. I was chuffed to be playing in the Premier League and I had worked with Ian Branfoot before at Reading.'

Hurlock's arrival at The Dell summed up the down-to-earth nature of a man so far removed from the image-conscious stars of the modern era.

Back then, journalists were still allowed on club property rather than being kept at a distance by gates and security guards, and so a crowd of media men were waiting in the car park for the new signing.

Television cameramen captured every luxury car which pulled in, only to stop filming as soon as they realised that Hurlock was not in them.

No one paid any attention as a battered old brickie's van drove in and pulled up in front of the main entrance. The back doors opened and out climbed Hurlock in a Hawaiian shirt, calling: 'Alright lads?' before vanishing inside as the cameramen scrambled for their equipment.

'I am just as happy in a posh car or a van. It doesn't bother me what I am in as long as it gets me there. Of course, I like having nice things but when you are brought up with nothing, then it's easier to adapt.

'Some people have a silver spoon and find it hard in the real world, but when you have nothing you can adjust.'

That earthy attitude was just right for Southampton, a club with no airs and graces and who were struggling on a limited budget against rivals whose ground capacity was often three times that of The Dell.

'Southampton are a terrific club and I loved my time there. And The Dell was a great ground with a fantastic atmosphere.

'We used to share the toilets with the opposition and I remember standing next to Ryan Giggs and saying, "If you go past me, you will regret it." But it didn't stop him. He was like a gazelle and I couldn't catch him!'

'We had a good side. In particular, Matthew Le Tissier and Alan Shearer were a joy to play with, two of the greatest footballers England ever had.

'Ian Branfoot wanted Tiss to work a lot harder, which was the way he used to like players. Even when I was with Ian at Reading, we used to work hard.

'To give him his due, Tiss always trained very well as long as he had a ball but the more you ran him, the more his ability dried up. Maybe you have to give him a free role and just let him do something special.

'I didn't mind doing the extra running to cover for him as long as he was producing. There was a lot of aggro between him and Ian Branfoot, but he was special. He could put the ball on a sixpence. I still watch videos of his goals even now and marvel at how unbelievable he was.

'I could tell that Alan Shearer was going to be special, even as a youngster. He had fantastic ability but could look after himself on the pitch.'

Hurlock was 35 when he left The Dell in February 1994, one of the first victims of Branfoot's departure. New boss Alan Ball was determined to distance himself from anything to do with the loathed long-ball game and so sent Hurlock on trial to Millwall.

'Mick McCarthy was manager there. I did really well and we reached the play-offs, but we didn't go up and he decided not to sign me.

'Fulham came in for me, which meant linking up with Ian Branfoot for a third time, but it was the same old story, with me getting booked every other week. I missed literally half the season and yet I didn't get any injuries. It was purely suspensions.

'Then we played my old club Brentford in pre-season and I broke my leg and that was the end of me.'

If ever there was a case of live by the sword, die by the sword, then this was it, as a bad tackle by Martin Grainger put one of the game's great competitors into retirement.

'I was always taught never to go into a tackle half-heartedly or else you will get hurt – and that is what happened to me against Brentford.

'I pulled out of the tackle because it was a friendly and it is an unwritten rule that is what you do before the start of the season. But he followed through and broke my leg in two places. It was 18 months before I could walk properly and that was me done. I had the hump at the time, but it is all done and dusted now.'

Hurlock has clearly mellowed in middle age, with a shy reluctance to talk about some of the more lurid incidents away from the field, not least because he does not want to alienate Saints fans for whom he still has a high regard.

Instead it is left to his pal Groves to tell how it all kicked off in the Captain's Table pub after Hurlock was deliberately targeted and provoked.

He recalled: 'We had been in the pub minding our own business when three or four lads started giving Terry some real stick – it was vile stuff, horrible lies. They accused him of being a nonce and liking young boys in the showers, which was the worst thing they could have said.

'I thought "Here we go…" but the landlord managed to split them up. Terry said he couldn't let that go and he would get it sorted.

'A few days later, we were at home to my old club Arsenal and Terry was after some extra tickets as he had some friends coming down. I just assumed it was because it was a London club and they wanted to watch the Arsenal.

'We won 2-0 and afterwards he suggested a drink with his mates in the Captain's Table. They were proper heavies, but even so I didn't think too much of it… until these lads walked in and the doors were locked.

'I was ushered into the kitchen, which suited me. I'm a lover, not a fighter! Tel said "You don't want to see this." Then it all kicked off like a Wild West brawl. There were punches everywhere and bodies on the floor.

'Someone must have opened the door because it spilled out into the street before it died down. Of course, it made the papers and Nigel Winterburn and Paul Merson both made a bit of money out of it as they were named and weren't even there.

'Merse had headed off to New York's nightclub and Nigel had gone back to London with the Arsenal team. Apparently, one of the injured had given his name as Nigel Winterburn. I think they got about 15 grand, not that I saw any of it!

'I just got hauled up to see Ian Branfoot, who must have thought he had signed a whole heap of trouble. I explained it was nothing to do with me.'

Groves was one of four signings made with the £3.6m British-record fee received from Blackburn for Alan Shearer – and three of them did not work out.

By his own admission, Groves was one of them and it is one of his biggest regrets in football that Saints fans did not get to see the best of him after joining from Arsenal in August 1992. A serious injury restricted the winger to just two starts and six appearances from the bench, scoring twice.

He said: 'I will be quite honest, I was a waste of money for Southampton. They paid something like £750,000 for me and I was really excited. I was 27 and coming into my prime and I wanted to really establish myself.

'I was looking forward to it. Southampton had a good team with the likes of Matt Le Tissier – I thought he would make me look good! In fact, he made one of my goals with a 60-yard raking pass from left to right in a 1-1 draw at home to Leeds.

'On paper, it looked a good deal getting four players for less than half of what they received for Shearer. The club brought in me plus David Speedie, who seemed to find it hard to get on with people, Kerry Dixon whose goalscoring form deserted him, and Ken Monkou, who was the only success. He did well.

'I loved the area and the club and I felt good about the move, but then I snapped my Achilles tendon and that ultimately finished my career at just 27, so I didn't enjoy my time at Southampton as much as I should have done. I just felt like a spare part as I was unable to contribute.'

The injury came just five months into his stay at The Dell in a 2-1 defeat at Middlesbrough, where again Hurlock features in the story.

Groves recalled: 'I came off very early in the game. I thought someone had kicked me on the calf, but it turned out I had snapped my Achilles tendon.

'I was sitting in the bath feeling very depressed, although I still didn't know quite how bad the injury was. It was a midweek game and it wasn't diagnosed until the following Monday, so I had a floppy foot for six days.

'Anyway, after about ten minutes, I heard the clatter of studs on the tiles. The door was booted open then in came this mane of hair – it was Tel. He said, "Bloodnut (that was his nickname for me because of my ginger hair), I've only gone and done him. That Willie Falconer, he had to have it so he got it and here I am!" Both of them had been sent off and there was only about 20 minutes gone.'

However, Groves is more than happy to confirm the widely held view that Hurlock was not simply a hard-man but also a very different character off the field – and a very good footballer.

'The thing about Tel is he was a far better player than most people recognised. They wouldn't see past the hair and the physical attributes, but he could actually play.

'His passing was excellent and in the modern game, he would be the perfect holding midfielder. A lot of players just pass it sideways to keep possession, but Tel loved to play the ball with the outside of his right foot and ping it forward.

'It was very easy for people to label him as just a hard-man and to dismiss him as someone who just kicked people. And he was certainly brave – if there was a tackle that was 30-70 against him, he would turn it in his favour. I don't know if his Seventies rock hair and image went against him. It definitely didn't earn him the benefit of the doubt from referees. But he could certainly play.'

There was even talk at one stage of a possible full England call, and while that might have been merited on both his passion and passing, it is easy to imagine the FA running scared of Hurlock's image and the negative press he might have attracted.

Yet one cast-iron certainty is that he would have played with all the heart and commitment demanded by the fans and which has so often been lacking from a succession of England teams.

Groves added: 'Terry got one cap for the England B team – and he was so, so proud of it. He was given a tracksuit and all the gear and he used to wear it to the training ground.

'With anyone else, you might have thought they were being flash, but not Tel. He was just honoured to have it. He would punch his left breast and say "Three Lions, Bloodnut!" It meant the world to him.

'Fans loved his passion and his endeavour. He was a proper cult hero in Glasgow when he was with Rangers, because of the way he played the game.

'Yet off the pitch he is the gentlest, nicest person you could wish to meet. He is polite and courteous, a genuine nice guy and probably one of the funniest.

'He was just so likeable that he got away with all sorts of mad-cap stunts, like the time we were supposed to be taking our wives out for an Indian meal and he asked if I wanted a quick drink at his local.

'He lived near the Cleveland Bay in Chandlers Ford and we often used to drink there, so we came out of The Dell and jumped in a taxi, which went up the Avenue. I expected it to turn off at the Hilton – but it flashed by.

'Next thing I knew, we were heading up the M3 to his local – in Walthamstow! We ended up in a drinking den near Blackfriars tube station, then had a kebab and about 3am we got an unlicensed taxi with a coat-hanger for an aerial and it took us back to Southampton.'

They may be great memories but Hurlock is not one for reliving them, at least not in public. Similarly, he declines to go into detail about the infamous bust-up with David Speedie in Jersey, saying: 'I don't want to talk about Jersey – I'll let others talk about that.'

But there is a rare flash of the old spark as he adds: 'But if I ever meet him, I wouldn't hesitate to punch him and finish it off as I should have done all those years ago.'

Bruce Grobbelaar

ON HIS wall in Ottawa, Bruce Grobbelaar still has a framed cheque for £1.

It is the reduced damages from *The Sun* newspaper, whom the goalkeeper sued over the match-fixing allegations, which hit the headlines just three months after he joined Southampton.

The Zimbabwe international says: 'I look at it every day. It reminds me to be humble.'

It is all that is left of a rollercoaster experience which threatened to undermine all his considerable achievements in the game, quite apart from costing him a small fortune in legal expenses.

The scandal also looked like it was going to rob him of his reputation as one of the game's great characters, though he insists to this day that he was the innocent victim in a set-up which backfired badly.

The story broke just days after a thrilling 3-3 draw at Manchester City in November 1994, when the newspaper published secretly taped conversations between Grobbelaar and his former business partner Chris Vincent.

It looked grim for the goalkeeper as he was filmed accepting £2,000 in cash, supposedly as part-payment for him to throw a match. Grobbelaar has always maintained right from the outset that he, in turn, was trying to set up Vincent.

The pair had fallen out just before the former Liverpool star signed for Saints in August 1994. Times were very different then. The club were on tour in Holland and only had the team coach for transport – and that was needed to take the players to a friendly.

So, when Grobbelaar flew into Amsterdam, manager Alan Ball asked an *Echo* reporter and photographer if they would mind taking reserve team boss Dave Merrington to pick up the new signing from the airport. Imagine the chances of that happening now.

The big-name free transfer looked taken aback to be met by the press, but still spent much of the hour-long journey to the match ranting about how he felt he had been stitched up and had lost a lot of money.

Grobbelaar recalls: 'It was a bit weird getting a lift from a reporter, but I do remember talking about Chris Vincent and how we had fallen out. He had just done it to me, so I was not happy and I went on my own little espionage trip to try and get more information out of him.

'I needed to know from him where my money was and he did not come up with any plausible explanation.'

The then 37-year-old set about trying to recover his losses and to get some measure of personal revenge over the man he felt had cheated him. So when Vincent approached him with an offer to throw matches for money, Grobbelaar insists he saw it as a chance to set up the man who had wronged him.

All along, he was adamant that he had no intention of keeping the cash he was handed on camera – and he is equally forthright in stressing that he made up stories of deliberately conceding goals or accidentally saving shots in order to make his legend look convincing.

He stated that he was trying to entrap Vincent – only to find his plan backfired spectacularly when it emerged that his former friend was working with *The Sun*.

He says: 'It turned out to be detrimental to myself. I was innocent and if I had gone to the authorities and reported it straight away, then I would not have had to go through the court. But it was a big learning curve for me.

'He had been a friend – or at least I thought so. But he was a good con-man, very good. I thought I had met him in the army, but he was never in the army at the same time as me. I was out in 1977 and he was in active service in 1978.

'When the scandal broke, I was actually at the south side of Gatwick Airport with Sky TV negotiating to do six cooking programmes from the Solent. I was going to be on a boat to Cowes and prepare a dish a day: prawns, sea bream, that sort of thing.

'I was sorting out a six-episode contract with Sky and then I walked across from the south terminal to the north and that's when

The Sun showed me the pics they were going to publish the next day.

'I felt sick, I said "I know exactly who has done this, it is Mr Vincent," and I was right. I spoke to the editor and I said if you put this in then I will sue you because there is nothing in it.

'Everyone thought I was going to go to Zimbabwe, but I went through the airport as if I was flying out and then got in a car and met my wife. I sued the paper at 11 o'clock that night.

'The story came out in the papers the next morning and by then I had already explained to my lawyers it was a load of rubbish and I wanted them to sue.'

The Sun's evidence also implicated former Wimbledon duo John Fashanu and goalkeeper Hans Segers, plus Malaysian businessman Heng Suan Lim, who was alleged to have been the middleman in a Far East betting syndicate. All denied any involvement.

Their trial began in January 1997 and with all parties pleading innocent, the jury were unable to agree a verdict, prompting a re-trial, at which all were cleared.

Grobbelaar was then able to pursue his own legal action, suing for libel and being granted £85,000 in damages in July 1999. However the amount was reduced to just a nominal £1 on appeal, with three High Court judges dismissing his explanation.

Lord Justice Simon Brown concluded: 'One is left with an inescapable core of fact and circumstance which, to my mind, leads inexorably to the view that Mr Grobbelaar's story is, quite simply, incredible. All logic, common sense and reason compel one to that conclusion.

'It is, of course, understandable how a jury, skilfully deflected from the path of logic, could have accepted Mr Grobbelaar's story or at least been left undecided about it – a result fatal to the defendants upon whom the burden lay.'

Grobbelaar was ordered to pay costs of £500,000, forcing him to declare bankruptcy. Although the scandal blew up early in his two-year stay at The Dell, the former Liverpool keeper still looks back fondly on his time with Southampton.

Even at 37, the clown prince of football was still a real coup for Ball and his Director of Football Lawrie McMenemy, who had made such a success of bringing in big names towards the end of their careers and getting the best out of them.

He had won 13 major medals in as many years at Anfield, including a European Cup triumph in Rome when his wobbly-leg antics famously helped the Merseysiders to a 4-2 penalty shoot-out victory over hosts Roma following a 1-1 draw.

His extrovert personality and flamboyant style of goalkeeping made him a huge fans' favourite and his arrival gave Saints real strength between the sticks, with England international Dave Beasant still in fine form.

Grobbelaar says: 'The scandal did not cast a shadow over my time at Southampton because I know I never did anything wrong during my time there and for Alan Ball.

'When the scandal broke, Alan Ball asked me six times if I had done it and I answered "No" each time. He said, "That makes the decision for me. I will play you in the first team." And that's what he did.

'He said there was no question I would be in goal and the knowledge that I could keep playing while I was going through the court cases really helped me to get through it all.

'In that 1994/95 season, I played probably 80 per cent of the games and we finished tenth. If Bally had had any doubts, he would not have played me.

'The judge asked me if it was scary coming to court each day and I said it was like a football game in many ways. The opposing barrister would be the opposition captain and his legal team would have made up a full side.

'We had a similar-size team. I said the judge would be the referee and his clerks would be the linesmen – but there are only about 40 to 50 spectators.

'I said, "Imagine going out on to a pitch in front of thousands of people in Zimbabwe, where you are the only white man on the pitch and if you do anything wrong they will all want to kill you – that is daunting." He said, "I see what you are saying!"

'Playing in matches was a release for me, so it was not hard to focus on the football. The legal stuff was just something I had to get through but I don't think any other person could have done it.

'I had gone through a war and seen tragedy after tragedy, so I was tough and my faith that I had never done anything wrong kept me going.

'The need for the truth to come out kept me going.'

As the scandal broke, it threw the club into turmoil. As senior statesman, Lawrie McMenemy handled the insatiable media demands, leaving Ball free to work with the players at Staplewood.

However, the training ground inevitably became a magnet for photographers desperate to get a picture of Grobbelaar in action.

He recalls: 'Matthew Le Tissier and I used to go out on to the training pitch for some shooting practice because he would really test the goalkeepers.

'Suddenly, he smacked a shot high and wide into the trees, which was so unlike him I could not work it out... until I heard a photographer cry out. He had been hiding in the bushes taking pictures, Matt had spotted him and had the ability to pick him off.

'There were a few of the paparazzi who would hide in the trees and try to snatch photos until Tiss started doing that. He had the skill to put the ball wherever he wanted. He was such a good player.

'He would have walked into my Liverpool side – he certainly would not have run into it! Mind you, we already had one like that in Jan Molby – imagine the two of them together!'

Having been assured of the player's innocence, Saints gave him their full support – and the fans added their own backing with a touch of humour.

They turned out in force for the next match, a home clash with Arsenal, which inevitably drew a media circus to the south coast, crowding out the already cramped press box.

Almost inevitably, Grobbelaar emerged as the hero in a 1-0 victory, which saw the Gunners awarded a penalty. The fairytale script would have seen the eccentric keeper make a stunning save, but although it did not quite turn out that way, he still did enough to distract the taker.

He adds: 'I came back from playing in a World Cup qualifier for Zimbabwe and played for Saints against Arsenal. We won 1-0 and Paul Dickov missed a penalty against me.

'The Southampton fans were great that day, very supportive and with a bit of humour, which is often the best way. I will never apologise in life for having a smile on my face.

'I remember they were throwing money at me. I took a cap off one of the stewards and passed it around. They put money in it and I gave it to the steward and told him to divvy it up among his colleagues. He said "Bugger off, it's my cap" and he kept it all!

'I really appreciated all the support I got, both from the fans and the club. The fact Alan Ball had such faith in me helped me enormously and really kept me going.'

Grobbelaar had already shown his commitment to the cause, playing in a protective mask after being hurt in a 2-0 win over Everton – by one of his own players.

'The hardest player at Southampton was Francis Benali, who gave me a depressed fracture of my cheekbone in my first season at The Dell.

'We were playing Everton at home and, after about eight minutes, I came for a cross and Franny came in with the striker and his elbow connected with my eye.

'I went off to hospital and they tried to contact the face specialist, but he was out on the Solent sailing. So I said I was going back to watch the game and they should call me when he got there. And that's what I did. We won 2-0, which was great. Then I had the surgery that evening.

'Franny could literally run through brick walls, but all the guys I played with there were brilliant, a good bunch and some real characters. The beauty of Facebook and Twitter is I can see what they are all doing now and hear their stories.

'I really enjoyed my time at Southampton, especially the first year. Then Alan Ball left for Manchester City and Dave Merrington took over and decided to play Dave Beasant in goal. He said there must be some things on my mind and that could affect my focus.

'I played a couple of games towards the end of the season to help keep the club in the Premier League, but then Merrington went and a new manager came in.

'I had a one-year option on my contract and the club asked what I wanted to do. I said I wanted to stay, but Graeme Souness told me to bugger off.

'I did not get on with him at Liverpool because I had told him he could not manage. If he came into management now I think he would be one of the best, but then he tried to rule by fear and there is no way you can do that. Some players do need a kick up the backside, others need a cuddle.

'I think because of Liverpool, he felt it was not great for him to have a strong personality around and I accepted that. It was his opinion.'

After leaving The Dell, Grobbelaar almost linked up once more with Ball only to find the move blocked at the 11th hour.

'Signing for Alan Ball was the highlight of my time at Southampton because he had such faith in me. When I left Saints, he phoned me in pre-season from Manchester City and said, "Come and play for me, I've got a German who can't catch a ball." I got there the same night.

'Bally met me at the airport at 10.30pm and said, "I'm sorry but you have been blackballed by the chairman Stephen Boler." I knew why. I had stopped a cheque he was going to pay into my account for £6.25m.

'I said it was too much money for the soccer camps we were setting up. Apparently, £2.5m of that was going to be split three ways, but I was not comfortable with it.

'Bally was very apologetic but I knew how he worked. So, I phoned Neil Warnock, who had been chasing me for six or seven weeks to play for Plymouth.

'I asked if he still wanted a keeper and I flew straight down and signed. Next day I played for them in a pre-season friendly... against Manchester City of all teams. We won 1-0 and I said to Boler, "That's for you, just to show you should have signed me." You couldn't make it up.'

Grobbelaar made 36 appearances for Plymouth and spent short spells at Oxford United, Sheffield Wednesday, Oldham Athletic, Chesham United, Bury, Lincoln City and Northwich Victoria over the next two years before returning to South Africa.

There he coached a succession of sides before moving to Canada to become goalkeeping coach at Ottawa Fury, managed by Paul Dalglish, son of legendary Liverpool boss Kenny.

Now he looks back on the court case with a philosophical attitude, concluding: 'I took it as a learning curve in life. You do get highs and lows but while you can knock Bruce Grobbelaar down, you can't take away his dignity and the ability to make something work.'

Gordon Watson

GORDON WATSON has almost a million good reasons why he wishes he had never left The Dell.

The former Saints striker collected a record sporting injury pay-out of £959,000 after having his leg shattered in a tackle just two weeks after moving to Bradford.

And he would have given every penny of it to have been able to turn back the clock and reverse his impetuous decision to quit the club in January 1997, opting to move to Bradford for around half the £1.2m that Saints had paid to Sheffield Wednesday 22 months earlier.

He said: 'I do regret leaving, not least because of the way things worked out for me. I broke my leg two weeks later and that was effectively my career over.

'Egil Ostenstad had come in and I lost my place. I should have knuckled down and fought for my place – I could have got it back.

'There was a bit of interest in me from French clubs Metz and Caen and I made the mistake of telling one of the coaching staff. I thought it was in confidence, but by lunchtime Lawrie McMenemy and Graeme Souness were asking me where I was going.

'I felt I was pretty much done after that. Once the seed had been planted in the manager's head, it killed me. In hindsight, I should have stayed – that is my biggest regret in football.

'Bradford came in for me. I thought it was laughable because it would have meant dropping down a division and I knew I could still play in the Premier League.

'But I felt I was not wanted, especially when the manager told me he didn't think I was good enough to play.

'Bradford promised that if I kept them up they would sell me to a Premier League club in the summer... so I signed for them.

'That was mid-January and on 1 February, I broke my leg. We were playing local rivals Huddersfield and I remember passing the ball as Kevin Gray came in... and my leg was in bits before I hit the ground.

'I don't think he meant to cause as much damage as he did, but it was horrific. The physio came on and I just said, "Get me out of here, it's completely gone!" And it had. I had no control from the knee to the ankle. Both the bones were detached.

'Football pundit Jimmy Hill described it as the worst tackle he had seen in 50 years. It was brutal. And that was me pretty much finished at just 24.'

Watson struggled to keep his spirits up, following a series of unsuccessful attempts to mount a comeback. He worked tirelessly to try and regain fitness, but each time his body let him down.

The striker successfully sued Huddersfield and Gray but no amount of compensation could make up for the fact that his hugely promising career was over, almost before it had begun.

He did make a brief return to the Bradford side 18 months later, scoring twice to help them win promotion to the Premier League. But ironically, that success hurt his hopes of playing for them and he walked away knowing he was not fit enough to play in the top flight.

He had short stays at Bournemouth and Hartlepool but never recovered the finishing power which had won him two England under-21 caps and earned him a £1.2m move to Southampton from Sheffield Wednesday in March 1995.

He made an instant impact, adding a real spark and new energy and commitment to the attack. He scored three goals in 12 appearances as Saints staved off the threat of relegation to finish tenth, helped in no small part by Watson's poacher's finish as the team memorably beat Newcastle 3-1 despite trailing with just four minutes remaining.

Flash by nickname and nature, Gordon Watson thrived on the energy and enthusiasm of Alan Ball and was devastated when the bubbly manager was allowed to leave for Manchester City rather too easily at the end of the campaign.

'It was such a shame Bally left. I don't think people quite realise how close we were to pushing on and achieving something.

'We had ten players in the squad who were under 24 and the club could have built something good. Nine of us had under-21 honours and the oldest players in the squad were the keepers Dave Beasant and Bruce Grobbelaar, which is where you need a bit of experience. We were all just breaking through and starting to make our mark, but then Bally left – and Matthew Le Tissier in particular was never the same again.

'Partly that was down to the rapport he had with Bally, who gave him the licence to do as he pleased on the field, and Tiss repaid him with the best form of his career.

'The rest of us dug in and did his leg work in a very fluid system. Bally got the very best out of Matt – some of the goals he scored were unbelievable, especially considering his diet.

'Tiss was given a gold card by McDonalds. Can you believe that? It was literally like giving a child the keys to the sweet shop. If there was one player you did not want to give a gold card to, it was Tiss. But he was so good, he could do as he pleased.

'He could truly produce something out of nothing, so basically we would win the ball, give it to him and he would stick it in the net. Simples!

'It was a lot of fun and if the other team scored two, we would go and score three. That was the philosophy.

'I have no idea what possessed the club to allow Bally to speak to Manchester City. All he needed was to feel wanted and if the club had said no, that would have been the end of it. The manager would have stayed, Tiss would have flourished and we would have continued to grow and develop.'

Ball was very much a players' man, enjoying a night out as much as the next man – especially as the next man was often Watson himself.

'I was probably the worst. I would go and kick the arse out of it on a night out. I always wanted to be different, to be noticed – maybe it was insecurity on my part.

'As a coach now, I would say it was lack of discipline – but Alan Ball embraced that. And it showed in the way we played on the field too.

'I remember one trip abroad where Bally decided he was going for a swim and asked me to look after his wallet.

'I was absolutely the worst person he could have asked. Of course, I went straight to the bar and put his credit cards behind it and told the barman that the manager had said the players could have a drink.

'I think we ran up about £500 on his cards before he realised what was going on. It was an expensive swim!

'But Bally was a great character. He loved a drink and a flutter. I remember once we had beaten QPR 2-1 at The Dell and Bally was giving his team talk. It must have been about 4.55pm and he was in full flow when my phone went, which was a complete breach of club rules.

'He said "Oh, don't mind me!" But I explained that four out of five horses had come in for me and I stood to win £70,000. He told me to take the call and wanted some money putting on from him.

'Then we all listened to the commentary. I don't remember which horse won, but it can't have been mine. It is just as well we had beaten QPR, otherwise he wouldn't have been quite as understanding.'

Ball's replacement was the strict disciplinarian Dave Merrington, who had done an outstanding job as youth team coach bringing through the likes of Le Tissier, Francis Benali, Neil Maddison, Jason Dodd and Tommy Widdrington.

It was a logical step. Merrington had got the best out of them at a young age, developing them as players and people. The hope was that he would be able to replicate that success in the Premier League.

Instead Saints struggled and, after finishing tenth the previous season, they ended up fighting for survival on the final day of the 1995/96 campaign – ironically succeeding at the expense of Ball's City side.

But while Ball had encouraged flair and abandon on and off the field, Merrington believed more in rigid restraint, leading to more dogged displays on the field and curbing some of the excesses off it.

'Dave Merrington was the opposite to Bally. He was old school and ruled with a rod of iron and, because a lot of the players had come up through the ranks with him, they were still terrified of him.

'On trips abroad, most of them were in bed by the curfew. Dave had been brilliant for them when they were youngsters. The job he did there was faultless.

'In my opinion, he should never have been taken away from that role and given the manager's job – both from his and the club's point of view.

'I didn't think he was what we needed as a manager and crucially it took him away from doing what he did best, which was developing young players.

'He turned boys into men. The mental toughness he instilled was incredible. Look at the job he did with Alan Shearer, who struggled initially but then was ready to go into the first team at 17 and scored a hat-trick on his debut against Arsenal.

'Alan was my under-21 partner and I know he would only have been half the player he was without the mental toughness Dave instilled.

'So many of those young players have so much to be thankful to him for – but he found it difficult to manage, especially on such a tight budget. He changed the formation, so we had two solid banks of four with Tiss in the hole behind a lone striker.

'That formation killed me and it killed Tiss because teams could pick him up much more easily. The freedom and our attacking mentality had gone. It is such a shame because we could have been so good.

'The players were all Dave Merrington's boys from his days with the youth team and he continued to rule them with a rod of iron. It made for quite a boring time off the field, with no one really stepping out of line.

'The time under Bally was all about attacking flair. We didn't really have any hard-men or destroyers. The nearest would be Tommy Widdrington and Neil Maddison, but even they were good footballers.

'And for all his steel on the field, Francis Benali is the nicest guy off it, which is incredible really because he was tough. He trained the way he played and would give any of us a kick.

'We didn't have a Terry Hurlock or a Jimmy Case, but we had a freedom and an energy and everyone loved it.

'We did have a couple of characters in David Hirst and Carlton Palmer, both of whom liked the occasional drink. I remember them hiring a helicopter to pick them up from the training ground so they could get to the Cheltenham Festival.

'Dave was not allowed to spend very much and, although his style didn't suit me and I didn't agree with a lot of his decisions, I did feel he was harshly treated.

'He did manage to keep us up on the last day of the season – ironically at the expense of Man City and Alan Ball, who had – wrongly – heard we were losing at home to Wimbledon and told his team to play for a draw.

'By the time he found out we were also level, it was too late and they were relegated.

'After the match, we learned that Dave's wife Pauline was seriously ill in hospital with a brain haemorrhage. It turned out he had left her there and come in to The Dell for this final fixture.

'He had no idea if she would even be alive by the time he got back, but it was such a vital game that he still took the team, celebrated keeping us up and then went back to the hospital. His reward? He was sacked.'

The close season also saw the departure of goalkeeper Bruce Grobbelaar, who had been benched for most of the campaign, with Merrington preferring Dave Beasant.

It was a disappointment for Watson, who loved the colourful character alongside him in the dressing room.

'Bruce was a real larger-than-life character. I used to get changed next to him at The Dell. He was a lovely lad and had some great stories – but you never quite knew whether they were true.

'He had this bush hat with snakeskin around it and he told me he caught the snake with his bare hands, killed it and skinned it. I have no idea whether he actually did it, but it wouldn't surprise me.

'I remember we went to Guernsey to play a friendly and he was met at the airport by Oliver Reed's driver – and that was the last we saw of him for a long time. For the benefit of younger readers, Oliver Reed was a top-quality actor who was even better known for his hell-raising.

'To say he liked a drink is an understatement. He could put it away like no one else. Bruce went off with him and it was some time before he got back to the hotel. He had missed dinner so he decided to go into the hotel kitchen and started cooking himself lobster – as you do!

'I have no idea where he got the lobster from because it was not that sort of hotel. But he shoved it in a big pan of boiling water. It is a wonder he didn't end up scalding himself.'

Grobbelaar left when Merrington was replaced by the keeper's former Liverpool boss Graeme Souness, who declined to take up the option on the player's contract as he set about rebuilding the side.

'Graeme started spending a bit of money. He got a few foreign players in. Claus Lundekvam and Egil Ostenstad were good lads, Uli van Gobbel was as hard as they come, but I did not get on with Eyal Berkovic. He had a lot of ability but I didn't think he was a team player.

'After he went to West Ham, there was a fantastic picture in the papers of John Hartson kicking him in the head when he lost patience with him. I rang John and said he should have kept going!

'And, of course, the other notable player Graeme brought in was Ali Dia. We played five-a-side with him and I thought he had his boots on the wrong feet. I couldn't believe it when I found out he was on the bench for a Premiership game against Leeds.

'I was sat in the stands so you can imagine how that made me feel. You can tell how bad he was by the fact we are still talking about it 20 years later. I would still have been better than him… even after I broke my leg!'

Carlton Palmer

CARLTON PALMER thought he was a proper hard-man – until he came up against Jimmy Case.

The midfielder, who made his name with West Brom and Sheffield Wednesday before joining Southampton in September 1997, prided himself on his combative nature.

As a brash, self-confident youngster, he was ready to bully all-comers – until the day he ran into the brick wall that was Jimmy Case.

He recalled: 'True hard players are a bit of a dying breed now. But there is no doubt in my mind about the toughest – and I will never forget the first time I came up against Jimmy Case.

'I was a big admirer of him but I was young and cocky and thought I could show him what I was about.

'Early in the game I went into a tackle with him, opened up my body and he just came straight through me like a lorry. He sent me flying and then said, "I have let you off this time!"

'Then he gave me some advice. He said, "Don't ever tackle like that again or you will get snapped in half. Don't open your body like that, that's how you get hurt." I never forgot it.

'It was a big lesson for me in how to tackle. I learned then to be first to the ball – and if the opponent is going over the ball, then I would go over it first on them.

'I never set out to hurt anyone. I was hard but fair – but Jimmy taught me how to tackle properly.'

It was a lesson which stood the youngster in good stead throughout a career which brought 590 league appearances (45 of them for Saints) plus 18 full England caps.

He was known for his 'engine' – the energy and determination to get from one end of the field to the other. By his own admission, he was not the most creative of players but what he gave the team was continual drive and a ferocious competitive spirit – qualities which he still feels were not always appreciated by fans and pundits.

Even today, it still rankles that he is dismissed by many as merely a runner who could win a tackle but then not do anything with the ball. And it hurts when he sees his name included in 'fun' run-downs of the worst ever England players – especially given the recent woeful tournament displays.

Purists say it is one of the great injustices of modern football that someone with the skill of Matthew Le Tissier could hardly get a kick for his country, while a player with more limited technical ability can win 18 caps.

But Palmer stresses that is not his fault. All he did was make the most of what he had, giving everything for club and country whenever called upon, and he was hurt when he felt his contribution was questioned in Le Tissier's autobiography.

'As far as I was concerned, I wasn't aware there was any problem between me and Matthew Le Tissier. I certainly didn't realise that at the time.

'But then I was in a bar in Dubai and one of the guys asked if I had read Matt's autobiography. He brought it in and showed me this chapter where Matt had a go at me.

'I was quite disappointed that he hadn't tried to speak to me about it. I thought that was a bit disrespectful.

'There have been players who I would consider to be bigger than Matthew Le Tissier who always spoke to me first before saying anything. I took great umbrage at it. I tried to get hold of him, but then decided I was bigger than that and left it.

'I also heard him on TalkSport talking about England not doing well and again he had a pop at me. He said, "What do you expect when Carlton Palmer gets 18 caps?" That really pissed me off.

'There was a lot I could have said about Tiss at the time, about his fitness, his desire, the fact he did not train hard – but I didn't come out and say anything about that.

'People talk about him being a better player than me and everyone has a personal opinion – but the fact is I had a better career than Tiss. I achieved more. That is a fact, not an opinion.

'I won more England caps and went to the Euros, which he hasn't done. I scored for England, he hasn't. I have played in the FA

Cup Final and League Cup finals, while he managed just one Full Members Cup Final.

'I didn't have a go at him about his comments, but how can a player who has not achieved as much as I have then have a go at me?

'I am not slagging him off, just responding to what he said. It does hurt when a former team-mate has a go. I am probably an easy target because of my style of play, but he has seen me in training and seen how hard I work and he should know better. How can someone criticise me when they haven't had the career I have had?'

Palmer is happy to acknowledge Le Tissier's superior skill and is convinced the Southampton legend would have achieved much more if he had not shown such loyalty to the fans who adored him.

'I have never said he is not a talented player. He was a fantastic footballer. But he only got eight England caps. Why?

'Especially with Glenn Hoddle as manager at the time, there has to be a reason why he only got that number of caps. He was a luxury player, albeit one with fantastic ability.

'I am not arguing with his talent and ability, but if he had wanted to be the best, he would have done what Alan Shearer did and gone to a bigger club.

'It is fine for him to make a big thing of being a one-club man – and if that one club was Chelsea or Arsenal, then I would take his point.

'No disrespect to Southampton, but he was comfortable playing here. I think it was a lack of ambition on his part.

'You look at the players Southampton have moved on. Alan Shearer in particular could have stayed. In my opinion, he is a bigger cult hero than Le Tissier. But he moved and won the title.

'If Matt had been ambitious and wanted to do well, then he would have moved. He would probably have got more England caps – but he might also have been found out.

'I am not saying he didn't have a good career. He had a very good career and he has done well for himself in the media.

'But it is easy for him to have a go at someone like me and not look at what he achieved in the game. I might not have had as much skill as Matt but I made the most of my ability and achieved more than he did. What upset me was that I wasn't aware that Tiss and I had a problem. He never said it to my face, so I find it hard that he came out with those comments after all these years.

'I am not sure he really believes what he said about me otherwise he would have said it to my face. Instead he put it in a book to sell to the Southampton faithful.

'I don't want to make an issue out of it or dwell on it, but he said what he said so I need to respond to it.'

Certainly Palmer's abrasive and antagonistic attitude made him one of those players fans loved to hate – and yet most would want him with them rather than against them.

It was often a question of perception. Doubters would dismiss him as awkward and argumentative, merely a destroyer who stopped the Le Tissiers of the game from flourishing.

Yet those same qualities were seen as athletic, assertive aggression by the managers who bought him – and then tried to re-sign him at other clubs.

'People say I was abrasive. Was I argumentative? Well, if I didn't agree with a manager, I would say so – but every manager I ever played for tried to re-sign me – apart from George Graham. So I must have been doing something right.

'To call me a bully is totally not true. I just wanted to win. I got about people and was in their faces – yes, I could be abrasive at times. But I was a winner.'

It was that ferocious determination which Dave Jones required to help keep Saints in the top flight. The team had lost six of their first eight games of the 1997/98 season and were rooted to the foot of the Premier League, with relegation already seeming certain.

The manager needed a steel core and paid Leeds £1m for the then 31-year-old, who quickly realised what was needed as the team held firm for 75 goalless minutes on his debut at Derby... only to lose 4-0.

That was not what Palmer signed up for and he let the rest of the players know it. Some saw it as loud-mouthed arrogance. Others recognised it as a refusal to accept failure.

'When I signed for Saints, they were seven points adrift. It was not Tiss dragging them out of it. Dave Jones needed to bring in someone like me to sort it out.

'I was frustrated with him when I went to Southampton. He was the one with all the ability but I said to the manager if you don't leave him out, we won't win matches. He said if he did leave him out, he would get the sack. In the end, Tiss toed the line with the rest of the squad and became fitter and part of a good team. We had a good bunch of lads and it was an enjoyable time. I don't want this to sour that.

'The thing is you need a balance of hard workers and skilful players in a team. You could not have a side of all Carlton Palmers, just as you could not have all Matthew Le Tissiers. You need a blend.

'At Southampton, we had a system where Kevin Richardson, Matthew Oakley and I would do his work and he played in a position which allowed him to have space to perform. And I would never deny that he had unbelievable ability, but I would argue I had my own strengths.

'I had better technical ability than I was given credit for. I remember Chris Waddle saying it was rubbish to suggest I could not play because I could pass the ball as well as anyone and get up and down the field.

'People in the game would notice my contribution and appreciate it. Fans or the media might focus on the final ball or the finish, but they wouldn't see the tackle in midfield which won the ball and started the move.'

Palmer's presence was hugely instrumental in steering Saints to safety with comparative comfort, considering they had taken just four points from their first nine fixtures, causing them to be widely written off.

There was no need for one of the famous last-day great escapes as Southampton remarkably finished eight points clear of the drop zone. Palmer takes great pride in the part he played and looks back fondly on his 16-month stay on the south coast.

'It was never on my agenda to go to Southampton – but it was one of the best things I ever did.

'George Graham had just taken over at Leeds and he made it clear I wasn't part of his plans. I just wanted to play football, so I decided to leave. Everton and West Ham were in for me but he made it clear he did not want to sell me to them, so he told me I could either drop into the Championship or join Southampton.

'I met Dave Jones and I really liked him. He told me about his future plans, the players he wanted to bring in and his ambitions.

'Saints were seven points adrift at the time, but there was plenty of time left so I signed – and I had a great time there. I really enjoyed it. It is a great part of the world – and the weather is ten degrees warmer than Sheffield.'

Palmer now regrets his decision to move in January 1999. It was another season of struggle for Saints, who once again looked doomed. When relegation rivals Nottingham Forest came calling, Palmer took the chance to move nearer to his family.

Saints not only made a slight profit by selling him for £1.1m but also went on to secure safety despite being in the bottom three for the entire campaign until the final three fixtures of the season. They won them all to stay up at the expense of Forest, who finished bottom.

'It was a successful time for me at Southampton. We had a good team and I should never have left. But when Ron Atkinson took over at Nottingham Forest, it was a chance for me to go back north.

'I was about to move my family down but that same day I learned we were expecting our third child, so I decided to keep the place in Sheffield and I moved to Forest.

'It was a big mistake. Forest didn't go well and I would have been better travelling down as I had been doing. But you make a decision which you think is right at the time...'

Despite fighting relegation for much of his time with Southampton, Palmer has nothing but praise for manager Dave Jones, whose tenure ended amid totally unfounded accusations of child abuse. He was completely cleared in court, but the midfielder never had any doubts at all about his innocence.

'I had a fantastic time with Saints. I always had a good feeling about Dave Jones and it is sad the way he lost his job. I thought it was scandalous the way he was prosecuted over those unfounded accusations of child abuse.

'I knew straight away he was innocent. You just trust your instincts on something like this and Dave was the most mild-mannered man you could wish to meet.

'I never heard him raise his voice, not even in the dressing room. He used to say, "If I have to tell you something more than once, I will leave you out." He wasn't one for shouting or getting irate, but he would make his point very firmly and calmly.

'When those allegations came out, I rang him straight away to offer my support. I know it devastated him and his wife, not only having to go to court but being placed on gardening leave, which compounded things. I do feel they should have kept him as manager.

'Unfortunately, the world we live in means you are often seen as guilty unless you can prove your innocence, so his name shouldn't have been released unless he had been found guilty – and that was never going to happen because he is a decent man.

'He is straight up and honest and I really felt for him. But he came through it stronger than ever. He is a good bloke and if I had the opportunity to work with him again then I would do.

'When he was manager of Sheffield Wednesday, I used to go and support them and I was gutted when he lost his job. It felt a bit harsh but when you get different owners, it often happens.'

Palmer had his own unsuccessful attempts at management with Stockport and Mansfield and then did media work for the BBC and then in Dubai before making the unlikely move to China, where he is now academy director at the upmarket Wellington College International in Shanghai.

And despite the cultural differences, he is enjoying life with no immediate desire to return home – and no thoughts of trying again to break into management here.

'It has been quite a journey getting here – it has all been a bit surreal. If someone had told me ten years ago that I would end up coaching in China, I would have had them certified.

'To cut a long story short, I had been doing media work in Dubai, looking at the Premier League and the Championship. I was asked to help with some soccer academies there and I got on really well with one of the guys organising them.

'When he moved to Beijing, he invited me to come with him and then when he opened up a centre in Shanghai he asked me to run it, so I came over and set it up.

'Now we have 60 programmes and I am in charge of all of them. We do after-school sessions and weekend clubs. It is hard work but I am enjoying it.

'Sometimes I think about coming back but we'll see. Opportunities come at different times. The kids had just gone to university, so it felt like the right time to come here.

'I have just signed a three-year contract here, so we'll see what happens after that. I will probably return when the kids are ready to settle down.

'We do miss our friends and family but I don't think I would come back to work or coach here because it is all different now. You see managers and coaches getting changed so regularly that it is not something I would want to do.

'We live in Shanghai now. It is like any big city, there are a lot of expats. The language can be a barrier because the Chinese don't speak a lot of English, but we have picked up a bit of it and are aiming to have proper lessons.

'The lifestyle is good and there are a lot of nice places within easy flying distance, such as Hong Kong or Japan. The only downside is being so far from some of the family and the time difference if we want to talk to them.

'I worked hard and I played hard – and I still do. I work very long hours in Shanghai but when I have the time, I do relax and make the most of it.'

Palmer has used his down time in the Far East to write his own autobiography, which he hopes to have published soon and contains the same brutal directness that characterised his play and his loud voice in the dressing room.

'I have written a book about my career, which is a very honest account, and I think it is a good read. I talk about racism and getting divorced – it is not your typical football autobiography. I have been very open – there is no point in doing it otherwise.

'For me, it is about closure on the first 50 years of my life – it is not about money. Some of the proceeds will be going to the Cavcare cancer charity in Sheffield, which is a cause very close to my heart.

'I don't feel I have to justify what I did in the game. I finished playing at 38 and could have carried on longer, but I chose not to. I had achieved everything I needed to, so I have been able to move on with my life. I got the maximum out of my career and I have absolutely no regrets.'

Graeme Souness

YOU CANNOT have a book entitled *Saints and Sinners* without mentioning the infamous Ali Dia.

By no stretch of the imagination could he be described as a hardman – and it is arguable whether he could even be called a Saints player.

Nonetheless, he has gone down in football folklore as a sinner after supposedly conning his way into the Southampton first team via claims that he was the cousin of former World Footballer of the Year George Weah.

Saints were seen as a laughing stock for being taken in, but there is a very different version of events from Graeme Souness, the manager who sent him on against Leeds – and hauled him off 53 minutes later.

'Much has been written and said about him, but the truth is someone at the club got a call from someone who said George Weah's cousin was available to come and train, so we made arrangements to take a look at him.

'It was the sort of thing we used to do all the time, with all sorts of players. If you get that kind of opportunity, you can't afford not to take a look – so we got him in.

'But within the first ten minutes of the very first training session, I made up my mind he was never going to be good enough for us and we let him train with the kids.

'But as the week went on, we had players dropping like flies. We had hardly any fit strikers and Terry Cooper said we might have to put that fool on the bench. He said he was quick, he would run forward and would at least be a nuisance.

'As more players dropped out one by one and we got towards the home game against Leeds, the decision was made – by me – to haul him into the group because we had no one else that remotely resembled a centre-forward.

'If you look at the other substitutes that day, we had Dave Beasant, Ken Monkou, Robbie Slater and Neil Maddison. We had no strikers at all and Matthew Le Tissier was carrying a knock. He came off with a thigh strain after half an hour or so and we had to put this lad on.'

Dia's first taste of action was to sprint clean through and it looked for a brief moment as though it was going to be an inspired gamble. But he missed the chance and then got worse and worse, chasing the game like a headless chicken.

Even so, Saints kept it goalless until eight minutes from time, when Gary Kelly scored and Dia was ignominiously replaced by Ken Monkou, only for Lee Sharpe to add a second in the final minute.

It was not the gamble which was so bad but the back story which unravelled in the days after Saints had cancelled his contract and let him go.

It turned out that Weah did not have a cousin, certainly not by that name, nor had anyone connected with him made a recommendation. The same ploy had reportedly been tried with Gillingham and Bournemouth. Dia was last heard of having a trial at Gateshead shortly after leaving The Dell, but has since succeeded in carrying off a vanishing act to rival that of Lord Lucan.

Countless journalists have tried to track him down without success. It is hard to know which is the greater achievement – wangling his way into the Premier League or managing to vanish without trace in this world of internet and social media.

Souness does not hide away from his part in one of the great football stories of modern times and now, as a media man himself, he recognises the entertainment value of the saga. But he insists he does not deserve to have his football judgment questioned.

'The story that we were conned could not be further from the truth. We knew in the first ten minutes that he was hopeless.

'But it has gone down in football legend that we were conned. I don't feel aggrieved about that – it made for a good story and that is the world we operate in.

'Truthfully, we knew straight away he was not good enough for the Premier League, but we were desperate.

'And it is common practice to get players in for a trial. We had players coming in on trial all the time – that was exactly how we got Eyal Berkovic. Someone recommended him, we took a look and ended up signing him.

'But there were a lot of others who were nowhere near good enough – but we had no money so we took a look at all sorts of players, hoping to find a gem.

'We gave a trial to Egil Ostenstad and Tore Andre Flo. They both played in the same closed-doors match at Staplewood. We managed to get Egil signed and he did really well for us, but sadly we missed out on Flo.

'We were in for him first but we did not have enough money, the deal became complicated and he ended up signing for Chelsea – and the rest is history. At the end of the season, I was told my budget was just £2m, so I knew I had to resign.'

It was that lack of finance for new signings, coupled with the reverse takeover of the club by Secure Retirement, which caused Souness to leave after just one season in charge of Saints.

He was followed out of the door by Director of Football Lawrie McMenemy, who had brought the former Liverpool manager to the club and therefore felt the honourable thing would be to offer his resignation.

It was a surprise when it was accepted but Souness never felt it was right for McMenemy to go too.

His own departure was less of a surprise. It was well known Souness did not see eye to eye with new chairman Rupert Lowe and, after keeping the side up despite a 1-0 defeat at Aston Villa in May 1997, his body language suggested it was a farewell wave to the fans.

'It was a shame because I have a lot of happy memories of Southampton, but it was a difficult time for the club. They had only just stayed up the previous season and we survived on the last day of the campaign again.

'It got a bit nervy towards the end of the season, but we came through and I never had any doubt that we would stay up. I enjoyed it and felt I was doing a good job – it is just a shame from my point of view that Rupert Lowe came in.

'When I agreed to take the job, I actually asked the board if they would be there for the duration of my three-year contract and they said yes.

'But then came this bizarre reverse takeover by Secure Retirement just a few months later and I knew I could not stay on.'

Souness, of course, meets the hard-man criteria for this book, even though Saints could never have afforded him when he was at his peak winning five league titles, three European Cups and four League Cups during his seven seasons at Liverpool.

During that golden era, he patrolled the midfield with a growling menace backed up by a certain Jimmy Case – no wonder few opponents got past them.

Yet the Scottish Braveheart was so much more than a midfield destroyer. His range of passing was sublime, his reading of the game superb. And his tenacious tackling and inspirational leadership made him one of the best – and most feared – players around.

'Yes, I liked a tackle but my game was a lot more than that. You don't get to win three European Cups and five league titles just by being aggressive. I played in the finals of three World Cups and captained my country there twice. That doesn't happen just by kicking people.

'People keep asking me if I could cope with playing in the modern game. Of course I could. It would be a doddle.

'The game has changed dramatically now. Until the late 1990s, referees were quite different. Before then, it had been quite important to have someone aggressive in the team because of the way the pitches were in those days.

'Nowadays the playing surfaces are like billiards tables, nice and smooth, allowing the ball to run true. Back then, pitches were bobbly and uneven, so players had to take an extra touch to bring the ball under control – and that allowed opposing players to make a challenge. And I certainly enjoyed that side of the game. I was never afraid to get stuck in… though I could play a bit too.

'And with slightly more lenient refereeing, it was part and parcel of the game to put in the odd meaty challenge – and you could see the crowd enjoyed it too. They loved a strong tackle as much as I did. It was a big part of the game.

'Nowadays it is more about being alert and intercepting the ball due to the changes in refereeing and the quality of the pitches.

'Whether it has made the game better or more enjoyable for the fans, I wouldn't like to say. Certainly the public like to see a bit of aggression.'

He brought those same qualities of fierce leadership and ferocious will to win into management first with Rangers, then Liverpool and then in Turkey with Galatasaray, whose flag he famously planted in the centre circle of bitter rivals Fenerbahce after his side had beaten them in the Turkish Cup Final. He then returned to England to manage Southampton.

'I had the same competitive streak as a manager, that same burning desire to win. You have to have a certain amount of aggression in the side if you are to be successful.

'We did not have a lot of "hard-men" at Southampton but we had Francis Benali, who would run through a brick wall for you. He was a real honest, tough man – and as nice as anything off the pitch.

'And we had Uli van Gobbel, who was built like a man-mountain. A real powerful man and physically very strong – you would not mess with him.

'But we had a lot of skilful players too and I really enjoyed my time at Southampton. It was definitely one of the better jobs I had.

'The supporters were realistic too. They knew there wasn't a lot of money and they let the manager get on with his job without being too critical. It was a great place to manage.

'I am only sorry that I got only one year there – I would like to have stayed longer. The fact I kept my house there for 12 years shows everything I felt about the area and I am still not far away.

'The decision was made for me when Rupert Lowe came along. I didn't get on with him – that's why I left. I quickly decided he was someone who seemed to know everything about everything and I felt in a very short space of time he could be wanting to pick the team. I couldn't have lived with that – not a chance.

'He was an expert on everything. Within a few minutes of being in the club, I think he felt he knew more than me and Lawrie Mac put together. We made a good team and could have done well there but it was not to be.'

Chris Marsden

IF JIMMY CASE was minder to Chris Nicholl's fledgling Saints, then there was only one logical candidate to fill that role for Gordon Strachan's side.

Chris Marsden was the perfect choice to protect the emerging Wayne Bridge at left-back.

Never mind the fact that the then 33-year-old had only ever played wide left once – and even then he had been substituted.

Marsden's tough tackling, his fierce will to win and his reading of the game made him supremely qualified to look after the youngster breaking into the first team.

Bridge loved to charge forward on surging runs, which were not only a threat to the opposition but also occasionally to his own side as it left a huge gap down the left flank, at least until he gained the experience to know when to go and when to stay.

That's where Marsden came in. He was able to tuck back to cover for the marauding full-back, giving him licence to overlap at will.

Strachan felt that Bridge's runs were being blocked if Saints played a conventional and static four-man midfield. But by moving Marsden 15 yards infield, it opened a gap for the youngster to exploit, with the security of the veteran midfielder there to cover.

It was a ploy which worked well all round. It gave Southampton one of the strongest left flanks in the Premier League and it enabled Bridge to develop into a future England international. It also established Marsden as a key man in Strachan's set-up.

Marsden recalled: 'Gordon was great for me. The best thing he did was let me have Wayne Bridge next to me on the left because he would run up and down that flank like a Duracell bunny and he made me look good.

'Inevitably, if you have an England international alongside you, it's going to make you look better – and he was a great player. He was a good defender who had great positional sense and could put in a tackle… and then next thing he would be up the other end of the field crossing it.

'I used to laugh at some of the analysts who would say, "Marsden is an intelligent player. Look at the way he hangs back to fill in for Bridge on his attacking runs." The truth was I couldn't keep up with him! I like to think I helped him, though. He was keen to learn and would take on board what I said to him. He has done OK for himself, marrying one of the girls from The Saturdays. I just hope he doesn't have any thoughts of recording a duet with her. It would be like watching Renee and Renato all over again!

'I only really ended up playing wide left by accident. I had always played in the centre but we had no one else that was left-footed, so I gave it a go. I scored against Ipswich with a diving header from one yard and did OK, so I stayed there.'

Bridge – a home-grown youngster who was spotted by Micky Adams – went on to make 161 appearances for Saints, the last coming in the 2003 FA Cup Final before a move to Chelsea for £7m plus Graeme Le Saux.

And he is quick to pay tribute to Marsden for his part in developing him into a top-class player who went on to win 36 England caps, including a World Cup finals appearance against Argentina in 2002.

Bridge said: 'Mazza was great for me, not just in the way he played but with the way he was as a personality and as a leader.

'He taught me so much. He was so passionate about the game and never minded giving you a kick up the backside if he thought you weren't giving your all. He always gave 100 per cent and he knew I would always give everything… but if he ever suspected that I wasn't, then he would turn into this raging madman!

'He was good to have around because he loved to be a hard-man and if anyone gave me stick he would look after me. He would be the first one there to have a go back – that was a big part of his game.

'He had real passion for the game – that came out in the dressing room. It would kill him if we lost and there were times you knew he was going to erupt. If that happened, it was best to be out of the firing line. He could be very scary, especially if you were playing against him. You would know he was going to get stuck in.

'He was someone you never wanted to get on the wrong side of, both physically and verbally, because he wasn't afraid to speak his mind to anyone. He wasn't one to back down.

'He was tough and he liked a tackle and he gave me great protection. If I had played with an out-and-out winger, then I wouldn't have been able to play the way I did. I would have been a lot more restricted.

'Mazza would cover me so I could get forward more, which was a part of the game I loved. In the early days, I would leave a few gaps but he would fill in and do as much as he could to help me.

'You have to have players who can work together and he definitely improved me. We had a good understanding. Getting up and down that left wing was a big part of my game and he helped me develop that.

'We had a good rapport off the field too. I always enjoyed a night out with Mazza. We would have a few beers and a laugh. He was a great lad off the field, especially if we had won.

'After a game, he would be dancing round the dressing room in his underwear singing songs – my wife made a career out of that, but she did it rather better!'

Bridge, famously, is married to his very own Saturday girl – Frankie Sandford from the pop group The Saturdays. But far from being an A List celebrity couple, the pair remain very down to earth.

Bridge added: 'I am still very grounded despite the fact I am married to a pop star; Frankie is the same. She is very good for me and, of course, my parents make sure I keep my feet on the ground.

'For the moment, I am just enjoying spending time with Frankie and the kids. I'm not sure where I am going to go with the next stage of my life yet.

'I might look at getting into coaching but I would want to work with people I trust rather than with someone I don't really know. Scott Parker has been on at me to do my badges and said he would try and sort me out.

'And when I was doing my rehab at Chelsea, Jose Mourinho said if I needed any help with jobs then to let him know, but it was not the right time for me.

'I had a good stint at Chelsea, things worked out well there. But then Manchester City didn't go as well after Mark Hughes had left. I got a few injuries and it was a difficult time for me. I had a few loan spells but it wasn't until I went to Brighton that I really started to enjoy my football again.

'I played well under Gus Poyet but then had problems with the cartilage in a knee. It was bone on bone. I had an operation, which didn't really help.

'At the moment, I am enjoying life but I have got to do something. I can't do nothing, so I will have to make a decision. But I was fortunate that I was playing when the big money came into the game. I earned quite good money, so there is no rush for me to decide.

'I get quite embarrassed thinking of the money I earned when you look at the likes of Matthew Le Tissier and how little he got paid by comparison. If he was playing now, he would be one of the richest footballers on the planet, he was that good.'

For all his wealth and fame, Bridge is still the same homely lad who grew up at The Dell and proudly won the club's Player of the Year award in 2001. His composed temperament and supreme fitness saw him claim a then Premier League record for an outfield player by appearing in 133 full consecutive matches.

The run started on 4 March 2000 and he went on to play 10,160 consecutive minutes without injury or suspension until he limped off in a 1-0 defeat by Liverpool on 18 January 2003 – a record eventually surpassed by Chelsea colleague Frank Lampard.

Although that move to Stamford Bridge made him financially secure and brought him Premier League, FA Cup and League Cup winners' medals, the Southampton-born star still found it a real wrench to leave his home-town club.

'I was genuinely devastated when I left Saints. I had been a fan all my life, my family were all Southampton supporters and it was the only club I had ever known.

'People think it was about the money – and I guess it was in a sense because it was about feeling valued. Saints said I was too young for them to pay me a lot. They did not want to offer me any more, which devastated me.

'Gordon Strachan didn't want me to go and I didn't really want to go, but it was hard to turn down. If there had been a different chairman, I might have ended up staying.

'It was a proper family club and I still miss it now. I have been back a few times but it doesn't feel the same. I would love to go back and for everyone still to be there. I loved it.

'I grew up as a Saints fan and my dad is a huge supporter. He loved Chris Marsden, both as a personality and as a player. He could see how good Mazza was for me in terms of my development. He sacrificed some of his own strengths in order to protect me and make me a better player.

'His hard-man image meant he didn't get as much recognition as he deserved because he could play. You only need to look at that goal he scored at Ipswich. We called him the new Ryan Giggs!

'He had stuff like that in his locker – he just did not get to show it very much because he was always tucking in and covering for me so that I could get forward.'

That leads neatly on to *that* goal, the one at Portman Road which earned him the nickname of Marsdinho or the acronym CMFG (Chris Marsden Football Genius).

It was one of the best solo goals seen in a Saints shirt since the prime of Le Tissier – and it came from the unlikeliest of scorers.

There looked to be nothing on as Marsden cut in from the left flank past Matt Holland. Almost before he knew it, he had darted past Jermaine Wright and then Titus Bramble towards the D of the penalty area.

By now in full flight, his momentum – if not his sense of direction – took him past Hermann Hreidarsson as he continued his run from left to right. There was just Andy Marshall in his way and Marsden rounded him before slotting into the empty net for a very special 'I was there...' moment that fans will never forget.

The excitement of the achievement seemed to make his legs turn to jelly as he hit the ball, and he laughed: 'It would be just like me to do all that hard work and then miss the goal. But it was a great moment.

'I have good memories of playing against Ipswich because I still get asked about that goal even now. I think I took on the whole of their team and the substitutes before I put the ball in the net. Even then, I nearly missed it – after all that hard work.

'I have no idea where it came from or how or why I went on that run, but you can see from my face afterwards just how much I enjoyed it.

'I didn't have the pace to outrun the rest of our lads as they mobbed me, which was probably just as well. Otherwise I would have kept running out of the stadium!

'It's a nice memory but I never really bothered too much about individual glory. For me, it was all about the team. That's why we did so well. We bonded as a really tight unit and battled for each other.

'I was competitive, hard-working... I would win the ball and give it to players who could do something with it. As I got older, I understood that more and it made me a better player.

'There was no point me trying to do things which were beyond me – although I did score from 40 yards against Tranmere in October 2002.

'I kept my game simple and effective. Similarly, there was no point Matthew Le Tissier running back and tackling – not that he ever tried it!'

When Marsden signed for Saints from Birmingham for £800,000 in February 1999, he was 30 and widely regarded very much as a journeyman midfielder, in the most honest sense of the term.

He had spent his career largely in the lower divisions with the likes of Huddersfield, Wolves, Notts County and Stockport, where he first played under Dave Jones.

At the time Saints were marooned in the relegation zone, where they had been all season after taking just one point from their first eight matches. At that stage, few fans could have predicted that Marsden would not only prove the catalyst for a successful survival struggle but that he would go on to become one of the most influential midfielders in the Premier League.

There was even talk of a possible England call, though Mazza always laughed it off with the same self-deprecating sense of humour and honesty which characterised his game.

'I joined from Birmingham just after the team had been beaten 7-1 at Liverpool. I couldn't believe what I had walked into.

'Most of my career had been spent in the lower divisions and I am sure there were a few raised eyebrows when Southampton bought me. But I thought I could play a bit. I felt I was a decent player – and then I found myself training with Mark Hughes and Stuart Ripley and Matthew Le Tissier.

'Oh my God! They were different class. I used to watch them in training and marvel at the things they could do, things I could only dream of doing.

'It was a massive learning curve. The gap was huge. Suddenly, I was up against the likes of Gianfranco Zola and Roberto di Matteo, proper world-class players. It certainly sharpened me up and made me realise that instead of poncing around thinking I was running the show, I needed to actually run.

'The other players were great and really helped me to settle in – and that tight team spirit really made a difference. One thing about Southampton is that even when we were near the bottom, the team and the fans stuck together. And I was delighted my goal in that key 3-3 draw at home to Blackburn played such a big part in keeping us up – and sending them down in our place.'

Marsden's move to The Dell saw him renew acquaintance with Francis Benali, having played against him at schoolboy level.

'I had already been to The Dell when I was 13 or 14 in a schools match when I found myself up against a certain Francis Benali. He was massive at that time.

'All these kids ran out followed by this huge centre-forward with a moustache. I thought he was at least 20. I genuinely thought they had played a ringer!

'He was like Chewbacca with hair everywhere and he just bashed everyone out of the way like a lorry. It was weird because, as everyone else caught up, he stopped growing and soon others were five inches taller than him. But at that age, he looked like a man-mountain.

'I certainly preferred playing alongside him rather than against him. Although he eventually lost his place to Wayne Bridge, the pair of us did add a bit of steel to the side. It goes without saying that you had to be prepared to put a tackle in.

'We had a decent team under Dave Jones. Then Glenn Hoddle took over and moved us up a level before he returned to his "spiritual home" and Stuart Gray took charge.

'He was really unlucky with the opening fixtures of the following season. We were away to Leeds and Spurs and home to Chelsea, all really tough games and we lost them all 2-0.

'The problem is that means you are playing catch-up right from the start. Before we knew it, we were in the bottom three and needing three wins to get out of it.

'Rupert Lowe did what he had to do and Gordon Strachan came in. He was absolutely fantastic. He gave the club a real lift and made us better both individually and collectively. Anyone who worked with him would say he improved them – with the possible exception of Agustin Delgado!

'He also made reporters into better journalists as they would certainly make sure they thought through their questions before asking them!

'The fact we managed to stay up that season was remarkable, especially as it was relatively comfortable in the end.

'He was one of the funniest guys too. He had a sharp sense of humour and always had a quip. But he was very prepared to let you know if he was not happy with you.

'It was great for me because he would go round the dressing room in numerical order – and I wore 4. So as soon as he had gone past me he would not come back, so I could relax and watch the others getting a bollocking.

'He was certainly the most colourful character I have ever worked with – and a very generous man.

'There were times things would fly around the dressing room, but he got the best out of us. He is Celtic's most successful manager since Jock Stein and he lifted Southampton to new heights.'

The pinnacle for club and captain was the 2003 FA Cup Final, which saw Marsden proudly lead the side out at the Millennium Stadium in the absence of the injured Jason Dodd.

It is still the Yorkshireman's most treasured football memory, especially after making such a major contribution with his hooked overhead goal in the 2-0 quarter-final win at home to Wolves. It was scrappy and scruffy and barely had enough power to cross the line but Marsden joked: 'By half-past ten that evening, it had turned into an overhead kick of Ronaldo proportions!

'I did not even realise it was my goal. I just got a toe to it and I think James Beattie unsighted the keeper and it bobbled in.

'The FA Cup run was incredible. We had a thumping win at home to Spurs in the third round and then the draw just kept going our way.

'We beat Millwall and Norwich and Wolves and suddenly we found ourselves in the semi-final with Arsenal, Sheffield United and Watford.

'No disrespect to the last two but I literally closed my eyes and kept muttering "Please not Arsenal" as the draw was made – and I am sure they were thinking the same!

'We got Watford, who were a good team, but we really fancied ourselves to make the final. And after 20 minutes of the game, I knew we would do... it was fairly comfortable.

'And so to Cardiff for the final, which was incredible. I could not believe it when we walked out and saw that wall of yellow at one end. Even now, Arsenal fans still talk about it.

'Reaching the FA Cup Final was phenomenal. It was only the second time the club had reached the final since 1902 or something, so that shows you just how much of an achievement it was.

'I was gutted that Doddsy was not fit because he was my mate and had been at the club for so long. He deserved to play. But it was a huge honour for me to lead the side out. It is just a shame I did not get to lift the trophy.'

For such a popular club icon, it was sad that his stint with Saints ended the following season in a fashion which did not reflect his massive contribution.

Southampton began the campaign strongly and were fourth in the Premier League going into Christmas following a 3-0 win at home to local rivals Pompey. But with Strachan announcing his intention to take a break from football at the end of the season and with no sign of a new contract being offered to the midfielder, who was then 35, Marsden opted to move in the January transfer window.

He made the unlikely choice to join Busan Icons, but it was not a good Korea move! After just two matches, he returned to England to link up with Sheffield Wednesday before injury forced him to quit.

His property-letting business in Spain did not work out, so he moved to Cyprus, where he now enjoys a relaxed lifestyle in the sun while still keeping in touch with the Premier League.

'I have a wonderful lifestyle now. I was hit pretty badly by the property crash a few years ago, but you just have to pick yourself up and go again.

'But when you live abroad, you don't need so much money. It is a completely different lifestyle. I wear shorts nine months of the year.

'But if I was going to live in England, it would probably be South-ampton – it is a great place. It is by the sea, the people are fantastic, they have beautiful weather… what's not to like?

'I remember when I signed, Dave Jones and Stuart Gray both said to me that if things went well, I would never want to leave the club and the area. And I did love my time with the club and I have really enjoyed watching them on TV over the last few seasons.

'It was the move to St Mary's which really saw the club take off. It is a lovely ground and it just shows how many clubs are held back by the fact they cannot relocate. Now you have women and families coming to games, the facilities are so much better – and Southampton have really kicked on.

'I get all the Premier League games out here in Cyprus and I watched a lot of them last season and it was a real joy, especially considering they had lost so many players.

'Ronald Koeman did a fantastic job with them – the transformation in recent years has been truly remarkable. They look a proper Premier League team.

'In my day, we had a team of hard workers and maybe two or three good players. If we were on top of our game, we could beat anyone on a good day or if the opposition were having a bad day!

'But Saints have been wonderful to watch in the past few seasons and I am delighted. I loved my time there and it is great to see them establishing themselves as a real force in the Premier League.

'I still see Jason Dodd when he comes out here and he told me about what happened to Claus Lundekvam, which was very sad. But finishing playing is one of the hardest things – that's why I still train a lot even now.

'I am only a couple of kilos heavier than my playing weight and although I still like to have the occasional drink, I don't miss the partying. I am too old for nights out now – I just have a beer in a rocking chair! Getting old is no fun!

'I don't talk much about my playing days. Occasionally, my son Matthew will see clips of great players and ask if I played with or against them and he finds it hard to believe that I did. So do I sometimes!

'The lifestyle is a lot calmer over here, you don't get any trouble. There is even a decent Pompey fan here, but don't tell him I said that!

'I am very proud of the fact that I never got beaten in a derby game. We played Pompey twice and we won both.

'I could not believe the atmosphere. I was used to the passion of derbies in Sheffield and the Midlands, but this was as vicious as anything I had known.

'I thought it was going to be OK, two nice seaside cities – but there was real animosity. The atmosphere was electric. It came as a real shock.

'It is a shame there won't be any south coast derbies for a while now – unless Pompey end up playing Eastleigh!'

James Beattie

AS A player, James Beattie was in a unique position – capable of hurting an opponent and then healing him!

The former Saints striker had been earmarked for a possible career in medicine until he was prescribed a very different course.

Academically gifted with nine GCSEs and As in three sciences and maths, he had high hopes of becoming a surgeon before adding a cutting edge, first to Blackburn Rovers and then Southampton.

It is a great irony that someone who once felt a calling to help those in pain then made a career out of inflicting it, both physically and in the football sense.

His power, skill and eye for goal brought him 68 goals in 161 Premier League appearances for Saints, earning him five England caps – and enough money to repay his parents for their sacrifices.

His father worked long hours as a truck driver to earn the money to give the young Beattie a private education at Queen Elizabeth Grammar School, harbouring hopes that his son would enjoy a distinguished career as a doctor.

And his devoted parents also took him to and from the local pool at unearthly hours as he trained for yet another possible career – as a swimmer with Blackburn Centurions.

At one stage, he was ranked second in the country in his age group for the 100m freestyle before suffering a serious shoulder problem. He was told by a specialist the cartilage had worn away and if he continued swimming, he could face serious problems in later life.

That made the decision for Beattie who, at 14, had already been spotted by Blackburn, the club he supported from the stands as a boy. To the envy of his school friends, instead of watching Alan Shearer, he was suddenly training alongside him, learning the art of physical play and finishing which came to characterise his game and earned him a £1m move to The Dell.

Beattie said: 'I don't regret not being a swimmer or a doctor. There is no money in swimming, but in any case the injury ruled it out.

'And while you can make a decent living from medicine, it is not like being in football so it was a good decision. The main thing I look back on is the sacrifices made by mum and dad to give me a private education.

'I was so happy that, through football, I was able to let my dad retire early. He passed away six years ago, but it meant I could give them the opportunity to travel together and see the world and do all the things they had missed out on while I was growing up.

'They sacrificed a lot of money and time taking me to swimming. I trained every morning and every evening, but it paid off because it gave me a very strong physique, which meant I always played football against older kids.

'My swimming meant I had a powerful build, so when I was a schoolboy with Blackburn I always used to play in the next age group up because they knew I could handle the physical side of the game. It helped toughen me up, which was important back then.

'The sport has changed in recent times. Players are pampered too much and don't really embrace the physical side of the game. Don't get me wrong, they are strong and powerful and fit, but it is hard for them to put themselves about as we used to.

'If we perceived a team to be a bit lightweight, then we would try to impose ourselves physically and use it to our advantage.

'If you could give the centre-back a strong challenge, then that would be in his mind for the rest of the game. He would have it in the back of his head that he might take a bang.

'I would still be fully focused, though, because it would be my play, my game plan, so I would totally concentrate on my game without worrying about getting hurt.

'But if there was someone you knew you could target and impose yourself upon physically, then it gave you a psychological edge even before kick-off.

'They would be concentrating on getting hurt by you. That thought would already be in their heads.

'I would just focus on my own game and getting into the right positions.

'I was never afraid to put my head in where it hurt or to go in for a tackle, but I would never intentionally try to hurt anyone.

'But I was always physical. I loved it. That first aerial challenge I would go in as hard as I could, which might mean a defender getting a knee in the back – or in their backside, which really hurt by the way.

'I would just hit them physically as hard as I could, so they would be thinking about challenges coming in rather than concentrating on the ball.

'I used to enjoy that side of the game – especially if I was playing against a centre-back who wasn't as keen on it.

'Arsenal's Sol Campbell enjoyed it, so did Craig Short of Blackburn. You would get proper physical games against them.

'I remember a game at Ewood Park, where I was having a right physical ding-dong with Craig Short. The ball was played up to my feet and he was tight behind me and jumped on my back just as I put my left leg down.

'The extra weight on my back made my groin pop. My muscle could not take the extra weight and I actually heard it pop. I did carry on, but it was proper sore.

'He was coaching at Blackburn when I was manager at Accrington, so we saw a bit of each other and used to look back to those times and share stories. That's how it was back then.'

Although modern rule changes have all but outlawed the kind of robust physical challenges Beattie enjoyed, he still hankers for the days when strong team spirit could counter superior skill.

And, like many across the country, he was delighted by Leicester's fairytale title win, which brought back so many good memories of his time with Saints, particularly the run to the 2003 FA Cup Final.

'We had a great side in 2003 with no real superstars but a group of players who banded together, both on and off the field.

'We were well drilled and knew what we were doing and we all got on great. That is something we have gone away from in England in recent years. Our game went too foreign. We tended to follow what other countries were doing rather than playing to our strengths.

'It is our game so we should dictate how we play it. I don't care how they play in La Liga or Serie A, we need to play our own way.

'Over the last ten years or so, everything has been possession-based. Everyone is used to being coached to play the same way and against teams of the same ilk rather than going more direct.

'It came back in style with Leicester winning the Premier League. It was brilliant to see a team with the lowest possession and passing stats going on to win the Premier League.

'They were lucky with one or two aspects, like the big teams not performing as well as normal, but the opportunity was there and Leicester took it.

'They had a tight group and a good core of English players and the manager was quick to embrace that. He saw a niche and made the most of it.

'They were a proper Band of Brothers who would go the extra yard or give that extra bit of fight for each other, knowing they could trust their team-mates both on and off the pitch. That means a lot in football.'

As he embarks on his own managerial and coaching career, Beattie is determined to focus on the strengths of traditional English values, encouraging unity on and off the field.

'These days, players can be a bit robotic. They train and then scurry off on their own. They never see each other away from that football environment, so they never create that bond.

'We had that under Gordon Strachan, who actively encouraged it. He knew there were no big-time Charlies in the squad. We were a proper team, not a group of individuals.

'Most of the teams in the league were better than us, but we knew if we performed together as a team then we were very, very hard to beat.

'We socialised together off the field, not necessarily going out drinking, although that did happen. Most of the stories are not fit for publication, though I remember one trip to Monaco when I walked into a bar and there was Carlton Palmer dancing on the table in just his underpants. It was one of the funniest things I have ever seen.

'But we also used to play golf a lot. There was a real golf culture at the club, though we made sure we used buggies to avoid any tiredness getting into our legs.

'We would go out for meals together and it was not just a few of us but everyone would get involved, so it was a very easy group to be part of.

'We took that same bond into training. It meant we were allowed to say what we demanded from each other. We could express an opinion without fear of anyone taking it personally.

'Senior pros and the younger players had massive respect for each other and Gordon Strachan knew how to get the best out of everyone, particularly me.

'I had huge respect for him because of what he had done in the game and how he treated us as individuals and as a group. He really pushed us and improved us.

'He enhanced things we had already learned and taught us a lot, in particular never to give up. We were incredibly fit and that was a huge weapon to have in our arsenal.

'If you know you are fitter than your opponent then it gives you a massive advantage, especially late in the game. If you run through or chase back and you are fitter than the man you are up against, then it will get to them. It really gives you a massive lift.'

Having modelled his game on his hero and fellow Saints hard-man Alan Shearer, Beattie thrived at The Dell once he had got over the initial disappointment of being sold by the club he supported.

Ironically, his chances at Ewood Park were limited because Rovers had splashed out £7.5m on another Southampton player in Kevin Davies. Although Beattie was not part of the deal, he was still seen by many as a replacement, putting him under pressure to perform despite being only 20 and still learning the game, with just four league appearances to his name.

Although he scored only five league goals in 35 Premier League appearances (13 from the bench) during his maiden season with Southampton, two of them came in the last three games of the season, when Dave Jones' men pulled out of the drop zone for the first time in the campaign.

It was enough to win Beattie the club's Player of the Year trophy, which he marked with two vital assists for new signing Marian Pahars as Saints completed an unlikely great escape with a 2-0 win at home to Everton on the final day.

He won the coveted award again in 2003 after netting 23 goals to become the leading English marksman in the Premier League. Although he won five full caps, he lost out to Emile Heskey for a place in England's Euro 2004 squad before moving to Everton for £6m in January 2005.

Beattie is keen to set the record straight about the switch, insisting he did not seek to leave St Mary's but was sacrificed in an ultimately fruitless bid to secure survival.

'It wasn't my choice to go. People think I went to Everton for the money, but I never asked to go. The fact is Harry Redknapp said he needed to sell me in order to get three or four players in to keep the team up.

'He said he could get a million or so for Antti Niemi, but I was his only really saleable asset. It wasn't my choice.

'I can't say I regret the move to Everton, but I wouldn't have wished for it. It was hard being away and seeing the club relegated – that hurt.

'I have no idea if they would have stayed up if I hadn't been sold – but it would have saved them a lot more money in the long run if it had worked out like that. It was a long road back to the top flight, but I am delighted they have made it and have done so well.

'I loved my time at Southampton and made some really good friends. It was a great place to live and things went well on the pitch until my final season, when it all went wrong. It all seemed a bit chaotic.'

Beattie was top scorer in his first full season at Goodison Park but then struggled to hold down a regular starting spot and moved to Sheffield United for £4m in August 2007, scoring 34 goals in 62 Championship games.

He had spells with Stoke, Glasgow Rangers, Blackpool on loan and Sheffield United again before becoming player-coach and then manager at Accrington Stanley.

Intelligent and articulate as well as passionate and knowledgeable, Beattie gave everything to the role – including his own money.

'Accrington was a very good place to start. It was hard work but it was great experience and you can never learn that on any course. No qualification prepares you for that.

'I loaned the club my own money because we had a transfer embargo and I needed to get someone in. I wanted Kal Naismith from Rangers and I couldn't sign him because we had a tax bill, so I paid it and he was our leading goalscorer.

'That shows the commitment I had to the club. It was very important for me and for the club to get him in and I just felt it was the right thing to do. I just wanted the team to be competitive.

'I owned some flats in Manchester, so I used them to accommodate players, which attracted them to the club, but it cost me a lot in income as they weren't paying rent.

'Our highest paid player was only on £700 a week – electricians can earn more than that. So we had a few that would have a proper job and then play part-time for us, but it was hard to entice players to join us if we were paying less than they could make from an ordinary job.

'It was an impossible situation and I had to call in a few favours from players and people I knew in the game. We didn't even have our own training ground, so I had to sort that out.

'We didn't win for 11 games when I got there and people said I didn't know what I was doing, but they didn't know I was driving round for three months trying to find somewhere for us to train.

'I eventually sorted something out at my old school and we drew the next game and then, over the last 31 games of the season, we were sixth in the league.

'I got a lot of credit from people in football for not just expecting to go in at Championship level but being prepared to get my hands dirty and work my way up from the bottom.'

He left by mutual consent in September 2014 and then teamed up with former Saints defender Garry Monk, first at Swansea and then at Leeds, where Beattie was named first-team coach in July 2016.

With the Yorkshire club's recent track record for a swift turnover of managers, it is entirely possible that Beattie could be on the move again between the interview and publication of this book. But he also knows the potential at Elland Road is enormous if the pair can make a success of the post.

'Leeds are a huge club, absolutely massive. I can't believe the response we have had since we came into the club. We went to Ireland on pre-season tour and there were literally thousands of fans wanting to see us.

'The club needs a bit of stability and with Garry there and with a bit of time, we can progress the team. We are under a bit of pressure because they promised to refund up to 50 per cent of season ticket money if we don't make the play-offs, but I am really hopeful we can do well.'

Beattie still has ambitions to be a successful manager in his own right but for the moment he is happy learning the ropes – although it still looks strange to see him in a collar and tie.

'I'm not sure it suits me but that is my life now. I am a tracksuit coach but I want to look the part as a manager – and I have to act the part too.

'It is just a case of doing certain things differently now I am on the other side of the fence, teaching them right from wrong, making them better players and better people. That means I have to set a good example.

'When I was a player, we had some great nights out – and I still do occasionally. But now I am the one setting the rules rather than breaking them.'

Claus Lundekvam

CLAUS LUNDEKVAM knows he is lucky to be alive.

Although a cultured and accomplished defender on the field, he was a party animal off it. And when he hung up his boots after 11 seasons with Saints, he went off the rails completely.

Without the routine of training and the banter that went with it, his life suddenly seemed to lack purpose. And with no real outside support, he fell into the depths of despair as his world became a blur of drink and drugs which almost killed him.

He said: 'I loved the atmosphere in the dressing room, the banter and the partying. It came naturally to me, so the lads very quickly accepted me when I signed from Brann Bergen.

'I have missed that so much since I retired. That has been one of the biggest challenges for me. Being without that camaraderie is the hardest part about finishing as a player – and for me it turned out pretty badly.

'I turned to drink and drugs, which was not good for me, but eventually I got the help I needed. It is still something I deal with day to day. I turned to Tony Adams' Sporting Chance clinic. I was in and out of the Priory three times and had 12-step treatment, which was literally a life-saver for me.

'But for that, I genuinely don't think I would still be here. I was drinking myself to death – and I didn't really care.

'I was so down and so depressed. I felt I couldn't cope without football. I missed the buzz and the adrenaline rush, so I sought highs in other ways.

'I had had that rush of being competitive ever since I was a kid, so when it was gone I made a few wrong choices and got addicted to alcohol and cocaine. It was very self-destructive.'

Like most addicts, Lundekvam struggled to accept he had a problem.

Former players like Matthew Le Tissier, Francis Benali and most notably Jason Dodd would try to shake him out of it.

Alarmed at the self-destructive path he was racing down, they tried to curb his drinking and his drug abuse. But he was in too dark a place to listen.

Frequently, his pal Mark Harris would pick him up after a night out and ensure he got home safely. Many nights, he or others would sit with him as he suffered the violent effects of the latest binge, often wondering if he would even wake up.

Dodd recalled: 'It is horrible seeing what has happened to Claus. Mark Harris and his dad, Colin, have been fantastic but there were many hours when I effectively babysat Claus, often for nights on end.

'I even had to pull in a couple of favours to get him arrested because I really thought he was going to kill himself. I managed to get him into the Priory – only to find another former Saints player in there. They only take a few people a month, so what are the chances of that happening?

'I am just pleased Claus is alive. I saw him at his worst. I used to go on holiday with him and Steve Strange and Claus would fall off the wagon over the summer. He would be a shambles when he reported back for training, yet by the end of pre-season he would be fit as anything.

'The way he was living was horrendous. He was in such a bad place, it was awful to watch it because he is such a nice guy.

'He is so generous and so honest – and maybe that was part of the problem. There were too many hangers-on.

'There were many times I thought he would not make it, but the good thing is he has come out of it and I just hope he can stay on the right path.'

Now clean and rebuilding his life back in Norway, Lundekvam can recognise how he was spiralling out of control, even though at the time he thought he was able to handle it.

He added: 'It was hard for me to admit I needed help and to accept that I was struggling without football. I had always been strong and I was not used to showing my feelings or being able to cry.

'That was my life for 25 years. I had been captain of Southampton and of Norway. I was supposed to be strong.

'It was a very, very hard thing to accept especially when your judgment is clouded by alcohol and drugs. The only way is to acknowledge you need help and just hold your hands up.

'It took me two and a half years to admit I had a problem, which just comes down to ego. I would tell everyone that I was in control – but I was not. Not at all.

'You have to admit that before it is too late and thankfully I did that. I was an extreme user and I hit rock bottom.

'I knew I could not carry on that way. If I had done, I would not be alive today.'

When he hit his lowest ebb, Lundekvam resigned himself to an early grave – and even set the wheels in motion to hasten the process.

He would drink and take cocaine at night and then take a fistful of sleeping pills the next morning to get himself right. Although he could cover up to much of the outside world, his family realised he had a problem. When he refused help, his worried wife moved the children away.

As raging paranoia took a grip, Lundekvam would reportedly prowl the bushes at night with a kitchen knife, convinced that paparazzi were spying on him. He removed all the light bulbs thinking they contained hidden cameras and even hid for hours in a cupboard.

'My wife left me along with our two little girls and I was left alone in a big house in Southampton, so I told myself I was going to drink myself to death. That was my destiny.

'At least that is how it felt. I was so low, I just accepted it. I booked a one-way ticket to Rio and had no intentions of coming back. I thought that was it, my final journey.

'I knew that in Rio I would find the things I wanted, a free flow of cocaine and lots of gorgeous women. That would have been fine by me. It wouldn't have taken long. Luckily, I never made it. I would not have returned.'

But fate intervened. Another drugs binge meant Lundekvam missed the flight. He still has the ticket – just to remind him of what might have been and how he can never return to such dark days.

'Thankfully, I ended up getting the help I needed. Because a lot of people tried, I went to the best psychologists, but none of them could help me. I owe so much to the Sporting Chance clinic because they saved my life.

'There were people there who really understood what I was going through. They are remarkable. I'm still not sure what convinced me to get help, but one night my head and soul gave in completely and I knew I just couldn't do it anymore.

'I was just so tired, I was so completely empty. I just couldn't take any more of it. And that made me very humble and I became incredibly sad. So I held my hands up and I asked for help.

'I was so depressed. When you use that much alcohol and cocaine, you get so paranoid. It turns on you and you become a liability to yourself.

'Pretty quickly, I ended up as a physical wreck and one night I completely broke down. I started to cry in front of my kids. I knew I could not handle it any more.

'I had to accept I was not in control and that I had hit rock bottom. That was my turning point – and that was the start of my recovery. And I am still recovering now.

'It is something I will have to deal with for the rest of my life, which is very hard and very sobering. I look at life very differently now.'

Now Lundekvam devotes a lot of his time to ensuring others do not fall into the same trap. Back in Norway, he speaks openly and honestly about his problems, warning of the dangers and helping players avoid the pitfalls which cost him his family and fortune.

He is far from the only player to have struggled with isolation, lack of purpose and depression after packing in the game. Former PFA chairman Clarke Carlisle attempted to take his own life as he tried to come to terms with life after football.

There have been other high-profile cases, from the success stories of Paul Merson and Tony Adams to the ongoing problems endured by the likes of Paul Gascoigne and Kenny Sansom.

And Lundekvam is adamant the PFA should be doing more to help players come to terms with the transition from stardom to humdrum.

He added: 'The PFA has come a long way since the 1990s and helps ex-pros, which is crucial because it is not easy to cope with life after retirement.

'One minute you are being cheered and applauded by thousands of fans who chant your name and stop you in the street, the next minute you are no one. At least that's how it seemed.

'Football was my life. It was who I was. Without it, I felt worthless and empty.

'I do think more could be done to support players when they hang up their boots. When your career is over, you need a team around you to help you deal with day-to-day life.

'It is a big problem and one which needs to be taken very seriously. I have not spoken to anyone who has found it easy to adjust after a long playing career.

'It is something I have been working on with the PFA in Norway. Hopefully, we can put in place some guidelines and support for players who have finished.

'Most players will experience some form of depression after they finish playing. It is something we need to look at and deal with because so many ex-pros have needed treatment for addiction to gambling or drugs or alcohol.

'It is a big thing and it needs to be addressed more seriously. The best advice I can give is for players to have something to go to when they stop playing – something to get up for in the morning.

'You have to still feel needed and important somehow. Of course, I was important to my family, but I could not see that. As a sportsman, I needed to be chasing something the whole time.

'I was used to performing and running out in front of 30,000 cheering fans every week and I missed it. I missed the buzz, the build-up, the banter. I missed the structure to the week preparing for the game with friends and a common purpose. I missed the adrenaline kick.

'I missed being recognised and being told I was doing a good job. Suddenly, that was all gone and it was very, very hard to take.'

Away from the glare of the spotlight and headlines, Lundekvam retreated into a solitary world of loneliness and isolation, getting through with increasing amounts of alcohol and cocaine.

He said: 'I just lay there with my own thoughts. It might sound cruel to say it, but my family took second place. I was so egocentric.

'I had enough money to be able to lie there and just order stuff.

'I would not blame anyone for what happened to me. It is just the way it was and I made a lot of wrong decisions. I kept chasing new heights the whole time. I was constantly looking for new ways to get that euphoria. For a while, cocaine helped me do that but very quickly it simply made me more depressed and paranoid.

'At first, it was a lifeline which gave me a buzz but after a few months it turned bad. I became anxious and paranoid. I could not handle days at all.

'I pretty soon found out it was literally a matter of life and death for me.

'It cost me a fortune financially. It cost me my family and I felt I could not show my face. I felt as though everyone could see through me and that I was having a really bad time.

'I stayed home but I had friends who would come by and check I was OK. A lot of players helped me. They rang me and said they were there for me – especially Jason Dodd and Matthew Le Tissier, who are still my best friends in football. Francis Benali helped too. They were there for me when I finished and tried hard to get me help. I will never forget that.

'Jason Dodd was superb. Colin and Mark Harris were my best friends at the time and they stood by me and helped me. I will never forget what they did. They were very concerned about me, but when you are an addict you don't think about anyone else, just where your next fix is coming from. That controls every minute of your day. It is an incredibly strong force.

'That is the honest truth. It is very powerful and I don't envy anyone who suffers like that. I would not wish it on my worst enemy.

'Now, though, I have a completely new life. I feel very lucky and I will use all my spirit and determination and ego to get through this.

'Things are good now. I no longer live with Nina, but our relationship is not a problem and I am great friends with the two girls. They are 13 and 16 now and they are the pillars of my life, the reason I get up every day.

'Of course, there is a lot of guilt but you cannot let it eat you up. That is why I have been to treatment back in Norway.

'I am not naive enough to think I am out of it, but I feel very lucky and privileged that I have managed to get this far.'

Lundekvam admits that it has been very therapeutic speaking about his problems and trying to turn them into a positive by helping others. He has written a book, which has yet to be translated into English, and regularly appears on television to open up about his trials and tribulations. Facing up to his situation so honestly has helped him come to terms with it and to focus on a way out of the darkness which enveloped his existence.

But he is also painfully aware that there is no easy road to recovery and this is a lifelong battle to control his demons.

'I do speak about my problems very openly and that has helped me a lot. I speak to others to try and help them avoid making the same mistakes as I did and I have been on a lot of talk shows and have written a book back in Norway.

'I know I am very lucky to be here to talk about it.

'I know I am not going to be able to cruise through life now. It is something I will have to deal with for the rest of my days. I have to accept I can never have another drink – that is part of it.

'I am always heartbroken if I have a relapse or cheat, but I have not had a drink for two years now.

'At my worst, I was drinking two litres of vodka a day and taking perhaps seven or eight grams of cocaine. I know I am very lucky to still be alive.

'I was lucky that I hit rock bottom quite quickly because my behaviour was so extreme. My suffering could have been prolonged by many years if it had been a more gradual decline.

'My parents have been involved with my problems from day one and have been so supportive. But they soon found out they could not help me. They knew I needed to help myself.

'They have been to treatment with me and learned all they could about the disease and how they could support me. They are very happy that I am now sober and clean and that I am feeling strong about life ahead of me.

'Now I want to help other players who hit rock bottom and who might be struggling with alcohol and drugs or depression. It is something I am really passionate about.

'Being honest and open is a crucial part of recovery. You have to get it into the open, even though so much guilt comes with it.'

For all his partying, Lundekvam is adamant that he would never have allowed it to impact upon his football, giving everything for Saints during a committed 11-year stay.

'I never took drugs during my playing days and although I had my fair share of alcohol, it never affected the way I trained or played.

'You can probably see the seeds of my later problems in those early years, but I always made sure I was right for the games. It never had an impact on my game. I was very professional and determined to be the best on the pitch every weekend.

'I was not going to let my partying affect that, so I made sure I performed in training and in games.

'But I was a big party animal. If something was happening, I was normally there. But I held back a bit because I was very aware I would be training the next day.

'There were some players who could get away with it and run all day regardless of what they put themselves through the night before.

'Things were very different in the mid-1990s. It was a very different culture from what it is today. The Premier League is now so much more professional and players cannot get away with it now, as they did then.

'I remember a lot of good times off the field. It was an important part of the game to bond off the field. It made us a lot stronger as a unit and we looked out for each other on and off the field. Christmas parties and trips abroad were such fun – I will never forget them. There was a lot of partying and inevitably a lot of alcohol.

'They were times when we felt we could let our hair down and really enjoy ourselves. When you are playing in such a pressurised environment you do need an escape valve, a release.

'You need to blow out and if you do that with your team-mates, then it is a real strength. In my first few seasons, we were always struggling to stay up but we had great spirit and togetherness.

'Not many other teams had that. We were probably one of the weakest teams in the division because we did not have a big budget to sign players, but we had the strongest spirit and that is what kept us up year after year against the odds.

'We survived because of our willingness to die for each other on the pitch – and those bonds were forged with trips to Amsterdam or Prague.

'We had a lot of players who loved it. Jason Dodd was the most professional player but he was a very social kid off the pitch and did a lot of the organising. And then there was Jim Magilton, who literally could not see anything after four beers. It was so funny.

'We had some great times. I remember organising a trip to Amsterdam before a game and we went ice skating in the middle of the night. It was crazy, especially with a match coming up.

'I would say 90 per cent of the squad had never been on the ice before. It could have been a disaster. Heaven knows how we did not pick up any injuries because we were all drunk.

'You had Rudi Skacel, who had been a professional ice skater and was jumping around while the rest of us were falling over. It would have made the headlines if anyone had got hurt.

'You could say I was on the slippery slope even then!'

Lundekvam signed for Saints from Brann for £400,000 in 1996. It proved to be a shrewd investment by Graeme Souness as the composed defender went on to make 403 appearances, mostly in the Premier League.

Famously, he scored just twice, against Wolves and Cardiff, who were both managed at the time by former Southampton boss Dave Jones, who took it personally! He also had the unlikely honour of scoring Norway's 1,000th goal in international football in a 2-0 win over Bosnia–Herzegovina.

And while many foreign players felt no allegiance to their chosen clubs, Lundekvam developed an immediate affinity with Southampton, staying for 11 years and making more Premier League appearances than any other Norwegian.

'Graeme Souness and Lawrie McMenemy watched me twice when I was playing for Brann. I was 22 and knew a few clubs had been watching me. I had been with the under-21s for three years and had just made my debut for the full international side, so I felt the time was right to move on.

'There were a couple of German clubs interested but the second time Lawrie and Graeme came over, they liked what they saw and I signed a contract that evening.

'A week later, I was making my Southampton debut against Forest – and it was a massive culture shock.

'I could not believe how physical it was in the Premier League and the tempo of the play really took me aback. I was known for being laid back and I was used to having time on the ball… but the English game was so much faster and tougher.

'I had to adapt very quickly and it certainly made me a better player. I had to do everything a lot more quickly because if you delayed or took an extra touch, the ball would be gone and probably in the net.

'My first few games were really tough. The tempo was much quicker – it was a massive difference. In Norway, I did not exactly stroll through games, but it was comfortable enough. Here, every time I came off the field, I was sore. I ached everywhere not just from running but from the battering I would take from opposing strikers. I was not used to that.

'I had to change my game and I think I adapted pretty quickly. I played it more simple and faster and I became more physical myself.

'The other players really helped. They showed me what was needed and I soon began to enjoy playing against more physical opponents, as long as they did not have the pace to get past me.

'I really enjoyed playing against the likes of Alan Shearer and Duncan Ferguson. Although they were hard, I was quicker than them.

'The toughest opponents for me were the likes of Michael Owen and Thierry Henry, who were both quick and intelligent.

'I had to learn quickly that I needed to give players a dig early on to let them know I was there and get their respect. That was something new for me.

'It was totally different from how I played in Norway. I had to be stronger, more physical and let them know I was not a pushover.

'I always had a good tussle with Alan Shearer and Duncan Ferguson, but it was always friendly enough. At the final whistle, everything was fine and we could shake hands. It was not always nice during the game, but we were all good afterwards.

'For each of us, it was a case of dishing it out but being able to take it too. I loved that part of the game.

'Henry was probably the best I played against. He was virtually unplayable. With his speed and intelligence, he would make you look stupid.

'I remember trying to analyse what I should do against him before a game at Highbury and thought, "I am going to show him who is boss." The first ball he received, I was straight in his back and gave him a good tackle from behind, but he just laid it back and then spun round me.

'Next time, I gave myself a few metres and he put the ball behind me and ran past. It was so humiliating.'

If Henry was the best player he faced, Lundekvam is in no doubt about the best he played alongside.

'Matthew Le Tissier is an incredible talent, way above anyone else in training. He is the best finisher I have ever seen with both feet. He is so natural. It is just a shame he did not really fulfil his potential. He could have gone anywhere if he had looked after himself better and if he had wanted to leave. He was unbelievably gifted in so many parts of the game.

'We accepted he did not do the dog work for the team, but that was OK because he would win games for us. He was great for Southampton, so down to earth and one of my best friends.

'The best defender I played alongside was probably Michael Svensson. With Antti Niemi in goal and Doddsy and Wayne Bridge on the flanks, we were a formidable unit. They were probably the best years of my career.

'Michael and I complemented each other well. He was a tough, ruthless defender who would run into every challenge – and everyone else would get hurt except him.

'He was the sort of player you would not go near in training because you knew you would get hurt. He trained as he played. Under Gordon Strachan, they were the most successful years we had.'

Twice Lundekvam almost left the club but both moves fell through and he went on to enjoy an emotional testimonial at St Mary's, which even now lifts his spirits when life gets tough.

'I came close to leaving on a couple of occasions. When Graeme Souness went to Benfica, there was talk of me following him but nothing came of it and then I almost joined Newcastle a few years later.

'The clubs had almost agreed a fee and, as I was 32 or 33, I thought I perhaps had one big move left in me. But then we played a pre-season friendly at Bournemouth and one of the defenders got injured, so the club said they could not let me go.

'I did dwell on it at the time but now I am really happy and proud to have been a one-club man here. That does not happen too often these days and I hope the fans regard me as a loyal player. I loved my years at Southampton and the club will always have a special place in my heart.

'I fulfilled my dreams here and I finished on a high with my testimonial at St Mary's, which is a night I will never forget. It was wonderful to come back one last time to thank the fans and the support from the crowd was fantastic. I was so emotional.

'I have never been so nervous before a game in my life. I had so much pain in my ankle that I did not know if I would be able to play, but it was an incredible night and it was wonderful to see so many friends there.

'The problems came after my testimonial, when I let my guard down. I had always kept myself fit and the fact I had a match to prepare for would ensure I did not go too overboard. I had a focus and goal.

'Once that was gone, I had nothing to hold me in check. I told myself I would enjoy life. That was my biggest mistake.

'I had three operations on my ankle and found myself drinking more and more.

'I thought I was prepared to retire at 35 and told myself I was very lucky to have been in the game so long. Then it hits you that there is no day-to-day routine, no training, no banter.

'It was a very lonely existence and quickly it became the start of my depression, which became a destructive cycle of chasing new heights.

'I went to a lot of parties and had a lot to drink and eventually I started to try drugs. The paranoia and guilt from that destroyed my life.

'Now my life is back on track. I have had a break from the media work to promote my book on talk shows.

'It is a very honest account – maybe a bit too honest for Norway. But it is one which people can learn from in terms of handling adversity and the fact it is possible to bounce back.

'You need to admit you have got a problem and are facing difficulties. It is not a short process. It takes years to adapt and I will never be completely free of it. But I am still here and still fighting. I am just so glad I never got on that plane to Rio.'

David Prutton

THERE IS only one place to start any chapter about David Prutton, which is a shame.

But he accepts he will forever be remembered not for the 25 England under-21 caps nor the 441 appearances for eight different clubs, but for one career-defining moment of madness.

By any stretch of the imagination, Prutton should not be in this book. Of course he was fiercely committed, tough in the tackle and sometimes overstepped the mark.

But a hard-man? No. He is articulate, funny, generous, down-to-earth and endearing, which makes it all the more astonishing that he lost his head in such a catastrophic way on 26 February 2005.

Saints, battling against relegation, were holding their own at home to Arsenal in a typically feisty affair when Prutton went steaming in on Robert Pires.

The warning signs had been there ten minutes earlier when he launched a reckless tackle against Mathieu Flamini, which earned him a booking.

The assault on Pires was probably a red card in its own right and Prutton now accepts he should have been grateful to Alan Wiley for only showing a second yellow.

Instead he flipped and committed the cardinal sin of pushing the referee as he furiously tried to confront the linesman.

'It is still the first thing I usually get asked when I meet someone. There are usually a few pleasantries and then they will say "What the fuck were you doing there?" And I still don't have an answer.

'I remember the before and after but I don't remember actually doing it. Of course, I have seen it on video but it is like an out-of-body experience watching it, as though it is someone else, not me.

'Sky show it from time to time when I am guesting and it doesn't bother me. I am not proud of it but equally I am not scarred for life by it.

'It's something I wasn't thrilled about but I don't want to dwell on it for the rest of my life and I won't.

'Literally the red mist came down and I just reacted. But I have no idea what I thought I was doing or what I was trying to achieve.

'I was a bit wound up even before the game. We were under a lot of pressure in a relegation battle and had just played West Brom, where I should have scored, so that was on my mind even before we kicked off against Arsenal.

'I'm not making excuses because obviously nothing could excuse what happened, I'm just trying to give a bit of context.

'The fact is I should have got sent off for the first tackle, which received only a booking. Instead of thinking I had got off lightly, I then went flying in on Robert Pires, which should also have been a straight red.

'But in my ridiculous, untempered view of the world, it seemed like all the unfairness of life was raining down on me and I was going to put it right.

'The linesman tried to stop me and I couldn't see why he was getting involved. I have seen the pictures and my face is contorted with rage – it is horrendous.

'I remember sitting in the dressing room knowing I had let myself and the team down, then Harry Redknapp came in and said we were playing well but one idiot had killed it for us. And I knew he meant me.

'I did everything I could to try and put it right. I wrote to Alan Wiley and to the linesman to apologise, I wrote an open letter to the fans saying how sorry I was and it was all genuine remorse.'

The rush of blood to the head had two major consequences for Saints. Most immediately, it left them down to ten men and saw them almost instantly fall behind to a Freddie Ljungberg goal on the stroke of half-time.

Thankfully, Robin van Persie also lost his cool and got sent off early in the second half to balance the numbers, enabling Saints to salvage a 1-1 draw.

But the longer-term impact was that Prutton received a record ten-match ban, meaning Saints were without a key player for eight crucial Premier League games.

'If only I had accepted the second yellow, I would have sat out just one fixture – and that would have been an FA Cup tie at Brentford.

'I had to appear before the FA, where three county FA officers with a combined age of 200 passed judgment. Mick McGuire of the PFA spoke on my behalf but he reeled off a list of my previous offences, so it sounded like I was an explosion waiting to go off.

'I said "Mick, what are you doing? You're killing me here." I think he was trying to show I was combative but not nasty, but it made me sound as though I had more previous than Reggie Kray.

'Harry Redknapp was there, getting more and more fidgety as the panel went off to deliberate. Eventually he said, "I've left the car on a meter, I've got to go." And off he went. Thanks for the support!

'I know I was out of order but I thought a ten-game ban was harsh. But I just had to take it on the chin and learn from it. It was my own fault. I regretted it as soon as I did it and for a long time afterwards.

'I let down myself and my team-mates and the fans and it presented an image that simply wasn't me. I got a lot of criticism, much of it justified, but some of it was way over the top.

'It was a really tough time for me and for my family, who were trying to fight my corner. I was vilified in the press. All I could do was keep saying how sorry I was and hope that time would heal the wounds.'

It has left Prutton – and Saints fans – with a lingering feeling of frustration. Although Southampton finished bottom with a woeful 32 points, they were just two adrift of safety.

And Prutton will always question whether his presence might have helped the team get the two draws they needed or whether his combative style might have helped them hang on to the 2-0 lead at home to Villa instead of collapsing to a costly 3-2 defeat.

'I will never know how life would have turned out if I hadn't done it. I do wonder if we might have stayed up. I had been playing well up until then and I like to think I would have maintained that form and it could have made a difference – although things must be bad if you are pinning your hopes of staying up on David Prutton!

'I would have loved to have been a part of the run-in but it was not meant to be. It was hard training but knowing there was nothing at the end of it as I couldn't play.

'It was tough watching the games, knowing I should have been out there helping – particularly the 4-1 defeat at our bitter local rivals

Pompey. I watched it in the gym until it got so embarrassing that I just had to go home.

'It is a really intimidating place to play and we were just too nice. It was probably a reflection of our season: the ability was there but the mental belief wasn't.

'I made sure I stayed as fit as possible in the hopes of playing in the final game of the season at home to Manchester United. That fixture had my full focus because I was desperate to atone for what I had done.

'It was a horrible day. I was thrilled to be back playing and although our fate was not in our own hands I really felt we could stay up, especially when Norwich crumbled at Fulham.

'It meant we just had to beat United, who were not really going for it. They had the FA Cup Final the following week and were there for the taking, but we just didn't perform.

'I think the bottom line is we were not mentally strong enough or technically good enough. In the end, it was like shooting an injured horse for United and they put us out of our misery.

'Some teams will respond to the pressure of having to win on the final day and the tense atmosphere that goes with it. And maybe Southampton teams of the past would have done that.

'But we didn't do that. It was purely down to belief and our mental approach – plus the fact we had left it too late.'

Prutton signed for Saints for £2.5m from Nottingham Forest in January 2003 with a big reputation as a promising talent and with a then record number of England under-21 caps.

After 143 appearances for his home-town club, Prutton felt ready to try his luck on the big stage and readily admits he was unprepared for the gulf in class.

'It was a real culture shock for me stepping up to the Premier League. I had done well at Forest and thought I was ready for the big-time, but it was a real eye-opener.

'I wouldn't say I had been a big fish in a small pond because Forest were – and still are – a big club in my eyes. But they were in the Championship and I knew that I would be playing pretty much every week.

'It was like playing with my mates because we had all come through the ranks together there, so I guess there was an element of being in a comfort zone in some ways.

'I came to Southampton and I couldn't believe what I was seeing – even in training. There were players I had never even heard of who were running rings round me.

'They were incredibly fit, strong and very talented. I couldn't get the ball off them.

'There were the likes of Paul Williams and Paul Telfer, who were proper seasoned professionals. They would look at me and ask what the hell I thought I was doing when I lost the ball.

'It meant I had to improve technically – and fast. We used to do some ballwork in a circle and I couldn't even get it, let alone do anything with it.

'Players were expected to keep it because if you give it away in the Premier League then it often leads to a goal. I soon learned that the speed of decision-making is paramount. You have to think very, very quickly.

'People say it is just football and you have time on the ball but you don't. The best players do everything by instinct without even thinking.

'A lot of it is down to confidence or self-belief too. If you are on top of your game, you don't think twice about running with the ball.

'It felt amazing to sign for Southampton. It was a chance to play in the Premier League with a club that was steadily on the up. After a succession of great escapes, they were getting some solidity in the top flight and establishing themselves in the top half of the table under Gordon Strachan.

'Even now, I am pretty proud that I got the chance to play for Southampton and I would not change it – the good, the bad and the indifferent.

'I remember the excitement of rushing down to sign. I didn't register in time to play in the next game against Manchester United, which we lost 2-0, and then I had to sit out the next fixture too as it was an FA Cup match against Millwall and I was cup-tied.

'I had already played for Forest against West Ham in the third round, so I missed out as Saints went all the way to the final – just my luck. Or maybe it was because I wasn't playing that they did so well!

'Even so, it was fantastic being part of the club and feeling the atmosphere around the city on that run to the final, which was an amazing occasion. The Southampton supporters were unbelievable that day.

'I remember walking out into the Millennium Stadium and seeing a wall of yellow and the noise was incredible. The Saints fans drowned out the Arsenal supporters even after the final whistle when we had lost 1-0.

'The fact that I couldn't play in the cup made it a bit of a stop-start time for me. The team was doing so well in the competition that there was a tendency to stick to that line-up for the league games, so I was in and out of the side.'

Prutton's hard running and abrasive edge meant he went on to become a regular in the side the following season as he began to adjust to the pace of the top flight.

'I guess I would describe myself as combative and energetic, which makes it sound like I just ran around and kicked people. But there was a lot more to my game than that.

'My aim was to get from box to box and to be as aggressive as possible without overstepping the mark.

'I had to learn to keep that aggression in check or at least to channel it in the right direction. I was not like a wild animal – despite what some people might have said or thought after the infamous red card against Arsenal.

'It was a case of applying it in the right direction and not letting emotion overcome what I was trying to do. I had to be fully focused, the concentration needed to be spot-on.

'It didn't always work. I think I picked up 12 red cards during my career.

'At first, when I got sent off, I used to say it was just a clumsy tackle but I have to accept that when you pick up that many red cards then they can't all be clumsy challenges.

'As I grew up, I realised that games were a lot more enjoyable if I wasn't always battling against the referee. I learned to introduce myself to them before the match, to chat with them and to ask how they were. It is human nature to perhaps react a little more favourably to someone who has gone out of their way to be nice or at least civil. It sounds obvious but it took me about 12 years to realise that!

'In the latter stages of my career, I even became something of a calming influence in the dressing room, which is a bit ironic really. But I would talk to the kids and I could see they were actually listening to what I had to say in the same way that I used to look up to the likes of Paul Telfer and Jason Dodd.

'Under Gordon Strachan, we were incredibly fit and we looked after ourselves. We knew how to have a good time but we never let it affect our game.

'Southampton is a city but it is also a place where everyone seems to know each other. If you were out on the town, people were generally great – at least when things were going well for the team!

'It was different when we were fighting relegation because the fans were understandably very wound up and didn't like to see you out on the town, even if you were just having a quiet drink.

'I remember towards the end of my time at the club, I got thumped on a night out. I got chatting to this bloke and we had a difference of opinion on my footballing ability until he ended the discussion with a smack in the face.

'I resisted the urge to get involved and my mate bundled him away. I am a lover, not a fighter – despite what Alan Wiley might say.'

It had all been going so well under Gordon Strachan but the departure of the 'Ginger Genius' sparked the start of a decline which took seven years to reverse.

At the time, only Arsenal, Everton, Liverpool and Manchester United had been in the top flight longer than Saints. But three managers in one season saw the club surrender their proud position in the Premier League.

Paul Sturrock departed after just two games of the 2004/05 season and was replaced by Steve Wigley amid initial confusion over whether he was permanent or caretaker boss.

It turned out to be neither. He was replaced in December 2004 by the unlikely figure of Harry Redknapp, who had just left Southampton's bitter local rivals Portsmouth.

It seemed a strange choice not just for the fans to accept, but also for chairman Rupert Lowe, who was keen to introduce a progressive coaching system. Other board members argued Redknapp – a much more traditional old-school manager – would at least motivate the team to stay in the top flight.

Not only did the move fail but the two footballing philosophies clashed again when Rugby World Cup winner Sir Clive Woodward was brought in to help him.

Prutton recalled: 'I got on well with all my managers at Southampton. Gordon Strachan was great for us and got the team into Europe – albeit briefly.

'When Paul Sturrock came in we had a nice little patch, but there was a lot of pressure on him, even down to the way he dressed, which I thought was tremendously unfair. I really liked him.

'Harry Redknapp coming in was just a ludicrous situation. He did not look like he was too enamoured to be there and I think he has said as much since.

'He never really looked comfortable here – even the red bench coat did not really seem to sit well on him. It just never felt right, especially coming straight from Pompey and given the fierce rivalry between the fans. Both sets of supporters were unhappy for different reasons.

'I think it was a real shock for him – and even more so when Sir Clive Woodward was brought in to assist him. Clive was very impressive as a man. He had a real stature about him and an aura of who he was and where he had come from.

'You couldn't fail to be impressed by him – he had won his country a World Cup. The problem was that it was for rugby rather than football.

'I wasn't one of those who instantly rubbished the idea. I am sure there are a lot of cross-over areas where football could learn a lot, especially on the science front. Football can be very insular but, of course, you can learn from other sports about better ways to do things.

'Clive was a great delegator, bringing in experts for specific areas. He was big on things like peripheral vision, diet, analysis – anything that could give just the tiniest little margin which might give you an advantage.

'But when he tried to have an input on the coaching side or in team meetings, we were left scratching our heads.

'Harry, though, was very different, an old-school manager. It was quite surreal watching them try to work together because they were complete opposites in personality and approach.

'From the comments in the press, you could feel Harry accepted it through gritted teeth. He was the manager and wanted to be in control, but suddenly he had to work with a complete outsider who wasn't even a football man.

'It was quite comical. I remember Harry storming on to the training ground shouting, "What the fuck is Clive doing sat in my office?" The chairman Rupert Lowe had moved them in together. I would love to have been a fly on the wall as they tried to work in the same room.

'I know Rupert divided opinion but he was great to me and I got on well with him. But bringing in Clive in that way meant we had to fight to be taken seriously as a club.

'If you have different factions pulling in different directions, then you look like a shower of shit – though it must be great entertainment if you are not a fan of the club. We attracted attention for the wrong reasons and it felt like people were taking the piss.

'Harry just let them get on with it and eventually left to go back to where he felt more comfortable. I don't think he looks back on his time here with the fondest memories.

'We found it tough in the Championship. We floundered and the club started losing a lot of money and there was a lot of political in-fighting – it was far beyond anything I could comprehend. It took a drop to League One, a change of owners, big investment and a complete rebuilding job for the club to bounce back. And it is great to see how well they have done since.'

Prutton returned to Forest on loan in January 2007 before moving to Leeds in the summer and then, via Colchester and Swindon, to Sheffield Wednesday where, after loans at Scunthorpe and Coventry, his career fizzled out at the age of 33.

He still felt he had something left to offer but with no concrete offers forthcoming he tried his hand at media work on Sky's popular *Soccer Saturday* show.

With his intelligence, wit and insight, it is no surprise that Prutton took to it easily – albeit with a lot of hard work.

He added: 'It was not a case that I intended to hang up my boots, it just sort of happened. There was no real interest from clubs to sign me.

'It all ended with a bit of a whimper really. It was not a conscious decision. It is not as though I had realised I was coming to the end of my playing career.

'I had a great time at Sheffield Wednesday, a big club with terrific fans, then I went to Coventry, who were playing their home games at Northampton at the time.

'That felt a bit weird but it was really intense and again it meant something to me. Again, they had great fans and hopefully they are now on the way back up.

'I thought things had gone well and at the end of the season everyone went off and I did not hear from them again.

'As the close season went on, nothing was coming up. I was offered a few trials but that didn't really appeal to me. For me, playing football is all-encompassing. It has to really matter.

'I have never done anything half-heartedly and if you do, then the fans see right through you. I also wonder if some clubs decided not to touch me in case they ended up losing a player for two or three months, even though I was never likely to push the referee again!

'So I called a producer at Sky to see if there was any chance of doing some punditry or analysis, just really to fill my time. It was all set up quite quickly and, as the season went on, I found myself doing more and more games.

'The more I was working and networking, the more producers I met and it snowballed. I was either a guest pundit or a co-commentator, which I enjoyed, and it was something I worked hard at.

'You can't just turn up at a game and say what you see. You have to offer the viewer something different. You have to offer an interpretation and it is a fine line to draw between being too simplistic or too convoluted. The information garnered in the build-up is invaluable. You need to do that research. After that, it is about presentation, being yourself, expressing an opinion and hopefully injecting a bit of humour where it works.

'If you set out to be funny then you will fall flat on your face. It has to come naturally.

'You have to be prepared to listen to feedback from people who have been in the industry a lot longer than you. Sometimes criticism might hurt but you have to take it on the chin and learn from it.

'Producers have to know they are bringing in someone they can trust, so it is about being professional, doing the hard graft and the research and being reliable.

'I'd like to think I could make a career doing television work. Sky coverage is increasing all the time, so it is up to me to try and establish myself through hard work and being professional – pretty much as I was as a player.

'A lot of players think it will be easy to go into TV when they pack up playing. They think it is a soft landing to fall back on – but it is a lot harder than it looks and it takes a lot of hard graft.

'But if you listen to feedback and learn from it and believe in yourself, then it is a great way to earn a living.

'People have said it helps that I am intelligent and articulate, but I just think of my old man saying how important education was. I'm glad it is finally coming in handy. I guess it is payback time now.

'I have a checklist of dos and don'ts when I am on air and right near the top is not to swear! People who know me will testify that does not come naturally to me – and it is very hard at times. I just do my swearing at home in front of the kids and keep it clean on air – proper northern parenting!'

Prutton looks back at his time at St Mary's with a good deal of fondness – and still has ties to the area.

'My four years at Southampton were fantastic both personally and professionally. It was a steep learning curve from a football point of view and I met my wife, Jenny, there – although I have to say I was a bit nervous when I discovered her father was Brian O'Neil!

'I have always been very appreciative not just that I could play football for a living but also of the clubs I was lucky enough to play for. I can look back and say I played in the Premier League – even though I did not cover myself in glory and will be remembered mostly for that one incident.

'I have met Alan Wiley many times in recent years and it is always lovely to see him. We make a joke about that incident. The fact is we get on much better now we are both wearing suits!'

Michael Svensson

IT IS impossible to write a book about hard-men and not include a player with the nickname Killer – even if he doesn't like it.

Like many of the game's toughest warriors, Michael Svensson is quietly spoken, gentle and easy-going – away from the pitch.

Once he crosses the white line, he becomes ruthless, unrelenting, cold and clinical – all the hallmarks of an assassin.

After signing for Saints from French club Troyes in September 2001, the 6ft 2in centre-back was surrounded by local media eager to quiz him on a nickname which immediately endeared him to the fans.

It was so good for headlines that there was no chance of them dropping it, even when he tried to distance himself from it.

He said: 'It came from my team-mates at Halmstad, who said they feared for their lives because of how rough and committed I was in training. I also had a tendency to get a bit angry, so they called me Killer.

'It is not a nice thing to be called. But I guess it was not personal and in the football context it was OK. It presented a tough image.

'I can't get away from the nickname – I have tried. So now, I enjoy it. I see it as being killer instinct rather than a murderer.

'I was certainly hard but I wouldn't say I was dirty. If you look at my record of red and yellow cards, it would suggest that I was tough but fair – or at least clever about it!

'I have to admit I did get away with a few things. I would say I pushed it to the very limit of what was allowed on the pitch. That was my strength – along with my ability to read the game and to put myself in a position where I could control the area.

'Gordon Strachan used to tell me, "Michael, you are a defender, so defend. Win the ball and give it to someone who can pass it." So that's what I did. It was quite simple for me to do my job.

'You see some players who play how they want to play rather than how they should for the good of the team or how they are instructed. I just set out to win the ball and get rid of it, passing it out if I could but otherwise just keeping it away from our goal.

'I was good at defending crosses, particularly in the air. I was strong in and around the penalty area – and you could say I was uncompromising in the tackle!'

Opponents and team-mates alike would confirm the modesty of that understatement. Players would literally bounce off the wiry but rock solid Swedish international, who won 25 caps.

He trained as he played, taking no prisoners and frequently antagonising colleagues and even close friends, not to mention those who barely gave him the time of day – like Agustin Delgado.

Svensson takes great pride in the fact that the Ecuador striker said only one word to him during the entire time he was at the club.

'I never held back in training, that's how I was and that's how I got my nickname. So I put in a proper meaty tackle on Delgado. It was hard but fair.

'He leapt to his feet and yelled "Idioto!" Even I didn't need a translator for that – it was the only word he ever said to me. It's kind of like a badge of honour for me!'

Delgado does not fit the criteria for this book as a hard-man, although, to be fair, it would be difficult to make a valid assessment as he played so little – only five starts in just under three years at the club.

But he could certainly be classed as a sinner, if only for the amount of trouble he caused manager Gordon Strachan, who inherited, rather than desired, the lanky striker. His transfer went through during the short time between Stuart Gray's departure and Strachan's arrival.

Since Delgado was widely regarded as a waste of £3.5m, no one has really claimed the 'credit' for the signing who arrived with a record of 29 goals from 43 internationals and with an exciting show-reel for the big screen at St Mary's.

Sadly, there were few Southampton additions to that CV. His stay did not start well as he arrived with a knee injury which required surgery and failed to heal quickly.

Ecuador were desperate for their talisman to be fit for the 2002 World Cup and it seemed that was the player's priority rather than getting himself right for Southampton.

Without telling Strachan – or indeed anyone at the club – he went back to South America for unauthorised surgery, which was described by Saints doctors as resembling something out of a horror movie.

Remarkably, he was fit enough to play in all three of Ecuador's group games and scored a header in a 1-0 win against Croatia before going under the knife once more.

He therefore missed pre-season to the annoyance of Strachan, who lost patience with the man who frequently went AWOL and whose complaints ranged variously from a bad back to toothache to hurt feelings that the club forgot his birthday!

Svensson recalled: 'I absolutely loved Gordon as a manager and I loved his quotes to the press. They still make me laugh even now. And my absolute favourite came when he was asked about the status of Delgado and said, "I have far more important things to worry about than Delgado. I have got a yoghurt on its sell-by date and that is my priority." I loved his quips.'

While Strachan had a quick-witted retort for any occasion, Delgado was quiet and withdrawn, possibly due to the language barrier, with his command of English hardly improving at all during his ill-fated 30-month stay at St Mary's.

He returned to his native country in June 2004, picking up a six-month ban for his part in a brawl during a domestic league match before, remarkably, being elected to the National Assembly in 2013 for the Pais Alliance party.

If Delgado struggled to adapt to life abroad, Svensson fitted in quickly and comfortably to life both on and off the pitch, embracing the English dressing room culture and the physical nature of the game.

'It was much more physical than the football in Sweden and even faster than I thought it would be, but that suited me. I came from French football, where we played three at the back and did a lot of man-to-man marking.

'Teams played through the middle. There were very few crosses coming in. But in England, I found myself constantly having to head the ball clear and that was a real strength for me.

'I learned the English game very quickly. One of my first away matches was at Bolton, where Dean Holdsworth started to give me a hard time and tried to intimidate me, swearing a lot.

'I quickly realised I had to be equally strong and I had to own that defensive area. I learned to put in a hard tackle very early on to perhaps soften up the striker. If you didn't do that, you knew you would be on the receiving end instead.

'Of course it didn't always work, especially against Alan Shearer. He was the hardest striker I ever faced. Colliding with him was like running into a brick wall.

'I remember the first time I came up against him. He got the ball with his back to goal, so I thought I would let him know I was there and went straight through the back of him.

'Absolutely nothing! I just bounced off him and he didn't flinch. He was incredibly strong and one of the best players in the world at holding up the ball then turning and shooting. He was amazing.'

Although Svensson was sent off in only his third appearance for his new club, there is some irony in that it was for handball rather than for any of his trademark crunching tackles.

'It was the last minute away to Spurs and we were hanging on at 1-1 when they got a corner. I headed it out but the ball was fired back in. I threw myself to block it but it hit my hand, so it was a red card and a penalty, which they scored. It was annoying – I spent all that time kicking people and got sent off for handball!'

The statistics would appear to support Svensson's claim that he was not a dirty player. He picked up eight yellow cards in his first season and nine the following year with just one more red card, which was the only talking point from a drab 0-0 draw at Bolton.

In a heated exchange, Svensson gently (by his standards) pushed away Mario Jardel, who fell to the ground as though he had been shot. It provoked a second yellow card for the Swede – and another memorable quote from his manager in support.

Strachan said: 'He's a big guy and at 15 stone to fall like that... my grandson weighs two and a half stone and he wouldn't have fallen because he's got more in him. He's a determined wee fella.

'I don't know how you face people after that, when you go home and speak to your family and they ask what you contributed to the game and you say "I fell, I fell like a big Jessie." It wasn't even a real push.

'It was a boring and scrappy match, so when the incident happened everyone was laughing. You have got to see it in slow motion to believe it. I'm not defending Michael, as soon as you put your hands on someone it's a yellow card, but it's not even a shove.

'It was embarrassing to watch. It's not hilarious for Michael but it's funny when you see it and it will keep me going for the five-hour trip home.'

Svensson added: 'It was a bit harsh but Gordon was great like that. He really looked out for his players.

'The English game is a tough league and I adapted quickly, mainly because I had good players around me and Gordon had faith in me.

'It was a great dressing room, full of characters and some really good players. You need good players around you to help and I was lucky to have that.

'The hardest of my team-mates was Chris Marsden, who was very tough on you if you didn't do a good job and he made sure you didn't make the same mistake again. I would class him as our toughest player – mainly because I didn't play alongside Francis Benali very often. He was the nicest guy off the field but unbelievable on it.

'I remember him saying he used to love playing at The Dell because the fans were so close to the pitch that you could literally kick opponents into the crowd. I would have enjoyed that.

'I loved a tackle but I only went for the ball – nothing else. Of course, there were times I took the man as well and that was good.

'But there were a few times I overdid it. We were playing away to Leeds and there was a situation just outside the area where all sorts of tackles were flying in. There was way too much going on for the referee to see it all. I was going for it totally and launched into a two-footed tackle on someone. Matthew Oakley pulled me away and told me to be careful as I would get sent off for that.

'I was lucky the referee did not see it but these days there are so many officials around the pitch all wired up and so many cameras that you wouldn't get away with anything like that now. But I did.

'I was quite good at reading situations. If it turned nasty, I could go in and out quite quickly and the referee wouldn't see it. That's how it was for everyone in those days. It was kick or be kicked.

'We played Chelsea away and I went in hard on Marcel Desailly. I went for the ball and I got the ball – but I got him afterwards with the follow-through. It was properly on the shin with my studs.

'I liked those sorts of tackles, where you take the ball and the man. If I was coming in at full speed and the opponent was stationary or was slower, then great. I would win the ball and he would have a bit of pain!

'It would rattle them and they would be looking for you for the rest of the match.'

Svensson's strength in the air and in the tackle became the cornerstone of the Southampton defence and played a key role in their charge to the 2003 FA Cup Final, which is still his most treasured football memory.

'When I signed, my objective was to become a good player in a good team and to have some success, which we did.

'We had a fantastic back line with Jason Dodd on the right and Wayne Bridge on the left and Antti Niemi in goal. Then, in the middle, I had a very special partnership with Claus Lundekvam.

'I have very nice memories of Southampton, despite the injuries I had. I loved the place and the club and I still go back there at least once a year to see old friends and to watch a game. The club are very welcoming and helpful like that.

'But, of course, the best memory was the FA Cup Final at the end of my first season. We finished eighth in the Premier League, which was then a club record, and it was just a great season.

'The FA Cup quarter-final was fantastic and then the semi-final was amazing. The supporters were incredible and it was a wonderful feeling to see them celebrating when we won.

'My abiding memory of the final is the unbelievable support we received that day. I don't remember too much about the game itself – in fact, I only watched it for the first time a couple of years ago. It was too painful to view it beforehand – and even as I was watching I still thought we were going to win. I kept cheering us on!

'But I will never forget coming out to warm up and seeing a wall of yellow at one end of the ground – and a huge spread of empty seats at the other.

'The Arsenal fans had not arrived by then – and they seemed to leave before our fans too, even though they won.

'Our supporters were absolutely incredible. Even though we lost 1-0, they out-sang the Arsenal contingent. It was deafening and it made the hairs on the back of my neck stand on end. I will treasure that for the rest of my life.'

Within a year though, Svensson was facing up to the beginning of the end of his playing career as he was hit by a succession of serious knee injuries.

Summoning all his trademark courage, resilience and determination, he endured five operations in four years only for his hopes to be dashed each time.

He sat out the whole of the 2004/05 campaign and watched in helpless frustration as Saints surrendered their proud place in the top flight after 28 years of mixing it with the big boys. It is a widely held belief that they would not have gone down if Svensson had been fit – and they would certainly have shown a bit more fight.

'It is nice when people say they are convinced we would have stayed up if I had been fit, but it is also hard to hear because it was so tough watching from the sidelines and seeing the club relegated.

'It was heart-breaking to know the club had been in the top division for so many years and then to get relegated while I was there, even though I could not play.

'The players and the physio staff were very supportive and kept me going through my rehab in the gym, but it was a tough time, especially as things were going so badly on the pitch.

'I always believed I would get back on the pitch and play again – and I did, but not for as long as I wanted.

'I hurt my calf in the warm-up at Portsmouth in March 2004. That put me out for a month and then when I came back my right knee went. I had hurt it in 1997, when I did my cruciate ligament, and the doctor said then that I would have problems with the cartilage.

'I ended up having a reconstruction of the posterior cruciate ligament and several other operations. I tried everything I could to get fit.'

Svensson made seven Championship appearances in the autumn of 2005 before breaking down once more. But again, he refused to accept defeat. Even though he sat out the rest of that season and the next two campaigns, he somehow got himself fit enough to captain the side at Cardiff in August 2008. But the comeback lasted just five games and he returned to Sweden, still refusing to accept his playing days were over.

'I did get back in 2011, when I played for two years at Halmstad with no big problems. I wanted another year but I was advised not to risk it.

'I felt OK in those two years and while I would not have been strong enough for the Premier League, I think I could have played in the Championship.

'It was a fantastic feeling when I finally did make my comeback after so long out. We played away to Helsingborg and I dominated the game. People said they couldn't believe I had been out for so many years.'

When he finally hung up his boots at the age of 36, he moved into coaching, working with the Halmstad under-19 side, as well as being assistant coach to the national under-18s.

He said: 'I am not really interested in going into management. There is too much pressure and the way managers are treated is unbelievable. You get so little time and never know what the future holds.

'It is much more rewarding to work with the youngsters and try to develop their skills and make them into better players. And I try to toughen them up.

'Swedish football is very different to the English game. You get a lot more time on the ball. But it is still important to assert yourself and to let the striker know you are there.

'The youngsters I teach don't know how to slide tackle because they have never been taught it. They are so clumsy and can hardly get on the ground to slide in for the ball. I want to teach them how to put in a hard tackle.'

If Svensson passes on his own qualities to those youngsters, then visiting sides could soon find themselves up against an army of well-trained Killers!

Rickie Lambert

RICKIE LAMBERT wishes he had never left Saints for Liverpool – but knows he would have regretted staying even more.

The England striker's dream move to his boyhood idols turned into something of a nightmare as he made just seven Premier League starts, with 18 all-too-brief appearances from the bench, managing just two goals.

It was a far cry from his golden years at St Mary's, where he was Southampton's own King Midas and everything he touched turned to goals. To be precise, 106 in 207 appearances from League One all the way through to the top flight.

That prompted a £4m bid for the then 32-year-old from his home-town club – and it proved too tempting for him to refuse, even though he was realistic enough to know he was unlikely to play as much as he had done on the south coast.

But if he had stayed and continued hitting the net in such spectacular style for Saints, then he would never have forgiven himself for not making the move.

He said: 'In hindsight, I do regret leaving. But it was Liverpool – my team. I madly supported them as a kid and even as an adult. Even when I was at Southampton, I still followed them and their results.

'They were very close to my heart, so when they came in for me it was absolutely impossible to turn down, especially with a few things that had happened.

'I left before Mauricio Pochettino but there were rumours he was going and there was some unrest. I didn't know quite what was going on. I don't want to go into too much detail, but there was a lot going on with me – I thought the way I had been treated wasn't right.

'There had been other opportunities for me to go when other clubs came in for me, but I never wanted to leave Southampton and felt very lucky to be there.

'But when Liverpool came in for me, I thought "I am 32, if I don't go for this now then I will never get the chance again." And imagine if I had stayed and things had carried on the way they had been going, then my regret would have been a lot higher because I would never have known how things would have turned out there.

'Even though things did not go as well as I had hoped, I would never have known that. The regret at not going would have been twice as big as the regret of going. And they say in life you regret the things you don't do more than the things you do... so I went.'

After just one season, Lambert was on the move again, this time to West Brom for £3m. But he fared little better, with just one goal from five starts and 14 cameo appearances as substitute.

His love for Southampton remained as strong as ever and was highlighted not just by his desire to feature in this book, but also on his return to St Mary's for Kelvin Davis' testimonial in May 2016.

The whole stadium rang to chants of 'Rickie Lambert, he wants to come home', drawing an appreciative acknowledgement from the big man, who said: 'I would not rule anything out in football. I enjoyed every day in Southampton with my family.

'My immediate focus is to get back as much of the fitness I have lost through not playing much in the last couple of years. I am working hard to get to a level where I can still be a success in the Premier League.'

That lack of first-team action – along with ageing limbs – also cost Lambert his coveted England place, although Roy Hodgson's side could have done with a fully fit and firing Lambert in France 2016.

He still treasures every second of an international career which seemed a wild fantasy when he famously worked in a beetroot bottling plant after being released by Blackpool in November 2000.

Four months later, he was given a chance by Macclesfield Town and began the slow slog through the lower divisions to the World Cup finals in Brazil – a Boy's Own story to warm the heart of all true football fans. Throughout, he remained a down-to-earth man of the people, prompting a genuine outpouring of affection from supporters of all clubs when he completed the fairytale rise by scoring with his first touch in an England shirt – at the age of 31 years and 179 days.

He had been told of his call-up for a Wembley friendly against Scotland just hours after the birth of his third child and, from that moment, he was swept along on a wave of emotion and magic.

Just shy of the 67th minute, Lambert came off the bench with the scores locked at 2-2. Two minutes and 46 seconds later, he rose majestically to thump home a trademark header, which proved to be the winner against the Auld Enemy.

It was truly the stuff dreams are made of, not just for the striker but for everyone who has ever kicked a ball in a park and imagined it was Wembley.

'I wasn't a Jay Rodriguez or an Adam Lallana, youngsters who could enjoy the moment and know they were young enough to get more chances. I knew I had to make an impact straight away or I might never get called back. I know I still had a short international career but to be involved in the set-up for over a year and to play in the World Cup is still the best achievement of my career.

'And the best moment is no surprise – it was scoring on my England debut against Scotland. It felt like my whole life had been building up to that moment.

'It was absolutely perfect. My whole family were there, the game was poised at 2-2 and I scored the winner with my first touch of the ball. Everyone could see what it meant to me.

'Afterwards, I sat in the dressing room and my head had gone. I felt like crying as I looked round and saw the likes of Wayne Rooney and Steven Gerrard and Frank Lampard, players I had always looked up to but had never really met before. Suddenly, I was not only alongside them but they were congratulating me – it was surreal. I have never really been able to put my feelings into words.'

His success shows just where hard work and real resolve can lead – and Lambert still wonders what he might have achieved in the game if he had adopted those principles earlier in his career.

After spells at Macclesfield, Stockport, Rochdale and Bristol Rovers, the then 27-year-old finally got the chance to shake off his journeyman tag when he was snapped up by Saints for £1m in August 2009. It was the start of a remarkable rise to stardom which saw him defy the doubters with every new high.

'I had scored 29 goals, so I was hoping a Championship club would come in for me – but no one had the bottle to do it. That was disappointing but I was still determined to play at that level.

'I began pre-season with Bristol Rovers and then, a week before the start of the campaign, I got the first inkling that Alan Pardew was taking over at Southampton and that he might be interested. Then it became official and I agreed terms straight away.

'Even so, it took a week or so for the clubs to agree. I thought Rovers were going to put a block on it, so I had to make it clear I wanted to join Southampton. And right from the start, it just seemed a perfect fit.

'I could see straight away they were a Premier League outfit in League One, so I knew they were capable of getting at least to the Championship. I knew they had fallen on bad times, going into administration and dropping down a couple of levels, but everything was in place for them to climb back up.

'The biggest obstacle I found was that a few of the players were used to losing. Just as winning can become a habit with the right kind of mentality, so can losing. And there was no way I was going to allow that to carry on.

'I was using Southampton to get me to the Championship – or beyond, although I was not thinking that far ahead at the time. I was 29, I had played all my career in the lower divisions and I was desperate to get to a higher level.

'I know people would have called me a journeyman because I had not played in the top two divisions and I was determined to get out of that league with Southampton.

'I never had an inkling then of just how well it would go, but I knew I would not have rested until I had at least had success in the Championship. I never envisaged doing it in the Premier League.

'It was not just me, we brought a couple of other players in. We knew we needed to start winning games to try and give the young lads confidence. I did that mostly by scoring goals.

'I knew I had to help change the mentality – what I didn't realise was I also had to change my own.'

Despite his initial success at St Mary's with seven goals in his first 12 games, he was stunned to be told he needed to improve and he needed to be fitter.

'When I got to Southampton, I hit the ground running in terms of goals. I started hitting the net regularly and thought I would just carry on. I thought I was doing quite well – until Alan Pardew called me in to see him and said I was not doing well enough.

'I was gobsmacked because I thought I was doing OK. But he questioned my diet, the shape I was in, my professionalism – he embarrassed me. It was a real wake-up call.

'He told me to sort myself out so I said "OK, tell me what I need to do." From then on, I would come in an hour early to training every day and would do some fat-burning and some boxing and other work to get myself fitter.

'I used to be a yard slower than everyone else but I got away with it because my brain was two steps ahead. Suddenly, I was just as fit as everyone else – and my brain was still sharper.

'The game became so much easier and I started to see the benefits of all that work. I began to thrive and I found I loved working to the maximum every single day. And I just carried it on from there.

'Until then, I had not seen the point because I was scoring goals and we were winning games. Part of the problem was that I had never been as professional as I should have been in terms of my lifestyle. I didn't really understand the benefits of eating and preparing right. No one had ever explained it to me like that.

'I wish I had started sooner – that's my biggest regret in football. I didn't have my head screwed on when I was young. I enjoyed going out. I didn't want to miss out on what my friends were doing.

'It was everything – diet, drinking during the week, not eating the right things. I know it sounds stupid, but I didn't understand how much it could help.

'I'm not talking about takeaways – more about the balance of protein and carbs, eating the right things and the right amounts and at the right time. I didn't know any of that. And I could not believe how much of a difference it made and I suddenly went up another level.'

Lambert not only did extra training but also worked hard at conditioning, diet and other fitness work and he will be eternally grateful to the Southampton staff.

'Nick Harvey, the fitness coach, was a massive influence on me and I owe him a lot. He really went out of his way to help me. Even in the summer, he would give up his time off to work with me and come training. He was a massive influence.

'So too was Matt Radcliffe, one of the Saints physios. My back and knee were not the best and I had bad technique. I could have carried on not sorting it out, but between them they got me right and I appreciate everything they did.

'They turned me into a machine and, for the first time in my career, I felt amazing. They made me into an athlete. When we went up into the Championship, I remember negotiating my contract with Nicola Cortese and I told him I was going to blow this league apart. He could see from the look in my eyes how serious I was.

'I was still being told by pundits that I was a League One player and that I would not carry on scoring in the Championship, but by the time I got there I had already changed as a person and as a professional and my expectations were much higher.

'So, it did not surprise me at all how well things went. I was a lot stronger both mentally and physically than I had been when I signed. I was speaking differently because I knew I was a lot better.'

Like Alan Shearer, Lambert realises the importance of being strong in the head as well as the body and he has used those who doubted him as his prime inspiration to succeed.

'Mental toughness is probably even more important than physical toughness. A lot is made of the lifestyle that the top players have – but the reason is they can handle the stresses and demands of the game. It takes time to hone your skills and you have to go about it in the right way.

'There is a lot of pressure to do well, but by the time I got to the Championship I had already played 400-odd games and I was mentally ready for everything. Before I even ran out for the first match of the season, I knew what I had to do and I was ready.

'I used to say it didn't bother me when pundits and fans and managers said "Nah, he's not good enough!" But it did get to me – and it made me even more desperate to prove people wrong.

'That became a massive part of how I succeeded. I used it as fuel every time I went out on a football field. I was determined to show people what I could do.'

That same mental toughness manifested itself through the entire squad as Saints rampaged straight through the Championship and into the Premier League at the first attempt, agonisingly missing out on the title to Reading by just one point.

While it came as a shock to many of the pundits who had said Southampton would do well simply to consolidate at the higher level, the players themselves were always quietly confident.

'We were not saying out loud that we thought we could go straight through to the Premier League, but we had a feeling among ourselves that it was possible. We thought we could at least get into the play-offs.

'We didn't quite envisage we were going to be the best team and blow the rest of the league away, at least until we were just pipped at the end by Reading. But as the season went on, the feeling grew that we could do it.

'To this day, it is still the most emotional I have been on a football field when we beat Coventry 4-0 to get to the Premier League. It was an amazing feeling, one of joy and relief and pride that we had got there.

'It was wonderful seeing how much it meant to the fans, to the club staff, to the players and, of course, it meant the world to me. All my career, it was something I never thought would happen.

'And to do it so quickly with Southampton was just unbelievable. It was the best feeling of my life at the time. I was so excited all over the summer. I couldn't wait for that first game.'

But for all his eager anticipation, Lambert was about to experience one of the most crushing disappointments of his career.

From the moment the fixtures were announced, he thought of little else than the curtain raiser, a match which could hardly have been tougher or more exciting – away to the champions Manchester City.

'I had looked forward to it so much and that made it very hard to take when I found I was on the bench for that opening fixture. Nigel Adkins has had a lot of stick from me over the years for that.

'He knows and appreciates how I feel about it. I couldn't handle it and I told him exactly how I felt before the game, I couldn't help myself.

'I could not believe what I had done to get to that point for Southampton – and then to be on the bench was a very hard pill to swallow.

'He went with Guly do Prado. I don't know if he was thinking to keep it tight and then bring me on to try and win it, but for me it sent a message straight away that he was not sure about me in the Premier League.

'Again, that drove me on. I just had to grit my teeth and go again and that moment when I came off the bench and scored against City is only behind my goal for England against Scotland as the best moment of my career.

'When the ball hit the net, I thought it would always be the highlight of my career – I didn't realise what was still to come.

'To play 400 games in the lower divisions and then finally get to the Premier League and score is a real fairytale, and even now I still struggle to find the words to fully express how I felt and what it meant.

'Running towards the fans and seeing them celebrating was such an unbelievable experience and I still get emotional thinking about it even today.

'We absolutely could have won that match. Steve Davis gave us the lead and I thought we might hang on, but we gifted them a couple of goals and lost 3-2.

'But we were still buzzing afterwards to have given the champions such a run for their money. We felt like we had shown we belonged at that level, but looking back it just showed our immaturity and inexperience that we could not see it out.

'It took us a good few games into the season before we found the maturity and know-how to handle the Premier League.'

Just as Saints started to find their feet in the top flight, the club stunned the football world by sacking manager Nigel Adkins, two days after they had fought back from 2-0 down to draw 2-2 at Chelsea.

It seemed a harsh decision, with Adkins seemingly set to steer Southampton to safety only to be replaced by the unemployed Mauricio Pochettino, who few had heard of – including Lambert.

'I was surprised when Nigel Adkins went – it seemed very cold. I didn't really understand it because we had gradually turned the corner and were starting to win games and gain points.

'We looked solid and I knew then that we were going to be safe – and they sacked him to bring in someone I did not know and had not even really heard of.

'I thought, "What are you doing? What's going on?" I found it very strange but as a professional you just have to get on with it and Mauricio Pochettino got a very good reception from the players.

'There were a few of us wondering, "Who are you? Are you going to push us on?" It was a weird situation because we didn't know that at the start, but he quickly gained our respect.

'I took to his personality straight away. He was very affectionate and loving. He would embrace you and shake everyone's hand, every day. It was a different culture but it was nice and it was refreshing.

'I remember he started to get his philosophy across straight away. He was very clear about what he wanted. He liked a lot of running and wanted us working our socks off. It was a real shock to us.

'The amount of work increased so quickly. We thought, "What's going on?" We would play 90 minutes on a Saturday and then come in on Monday for a full session of running.

'I was never used to that before in my life and I was not too sure about it. I was questioning him to the lads and saying, "What the fuck is going on?" I said, "I'm not having this, I'm going to go and speak to him."

'Jos Hooiveld and I went in to see him and said, "You need to calm down on a Monday, we are not used to this." He listened and finally he said, "OK, I understand, that's fine." We went out to speak to the lads, very pleased with ourselves.

'I said, "Don't worry, we've had a good chat. He understands and it's all good." The lads said that was brilliant and we trained normally and played on the Saturday.

'We went in on the Monday and he had us doing double the amount of running. That was him putting me in my place and letting me know he was in charge. From that moment, I accepted it. I was not going to try and change his mind again.

'He did lift us on to another level and as each week passed the lads realised he was very, very good. He was brilliant. We knew exactly what he wanted and it worked well for us. He believed in what he was saying and that if we did what he said, then we would be successful.

'It was a pleasure working under him and I am sure all the lads would say they were in the best shape of their careers. He pushed them to a different level in terms of technique, fitness, awareness – every aspect of the game. Even the young lads improved.

'And he was very loyal. He came to Wembley for my England debut and brought his family – but acted like he was part of my family. It was very touching to see how much he was affected by my goal. It meant just as much to him as it did to my family. I thought that was quality on his part.'

However, Lambert and his team-mates almost fell foul of the Argentine after breaking curfew during a pre-season tour to Austria.

'I could tell you a lot of stories about nights out with the lads, especially on foreign tours. But I am not sure it would be right to stitch them up. Maybe if I ever do my own book...?

'I can tell you one story. We had gone to Austria for Mauricio's first pre-season and we sneaked out of the hotel for what was supposed to be a few drinks, but we ended up staying out all night.

'When we got back, we found we couldn't get back into the hotel. They had locked everything up and it was well guarded, so we didn't know what to do.

'To make it worse the chairman, Nicola Cortese, was staying there, so we were absolutely shitting ourselves because he would have gone mental.

'Training was due to start at 8am and we had to get back in to get our training gear, so we had to break into the hotel. We ended up climbing up walls and over balconies to get to our rooms.

'Looking back now it was funny, but at the time it was very scary.'

It is just one of many fond memories from a truly magical five-year stay which will always secure a place in the hearts of all Saints fans – and vice-versa.

'To come from where I had been to suddenly scoring in the Premier League, I was living the dream. Those few years at Southampton were like a fairytale for me.

'I had that burning desire to keep proving people wrong. I have always been a man to try and push the club forward and it meant a hell of a lot to get Southampton to the Premier League.

'Once I got to the Premier League, the hunger to do well became even greater. I knew I was going to be a success because I was not going to work so hard to get to that stage and then not allow it to happen.

'Every year, I tried to improve because I felt I always had to prove myself to the coaches and the "experts" that I was good enough. I knew there were questions over whether I was good enough for League One and then the Championship… and then the Premier League.

'Then people said I would never do it for England – and it just started to get silly. I was on the crest of a wave and I just rode it and I loved every minute of it.'